PEARSON ILLUSTRATED

DICTIONARY

5TH EDITION

JUDITH DE KLERK
AMANDA MARASCO

Pearson Australia
(a division of Pearson Australia Group Pty Ltd)
459–471 Church Street, Level 1, Building B, Richmond, Victoria 3121
PO Box 23360, Melbourne, Victoria 8012
www.pearson.com.au

First published 1983 by Pearson Australia
2024 2023 2022 2021
10 9 8 7 6 5 4 3 2

Publisher: Gael McLeod
Project Manager: Suzy Freeman
Editor: Kent Wilson
Designer: Nina Heryanto
Copyright & Pictures Editor: Sian Bradfield
Illustrator: Wendy Gorton
Typesetter: iEnergizer Aptara Limited
Printed in Australia by Pegasus Media and Logistics

National Library of Australia Cataloguing-in-Publication entry
Author: De Klerk, Judith, author.
Title: Pearson illustrated maths dictionary / Judith de Klerk; Amanda Marasco.
Edition: 5th edition.
ISBN: 9781486009831 (paperback)
Target Audience: For primary and secondary students up to Year 10.
Subjects: Mathematics—Dictionaries, Juvenile.
Other Authors/Contributors: Marasco, Amanda, author.
Dewey Number: 510.3

ISBN 978 1 4860 0983 1

Pearson Australia Group Pty Ltd ABN 40 004 245 943

Acknowledgements
We would like to thank the following for permission to reproduce copyright material. The following abbreviations are used in this list: t = top, b = bottom, l = left, r = right, c = centre.

Alamy Ltd: blickwinkel, p. 164; RGB Ventures LLC dba SuperStock, p. 182; studiomode, p. 58t. Dreamstime: pp. 1, 2, 11, 17, 21, 22r, 23b, 24, 27, 30, 32, 35, 43, 46, 50, 51, 52, 54, 55, 56, 58bl, 58br, 59, 61 all, 68, 71 all, 73, 74, 75, 78, 79, 80, 88tr, 88br, 89, 91t, 93, 96, 98 all, 99, 100r, 101, 102, 108, 112 all, 116, 118, 121, 133, 137, 144, 145, 146tl, 146b, 147bl, 147tl, 147tc, 156, 157 all, 158, 159, 161, 163, 166, 167, 169, 170, 171, 176, 179. NASA Images: SA/courtesy of nasaimages.org, p. 183. Pearson Asset Library: Susanna Price \ Dorling Kindersley, 88l; Studio 8. Pearson Education Ltd, 22l. Pearson Australia: Alice McBroom, p. 57. Shutterstock: pp. 9, 23t, 41, 44, 49, 76, 91b, 100l, 131, 146tr, 147tr, 174.

Every effort has been made to trace and acknowledge copyright. However, should any infringement have occurred, the publishers tender their apologies and invite copyright owners to contact them.

Contents

Introduction

Mathematics is a language with an extensive vocabulary that often confuses students. It is important that the terms used to explain mathematical concepts have universal understanding, and the meanings of these terms are defined clearly and simply.

From the fourth edition written by Judith de Klerk with the assistance of her husband Louis de Klerk, this fifth edition of the *Pearson Illustrated Maths Dictionary* has been updated by Amanda Marasco to include all the mathematical terms used in the Australian Curriculum: Mathematics glossary, as well as many others relevant to the Years 5–10 curriculum. Photos bring a real-life aspect to the dictionary, colour tabs make word navigation easier, and a new design gives a fresh appeal. Definitions are written in clear and precise language, yet are simple enough for students to understand and are supported by examples and illustrations.

This dictionary is written for students from upper primary to Year 10, particularly EALD (English as an additional language or dialect) and literacy students, pre-service teachers, mathematics teachers, EALD and literacy teachers and parents. It will also be a useful acquisition for school libraries.

I believe that this edition will demystify many maths terms and thereby improve the understanding of mathematical concepts.

Gael McLeod
Publisher

A

See also **angle name, area, formula, line, point, vertex**

1 In formulas, the letter A stands for area.

Example

Area of a triangle

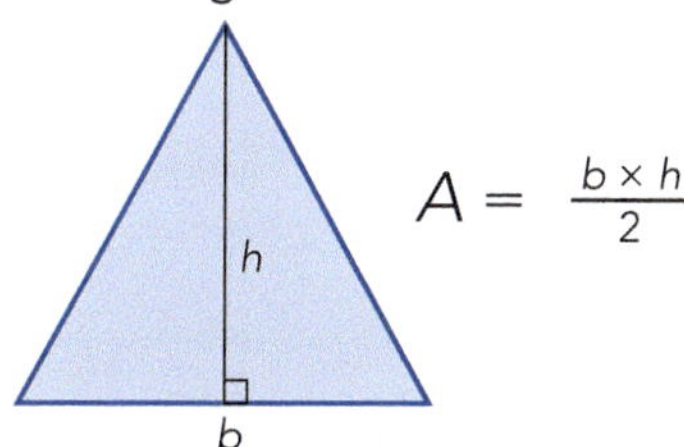

$$A = \frac{b \times h}{2}$$

2 A and other letters of the alphabet are used to name points, lines, angles and vertices (corners) of polygons and solids (3D objects).

Examples

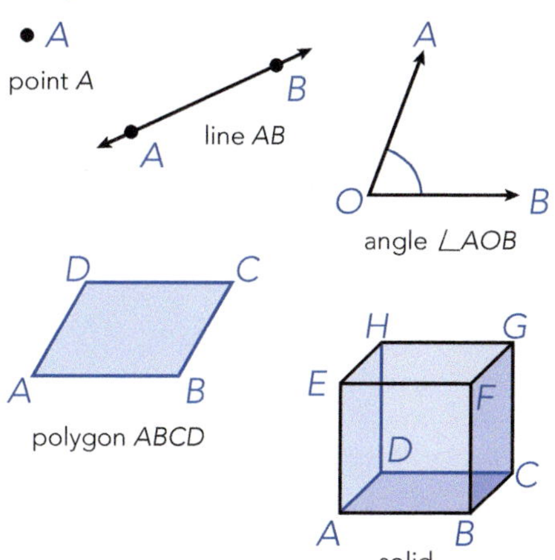

abacus

A board with spikes or a frame with wires on which discs, beads or counters are placed. Used for counting and calculating.

Examples

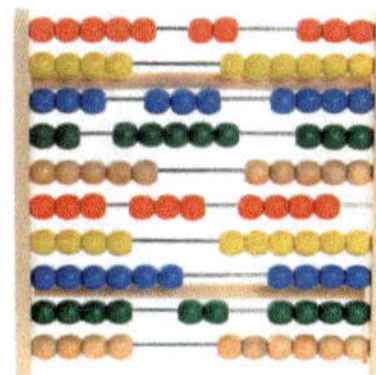

abbreviation

See also **symbol**

A shortened form of writing words and phrases.
When writing shortened forms of words, we usually put full stops after the letters.

Example

Victoria: Vic.

In mathematics, symbols are often used, for example, to show units of measurement. Although they represent a word, we do not write full stops after symbols.

Examples

m cm mm kg mL m^2 cm^3

abscissa

See also **Cartesian plane, coordinates, ordinate**

The horizontal coordinate of a point. The *x*-coordinate of a point (x,y) in a Cartesian coordinate system.

Example

For the point (2,3), 2 is the abscissa.

accurate

See also **approximately pi, surd**

Exact, correct, right, without error.

Example

The accurate answer to $1 \div 3$ is $\frac{1}{3}$ or $0.\dot{3}$. If it is written as 0.3, 0.33, 0.333, the answer is only an approximation. Calculations involving π (pi) or surds such as $\sqrt{7}$ must be left in this form to give accurate answers. Exact values must be used in calculations until the final step to ensure an answer is as accurate as possible. Anything that is measured is only as accurate as the equipment used to make the measurement.

acute angle

See also **angle, obtuse angle, reflex angle, revolution, right angle**

A sharply pointed angle with size between 0° and 90°.

Examples

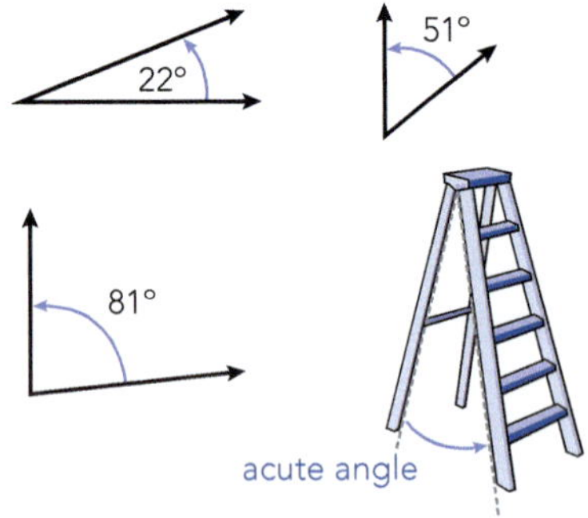

acute-angled triangle

See also **acute, equilateral triangle, obtuse triangle, right-angled triangle, scalene triangle**

A triangle that has three acute angles.

Example

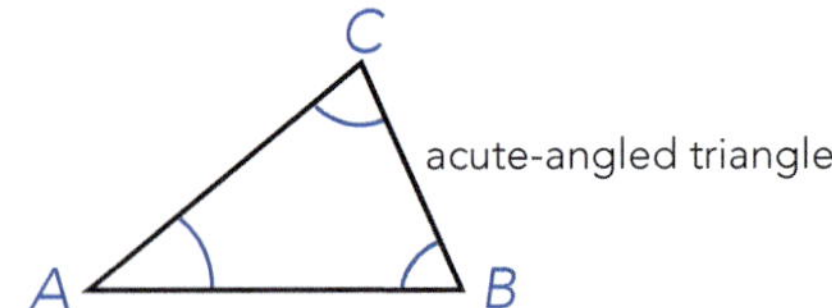

AD (Anno Domini)

See also **BC, CE**

An abbreviation of the Latin phrase meaning 'in the year of our Lord'. The number of years after the birth of Christ.

Example

The eruption of Mount Vesuvius in AD 79 destroyed Pompeii.

add

See also **addition, quantity, total**

Join two or more numbers or quantities together to get a combined total.

Example

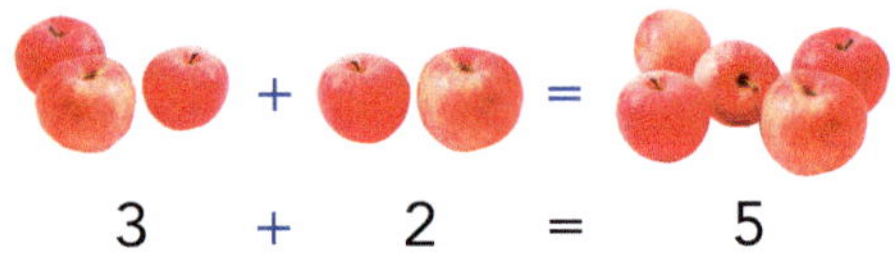

3 + 2 = 5

The apples were added together.

addend

See also **sum**

Any number that is to be added.

Example

$$2 + 6 = 8$$

addend ↑ addend ↑ sum ↑

In 2 + 6 = 8, 2 and 6 are addends, 8 is the sum.

addition (Symbol: +)

See also **algebraic expression, fraction, integers, number line**

1 Joining the values of two or more numbers together.

$$3 + 4 = 7$$

On the number line.

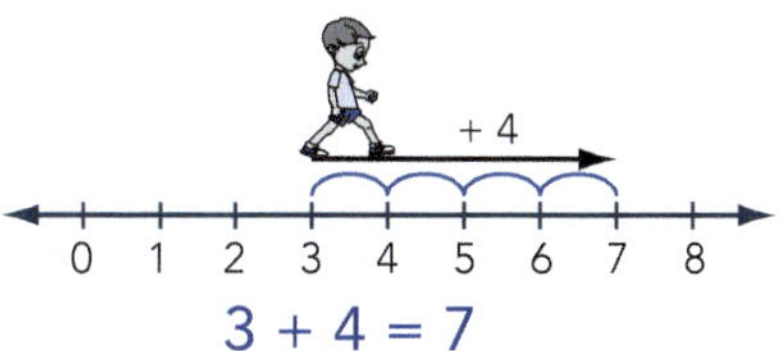

$$3 + 4 = 7$$

2 Addition of fractions.
Fractions must be converted so they have the same denominator before being added.

$$\frac{1}{4} + \frac{3}{5} = \frac{5}{20} + \frac{12}{20}$$

$$= \frac{17}{20}$$

3 Addition of integers.
Adding a negative integer gives the same result as subtracting a positive integer.

$$+5 + -7 = 5 - 7$$

$$= -2$$

4 Addition of algebraic terms.
Only terms with exactly the same pronumeral part can be added.

In a figure, two sides that have a common side.

$$2a + 3b + 5a = 7a + 3b$$

addition property of zero

See also **sum, zero**

When zero is added to any number, the sum is the same as the number.

Examples

$$4 + 0 = 4$$

$$0 + 12 = 12$$

additive inverse

See also **inverse, zero**

When we add a number and its inverse, the answer is zero.

Example

$$8 + -8 = 0$$

number ↑ inverse ↑

adjacent

See also **angle, arm of an angle, hypotenuse, vertex**

Positioned next to each other, having a common point or side.

Example

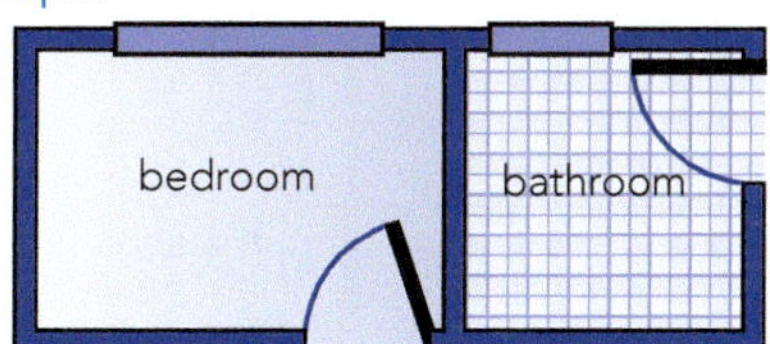

The bedroom is adjacent to the bathroom.

adjacent continued ▶

1 Adjacent sides.

In a figure, two sides that have a common vertex.

Example

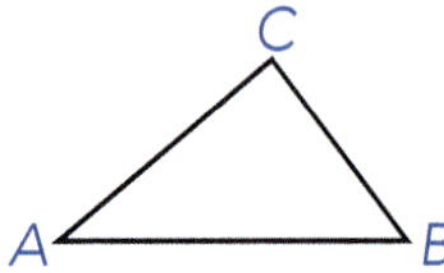

In this triangle, side *AB* is adjacent to side *AC* because they have a common vertex *A*. Side *BC* is also adjacent to side *AC*, with the common vertex at *C*.

2 Adjacent angles.

Two angles positioned in the same plane that have a common side and a common vertex.

Example

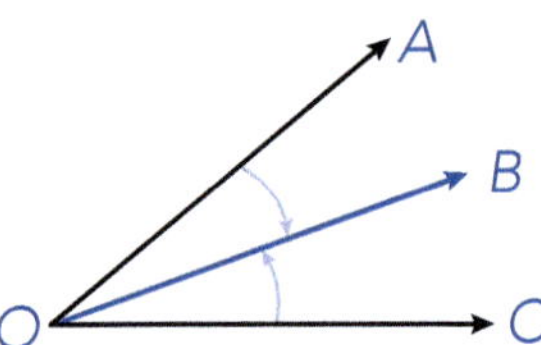

$\angle AOB$ is adjacent to $\angle BOC$ because they share the angle arm $\overrightarrow{OB}$.

3 In a right-angled triangle, the adjacent side is the side that is not the hypotenuse and that is next to the reference angle θ.

Example

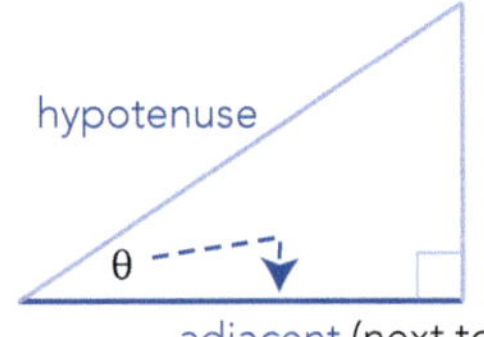

algebra

See also **algebraic expression, coefficient, pronumeral, symbol, variable**

A branch of mathematics that studies number systems, number properties, patterns and rules.

Letters and symbols called pronumerals are used as a 'shorthand' way of writing mathematical ideas, such as a formula or equation.

Examples

$2c$, $3x + 5z - 2$, $2a + 3a = 5a$

algebraic expression

See also **coefficient, numeral, pronumeral, symbol, value, variable, term**

Terms that are added or subtracted. They can all be algebraic or a combination of algebraic and numerical terms.

Examples

$5 - x$
$a + b + c$
$x^2 - 2xy + y$

algebraic fraction

See also **denominator, expression, fraction, numerator**

A fraction that has an algebraic expression as either the numerator, the denominator or both.

Examples

$$\frac{n}{3}, \frac{1}{2n+5}, \frac{x}{y+4}, \frac{a+b}{3a}, \frac{2x+1}{y+3}$$

Algebraic fractions follow the same rules for simplification as numeric fractions.

algebraic term

See also **algebraic expression, variable**

A number, a letter (pronumeral) or the product of a number and/or letters (pronumerals).

Examples

i a variable or number: a, x, 7, -3

ii the product of two or more variables: ab, xyz

iii a variable raised to a power: x^2, b^3

iv the product of one or more variables and a number: $4x$, $-6d$, $2ab$, $11xy^2$

algorithm

See also **backtracking, inverse operations**

A rule for solving a problem in a certain number of steps. Every step is clearly described. A flowchart or arrow diagram can be used to show the steps.

Example

Evaluate 7 × 3 + 4.

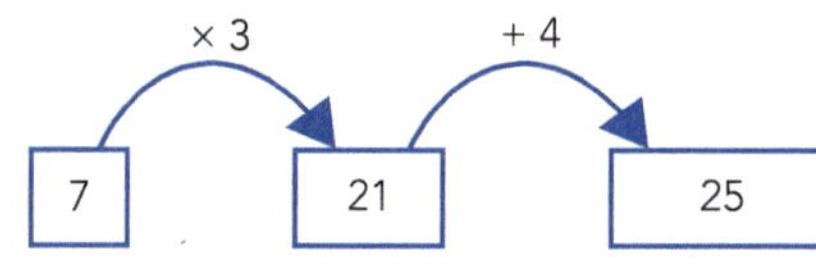

Step **1**: Multiply 7 by 3 to get 21.
Step **2**: Add 4 to get 25.

align

See also **line**

To place in a straight line.

Example

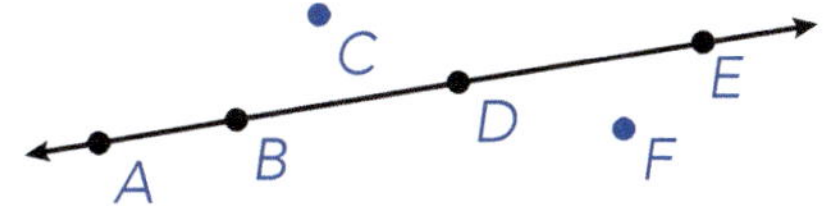

Points A, B, D and E are aligned; points C and F are not.

alternate angles

See also **angles, parallel lines, transversal**

When two or more lines are crossed by a transversal (another line), pairs of alternate angles are formed. The angles in each pair lie on opposite sides of the transversal and between the other two lines.

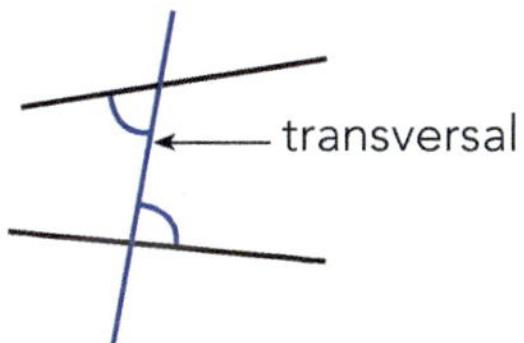

If the two lines that are crossed by the transversal are parallel, then pairs of alternate angles are equal. They can be easily remembered as 'Z' angles because of the shape they make.

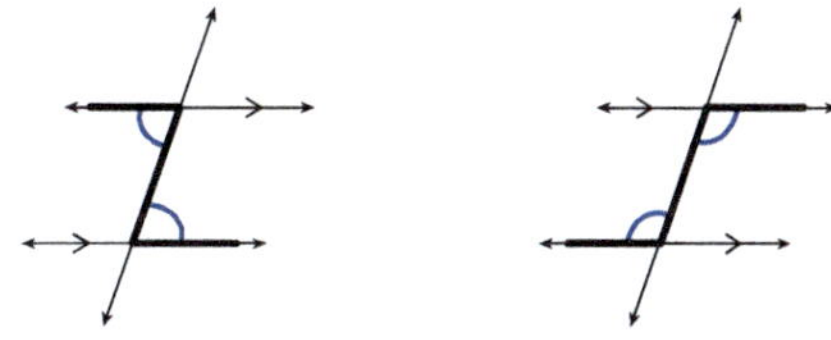

altitude

See also **height, perpendicular, surface**

Another name for height. How high something is above the surface of the Earth, sea level or horizon. In a figure, the altitude is the perpendicular height from base to highest vertex.

Example

i The altitude of this aeroplane is 9000 metres.

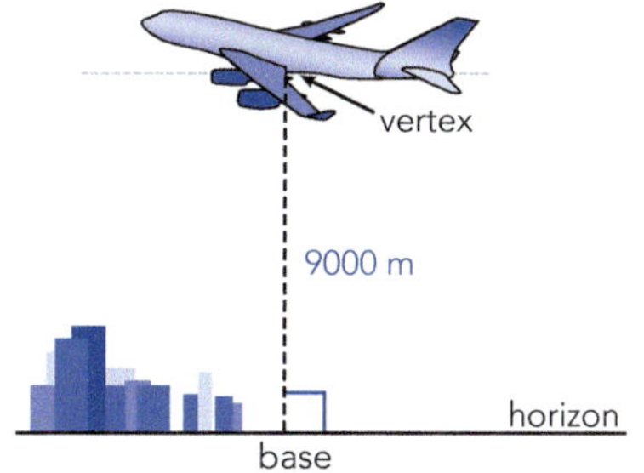

altitude continued ▶

ii The perpendicular height in this figure is the altitude.

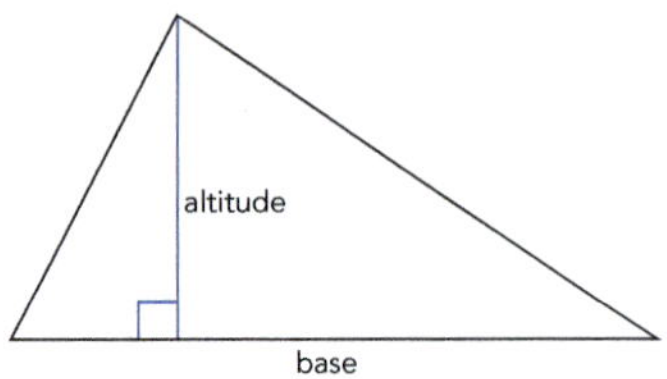

a.m. (ante meridiem)

See also **p.m.**

The time from immediately after midnight until immediately before midday. The term a.m. is used only with 12-hour time.

Example

The time is five past five in the morning.

It is 5.05 a.m.

amount

See also **quantity**

The total of something.

Example

The amount of money in my pocket is seven dollars and fifty cents.

amplitude

See also **cosine, sine, trigonometry**

The greatest displacement or height reached by a wave curve, perpendicular to the resting line.

The magnitude of an oscillating curve such as a sine or cosine curve.

Example

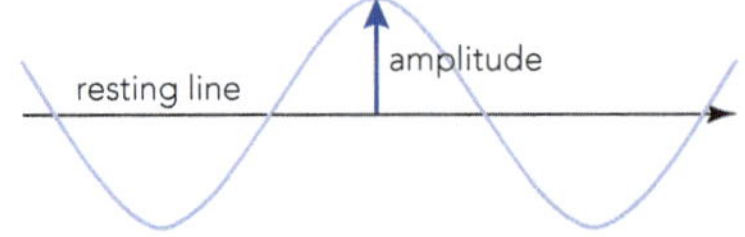

analogue clock

See also **a.m., digital clock, p.m.**

A clock or a watch that has numerals 1 to 12 equally spaced 30° apart, usually around the edge of a circular face, and two hands of different lengths attached at the centre, that rotate around the face. The longer hand indicates the minutes past the hour and takes 1 hour to complete one full 360° turn or revolution, and the shorter hand indicates the hour and takes 12 hours to complete one revolution.

Example

This watch shows twenty-five minutes past nine in the morning.

It is 9.25 a.m.

angle

See also **acute angle, arm of an angle, degree, obtuse angle, parallel lines, ray, reflex angle, revolution, right angle, straight angle**

The space between two rays that start at a given point. This point is called the vertex, and the two lines are the 'arms' of the angle.

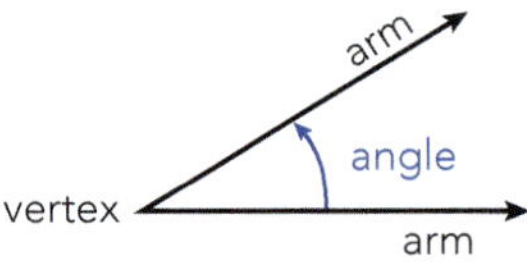

The size of the angle is the amount of turn from one arm to the other.

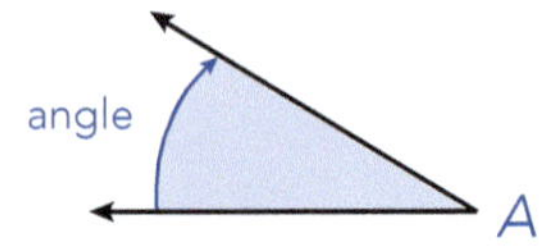

Angles are measured in degrees (°), minutes (') and seconds ("). There are 360 degrees in one full turn, or revolution. There are 60 minutes in one degree. There are 60 seconds in one minute.

Types of angles:

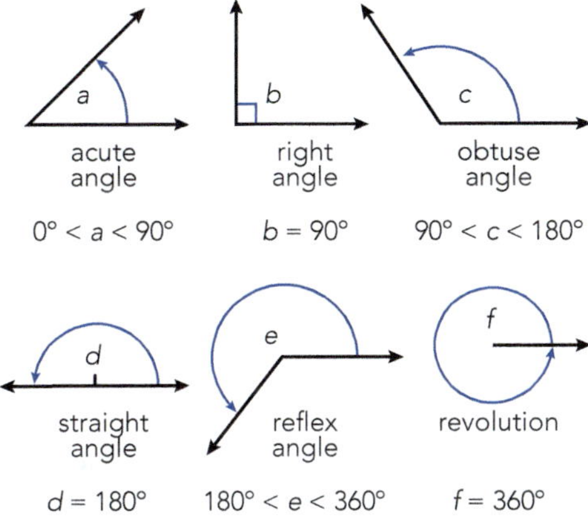

angle name

See also **vertex**

Angles are given names by marking them with letters.

Example

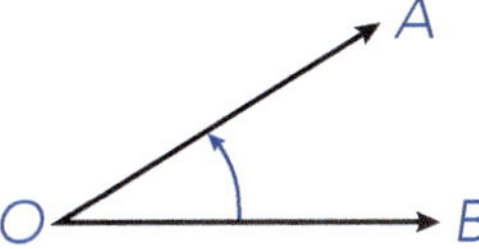

The name of this angle is $\angle AOB$. The letter O in the middle of $\angle AOB$ indicates the vertex of the angle.

angle of depression

See also **angle of elevation**

An angle formed between the horizontal line and the line of sight to an object below.

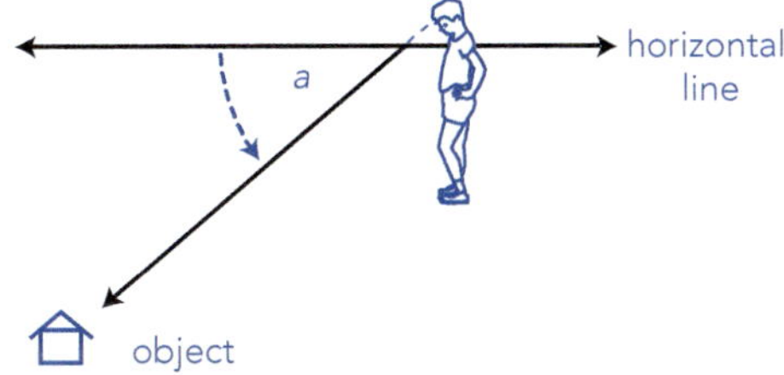

The angle of depression is *a*.

angle of elevation

See also **angle of depression**

An angle formed between the horizontal line and the line of sight to an object above.

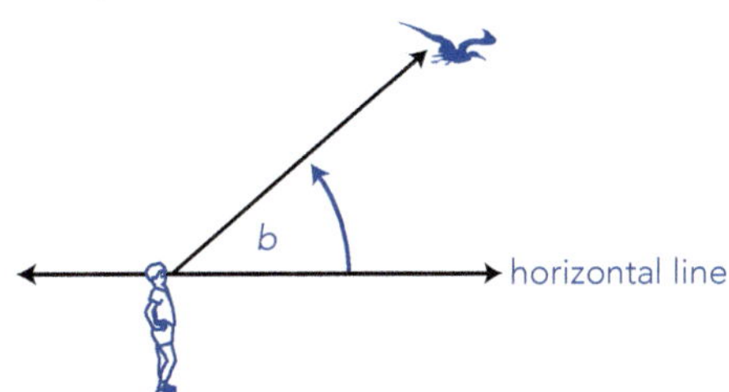

The angle of elevation is *b*.

angle sum

See also **polygon**

The total number of degrees in any polygon.

1 The angle sum of a triangle is 180°.

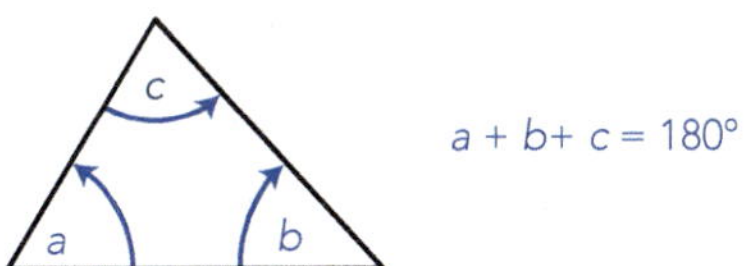

angle sum continued ▶

2 The angle sum of a quadrilateral is 360°.

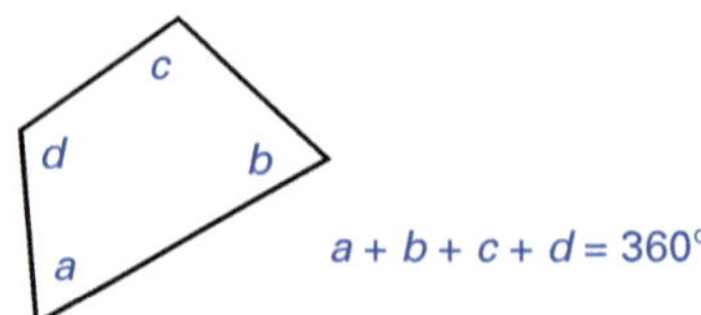

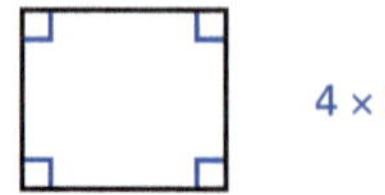

3 The angle sum of any polygon may be found using the following rule: number of vertices × 180° – 360° or (number of vertices – 2) × 180°

Examples

i the angle sum of a triangle

$(3 \times 180°) - 360° = 180°$ or
$(3 - 2) \times 180° = 180°$

ii the angle sum of a pentagon

$(5 - 2) \times 180° = 540°$

iii the angle sum of a hexagon

$(6 \times 180°) - 360° = 720°$

angles in a circle

See also **arc, circumference, diameter, subtend**

Angles formed by connecting three points on the circumference of a circle with straight lines, or connecting two points on the circumference with straight lines to the centre of the circle. Here are three circle theorems.

1 The angle at the centre of a circle is twice the angle at the circumference, subtended by the same arc.

Example

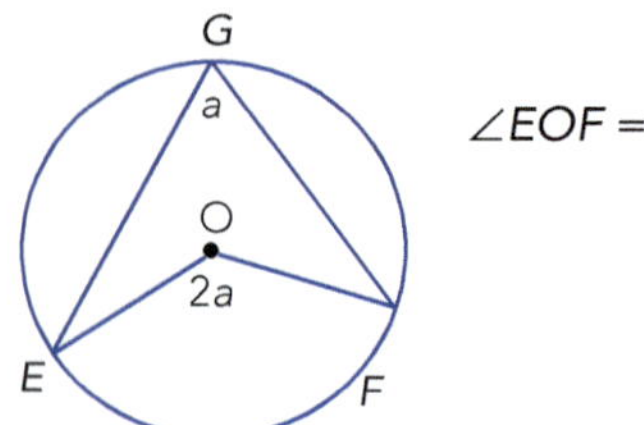

2 The angle in a semicircle is a right angle.

Example

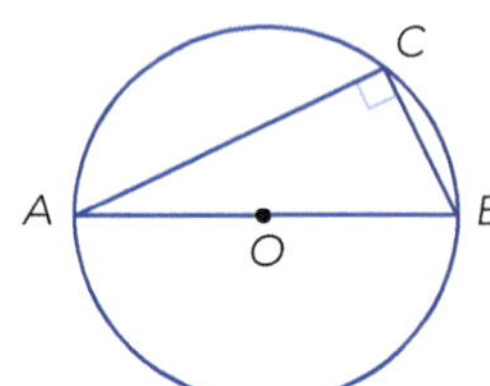

∠*ACB* is a right angle. The interval *AB* is the diameter of the circle.

3 Angles at the circumference of a circle that are subtended by the same arc are equal.

Example

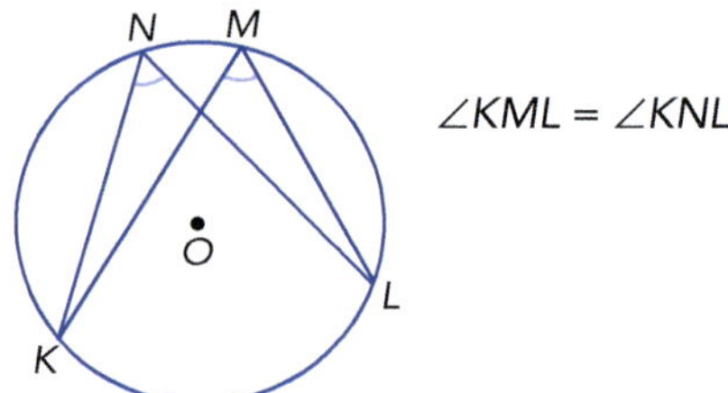

annual

See also **per annum**

1 Happening only once a year.

Example

Annual flower show.

2 Recurring yearly.

Example

Annual rate of interest is 6.5%.

annulus

See also **area, circle, concentric circles**

The shape formed between two concentric circles (circles with the same centre).

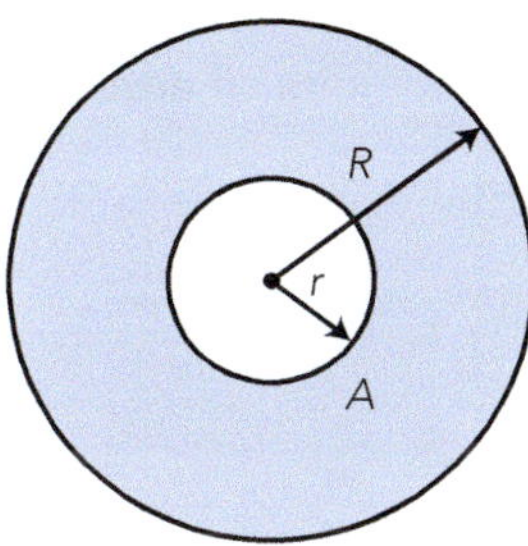

The area of an annulus can be found by subtracting the area of the inner circle from the area of the outer circle.

$$A = \pi R^2 - \pi r^2$$
$$= \pi(R^2 - r^2)$$

anticlockwise

See also **clockwise**

The direction opposite to that in which the hands of a clock travel.

Example

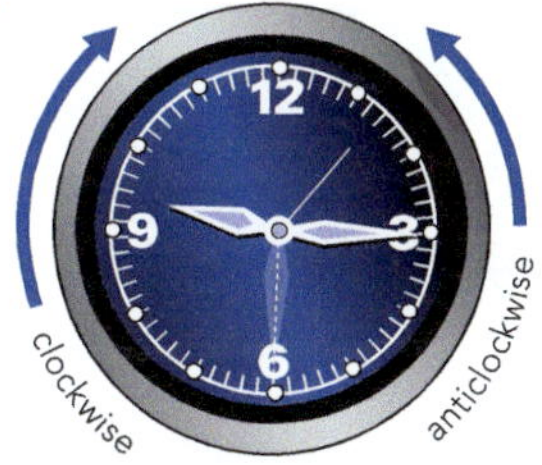

Example

Screws and bottle tops are loosened in an anticlockwise direction.

apex

See also **base, pyramid, vertex**

The highest point where two or more lines meet to form a corner of a figure or solid. The apex is the furthest vertical distance from the base.

Examples

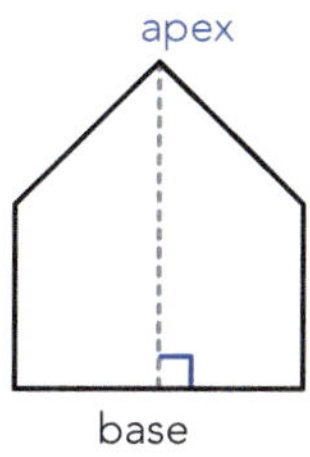

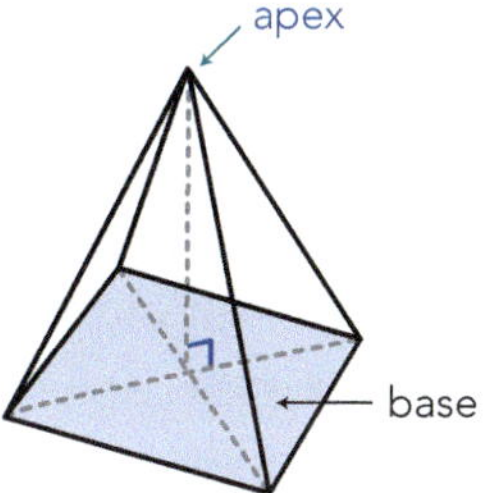

appreciation

See also **depreciation, interest, principal**

An increase in the value of an object over time.

Example

A painting bought for \$600 was sold at auction a year later for \$950. The appreciation over 12 months was \$350.

approximately (Symbols: ≈ ≑ ≃)

See also **accurate, rounding**

Nearly, not exactly, but almost. The symbols ≈ or ≑ or ≃ may be used for 'is approximately equal to'.

Example

The expressions

$0.97 \approx 1$ $\quad 0.97 \doteqdot 1$ $\quad 0.97 \simeq 1$

all mean '0.97 is approximately equal to 1'.

approximation (Symbols: ≈ ≑ ≃)

See also **accurate, approximately, rounding**

A value that is nearly exact. It is almost accurate. One method of approximation is to calculate with rounded figures; another is to round a final answer to a number of decimal places (d.p.).

Examples

i $798 \times 2.1 \approx 800 \times 2 \approx 1600$

ii $9.56 \times 4.725 \approx 45.2$ (1 d.p.)

iii The value of 3.14 for π is only an approximation.

arc

See also **circle, curve**

A part of any curve, but most often used to mean a part of a circle.

Example

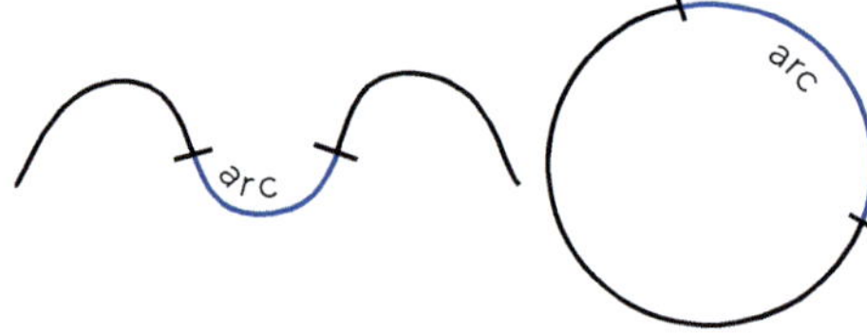

are

See also **area, hectare**

Unit of area in the metric system. It is the area of a square with sides measuring 10 metres.

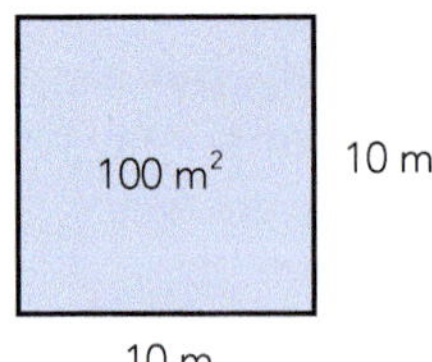

$100\ m^2 = 1$ are
100 are = 1 ha (1 hectare)

area

See also **conservation of area, surface, unit of measurement**

The amount of surface enclosed by a plane (2D) shape. Area is measured by counting squares of a suitable unit length. Metric units of area are:

square centimetre, cm^2

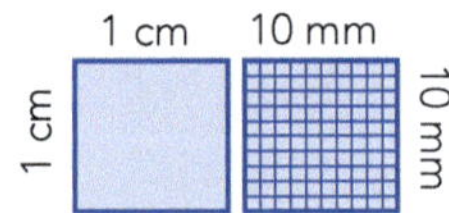

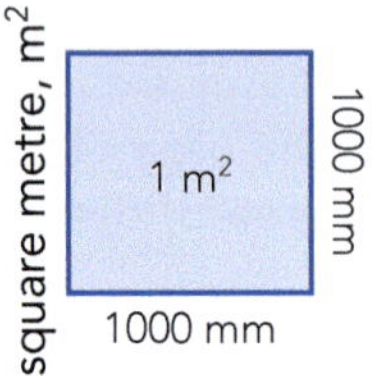

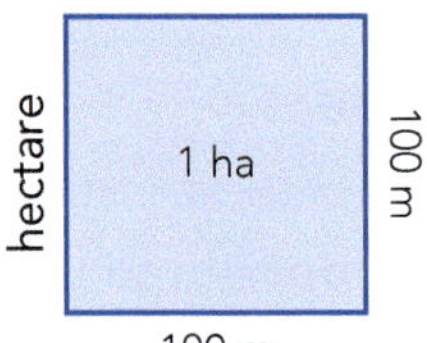

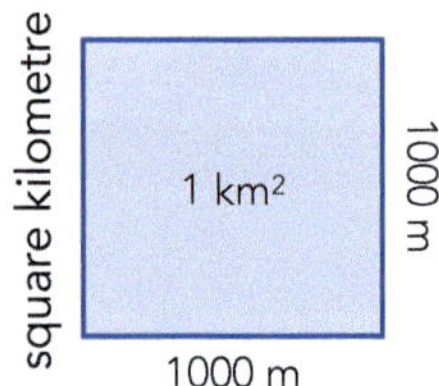

Example

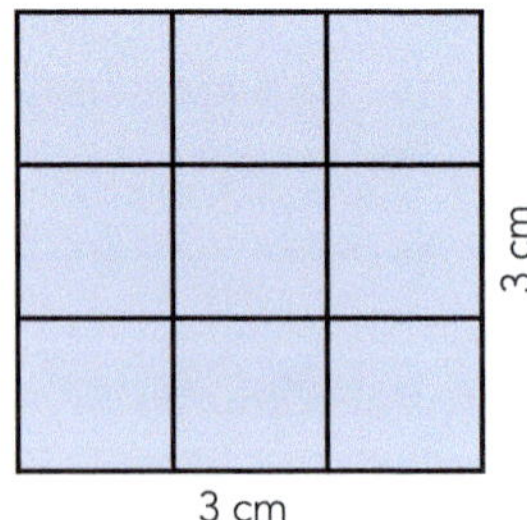

The area of this shape is $9\ cm^2$.

arithmetic
See also **computation**

The part of mathematics concerned with the study of numbers. Arithmetic is used for computations with whole numbers, fractions and decimals. The computations include addition, subtraction, multiplication and division. Arithmetic is also used for measurement, working with money and solving problems.

arithmetic mean
See **average, mean**

arithmetic sequence
See **sequence**

arm of an angle
See also **angle, vertex**

One of the lines or rays which form an angle.

Example

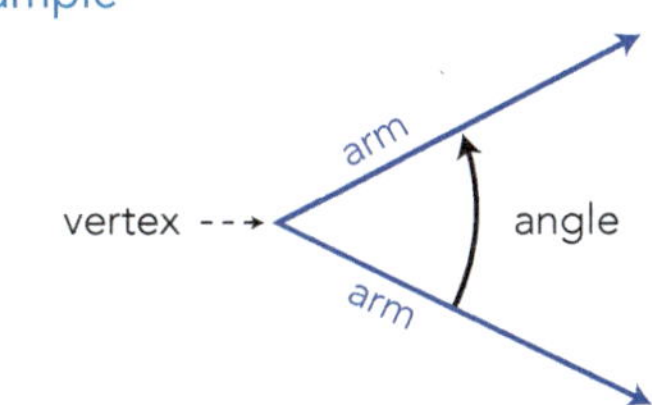

array

Arrangement of objects or numbers, in columns or rows.

Examples

An array of objects in rows and columns

3 7 12
5 8 10
4 16 32

These numbers form an array.

arrow

Used to indicate direction.

Examples

arrow diagram
See also **many-to-one correspondence, mapping, one-to-one correspondence, relation, set**

A diagram using arrows to show a relation (or connection) between one thing and another.

Examples

i Relation in one set of numbers

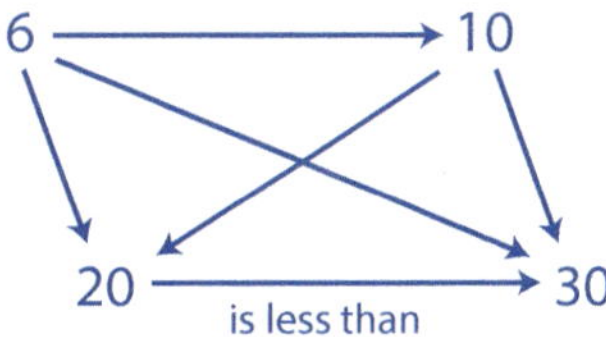

ii Relation between two sets

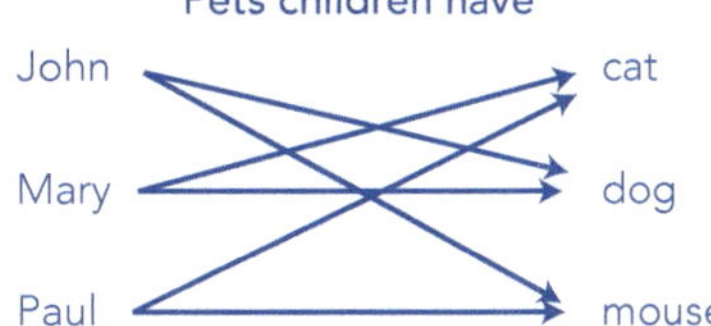

ascending order
See also **descending order, increase, order, pattern, sequence**

Going upwards or increasing in value. Numbers in ascending order increase moving from left to right, or down a list.

ascending order continued ▶

Examples

i These numbers are in ascending order:

0.1, 0.2, 0.3, 0.4, 0.5
↑ smallest ↑ largest

ii These lengths have been arranged in ascending order:

5 cm, 50 cm, 5 m, 5 km, 50 km
↑ shortest ↑ longest

associative laws

See also **commutative laws, product, sum**

1 The associative law of addition
The order in which three or more numbers are added makes no difference to the total sum.

Example

$$\begin{aligned}&3 + 7 + 9\\ &= (3 + 7) + 9 \quad \text{or} \quad 3 + (7 + 9)\\ &= 10 + 9 \qquad\qquad\quad = 3 + 16\\ &= 19 \qquad\qquad\qquad\;\; = 19\end{aligned}$$

2 The associative law of multiplication
The order in which three or more numbers are multiplied makes no difference to the final product.

Example

$$\begin{aligned}&3 \times 7 \times 9\\ &= (3 \times 7) \times 9 \quad \text{or} \quad 3 \times (7 \times 9)\\ &= 21 \times 9 \qquad\qquad\quad 3 \times 63\\ &= 189 \qquad\qquad\qquad = 189\end{aligned}$$

asterisk

A small star * often used to indicate multiplication. It is used as a multiplication sign in computer programs.

Examples

3 * 2 = 6 * means × (multiply)

asymmetry

See also **axis of symmetry, symmetry**

Not having line symmetry (reflectional, or 'mirror' symmetry).

An object which has no line symmetry is described as asymmetrical.

Examples

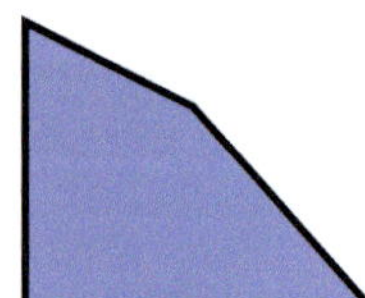

As these shapes have no axis of symmetry, they are asymmetrical

asymptote

See also **exponential, rectangular hyperbola**

A line or curve that another curve approaches but does not touch or cross.

Example

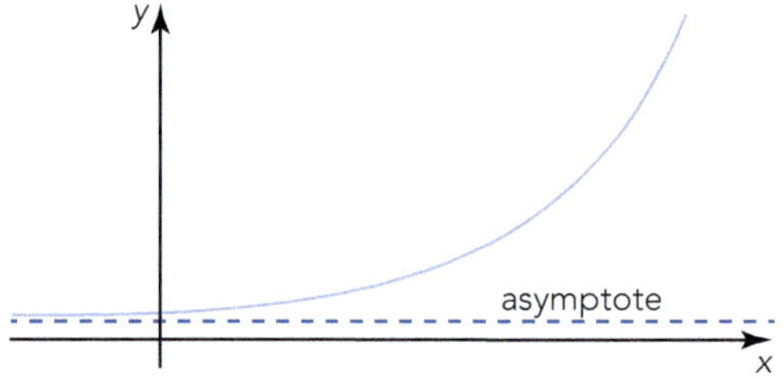

attribute

See also **classify, property**

A characteristic or property of an object, such as shape, size or colour.

Examples

i Attributes of shape: round, square …

round and thin

ii Attributes of size: thick, thin, small, large …

round and thick

iii Attributes of colour: black, red, yellow …

square and black

Other classifications different from the examples above are clearly possible.

average

See also **mean, measures of central tendency, score, sum**

A value which represents the whole collection of numbers or data values. Usually the word 'average' refers to the mean. The mean is found by adding all of the values and dividing the sum by the number of values that have been added.

Example

Find the average of 2, 5, 4, 6 and 3.

$$\text{Average} = \frac{\text{sum of values}}{\text{number of values}}$$

$$= \frac{2 + 5 + 4 + 6 + 3}{5}$$

$$= \frac{20}{5}$$

$$\text{Average} = 4$$

The average is also called the arithmetic mean.

axis (Plural: axes)

See also **coordinates, graph, horizontal line, intersection, origin, vertical**

The lines which form the framework for a graph. The horizontal axis is called the *x*-axis, the vertical axis is called the *y*-axis. Both axes are marked with equally spaced scales. The point where the axes intersect is called the origin (O).

Example

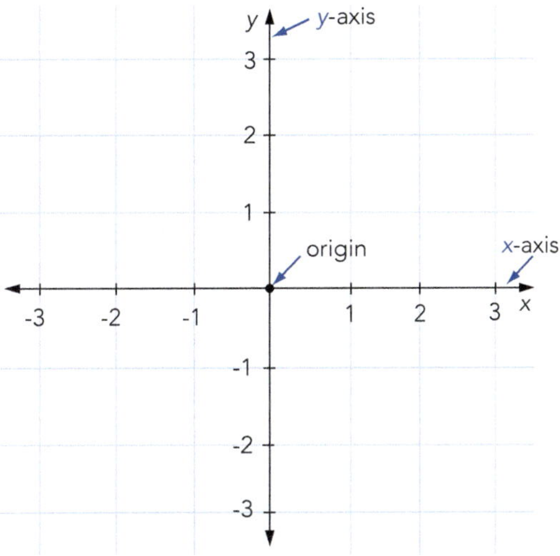

axis of symmetry

See also **axis**

The line that divides a shape or object in half so that one half is the mirror image of the other half. This line is sometimes called a line of symmetry. A shape may have more than one axis of symmetry. The number of axes of symmetry that can be drawn is called the order of reflectional symmetry.

Examples

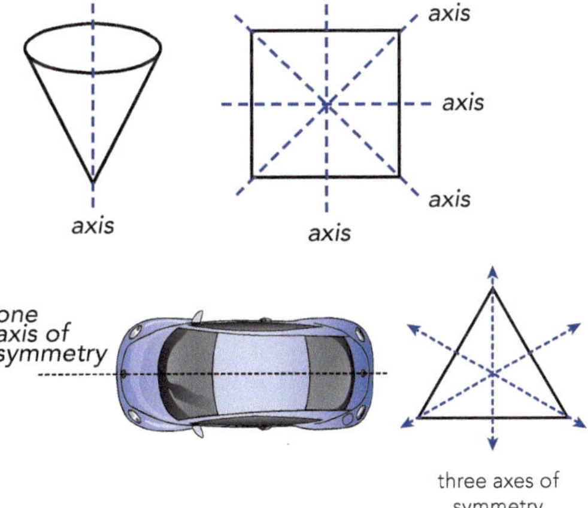

three axes of symmetry

back-to-back histogram

See also **back-to-back stem-and-leaf plot, data, histogram**

Two histograms drawn on either side of a vertical axis so that the data in the two groups can be compared. The histograms are drawn with bars and not columns as for ordinary histograms.

Example

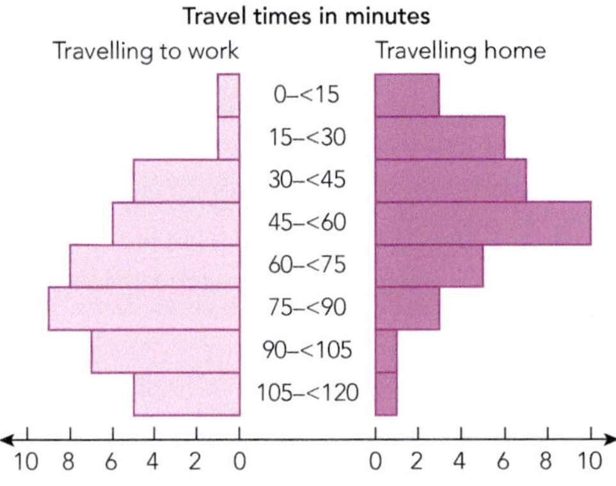

back-to-back stem-and-leaf plot

See also **back-to-back histogram, stem-and-leaf plot**

Two sets of data displayed on the one graph using stem-and-leaf plots so that the two sets of data can be compared. The 'leaves' are displayed on either side of a central 'stem'.

Example

Comparing the heights of 50 Year 7 students.

Boys	Stem	Girls
1	13_L	2 4
8 7	13_H	5 6 8
3 3 2 1	14_L	1 2 2 3 4 4
9 7 7 6 5	14_H	5 6 6 6 8 9 9
4 4 3 2 2 1	15_L	1 3 3 4
9 8 8 7	15_H	6 6
4 3	16_L	3
9	16_H	

backtracking

See also **flowchart, inverse operations, linear equations, solve**

A method used to solve simple linear equations by working backwards along a flowchart and performing inverse operations.

Example

Solve $3(x + 2) = 15$ using backtracking.

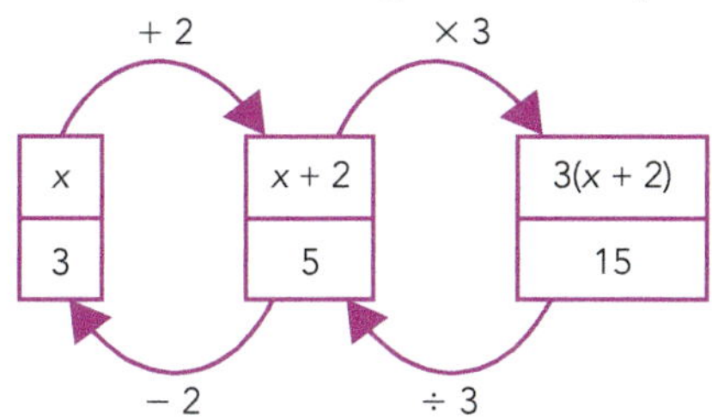

Build the expression:

Step 1 Start with x and add 2

Step 2 Multiply $(x + 2)$ by 3

Undo by backtracking:

As $3(x + 2) = 15$,

Step 1 Divide 15 by 3

Step 2 Subtract 2

Solution:

$x = 3$

balance

See also **equivalent equations, mass, scales**

1 An equal distribution.

Example

balanced unbalanced

2 Balance scales are used to measure the mass of an object by balancing it with an object whose mass is known.

Example

The beam balance below shows that seven apples are balanced by a 1 kg mass. This means that the mass of seven apples is equal to 1 kg.

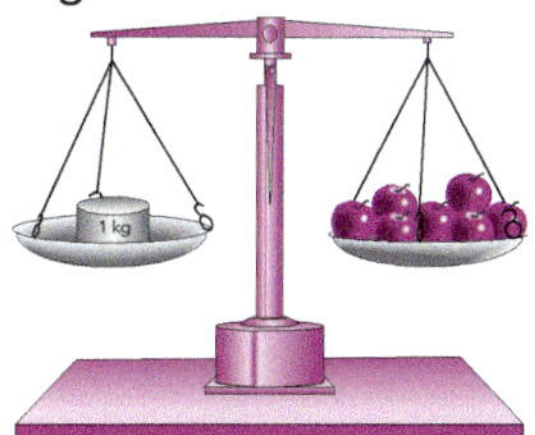

3 The amount of money in a bank account at any given time.

Example

Date	Description	Credit	Debit	Balance
2006				
02 Feb	Pay	350		350
05 Feb	ATM withdrawal		200	150
10 Feb	Rent		50	100
16 Feb	Pay	350		450
21 Feb	Rates		295	155

bar graph

See also **column graph, graph, pie graph, picture graph**

A graph which uses horizontal bars to represent categorical data. A bar graph with vertical bars or columns is called a column graph.

Examples

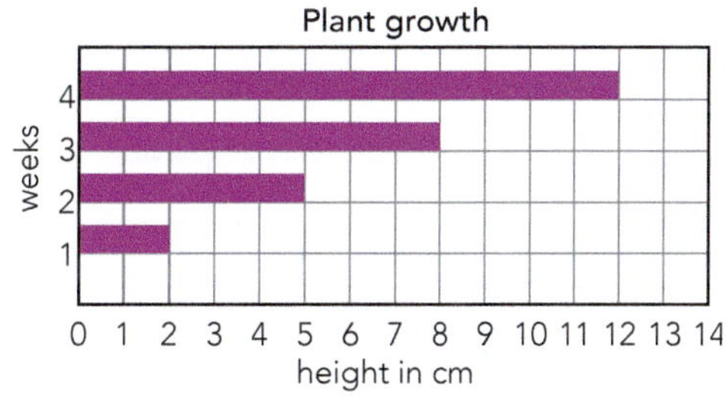

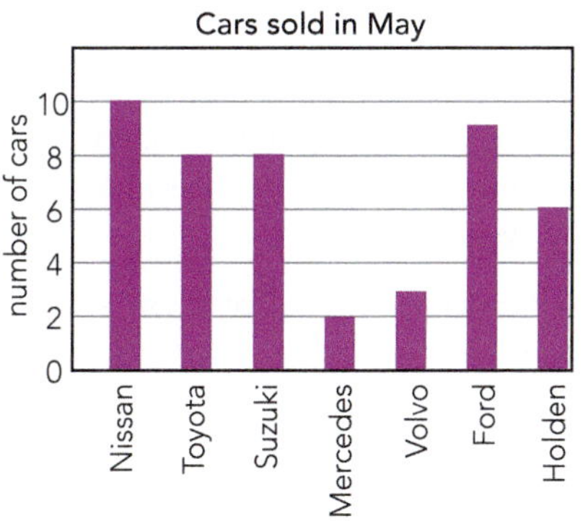

base

See also **decimal place-value system, exponent, index, index notation, Hindu–Arabic system, power of a number**

1 The face on which a solid stands. The side on which a shape stands.

Examples

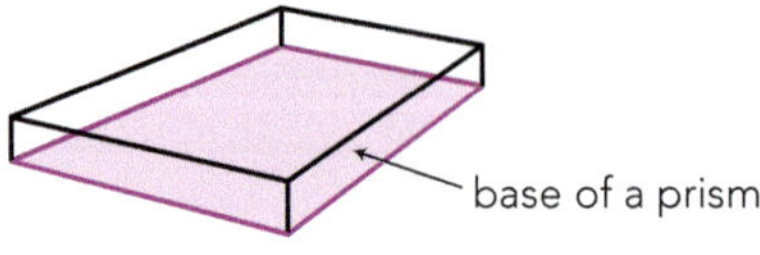

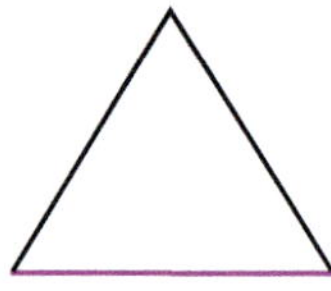

base of a triangle

2 The number on which a place-value system of numeration is constructed that has determined the system of numeration that has evolved.

Example

hundreds	tens	units	tenths
100	10	1	$\frac{1}{10}$

10× bigger

10× smaller

100× bigger

The Hindu–Arabic system is a base 10 system that we call the decimal place-value system.

3 A number, symbol or a variable used with an index to show an index notation.

Example

In index notation, the base is the number that is raised to the index. It is the number that is multiplied together by the number of times indicated by the index.

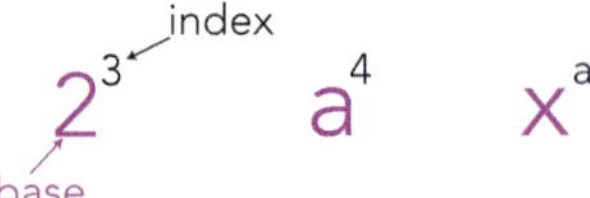

2^3 is read as 'two cubed'. 2 is the base.

base ten system

See also **base, decimal place-value system, decimal system, digit, index, index notation, multibase arithmetic blocks, power of a number**

A number system that uses 10 different digits to represent numbers.

Example

The Hindu–Arabic system is a base ten system because it uses 10 digits: 1, 2, 3, 4, 5, 6, 7, 8, 9 and 0.

basic numeral

See also **arithmetic, calculation**

The simplest answer to an arithmetic calculation.

Examples

7 is the basic numeral that represents the result of $(13 + 2 \times 6 - 4) \div 3$.

64 is the basic numeral represented by 4^3.

BC (Before Christ)

See also **BCE, AD**

The years before Christ was born.

Example

Egyptian Pharaoh Tutankhamen ruled in the 14th century BC.

BCE (Before the Common Era)

See also **BC, AD**

Indicates the same period as BC. BCE can be used in place of BC.

bearing

See also **compass, direction**

An angle used to specify the direction of travel required to move from one point to another. There are two types of bearings:

1. true bearings give the angle as a number of degrees clockwise from North
2. compass bearings give the angle as a turn from North or South (whichever is closer to the position of the point) towards East or West.

Examples

i true bearing: 035°T
compass bearing: N35°E

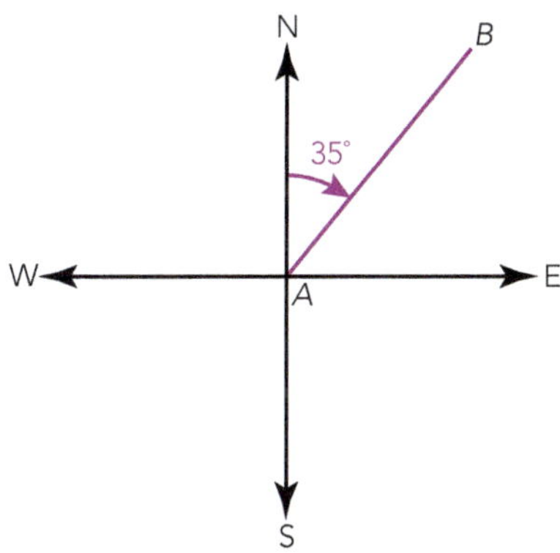

ii true bearing: 283°T
compass bearing: N77°W

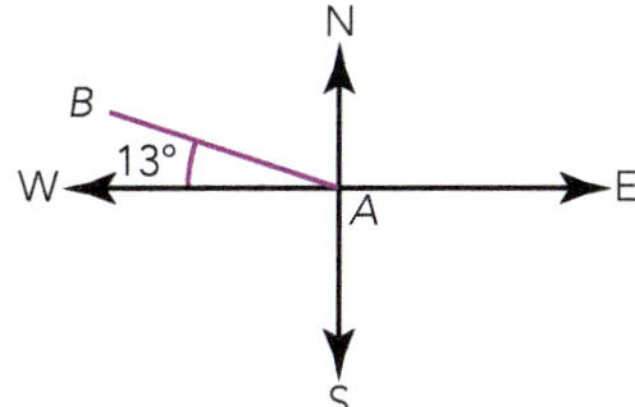

bi

See also **binomial, bisect, bisector**

A prefix (letters that stand in front of words) that means two or twice.

Example

A bicycle has two wheels.

bias (statistics)

See also **data, statistics**

A preference or a belief that has no evidence to support it. In statistics, it is a selection process that introduces favouritism or unfairness in the collection of data.

Example

Asking people at a football match whether they like watching sport.

billion

See also **million**

In most English-speaking countries, including Australia, a billion means 1000 millions.

1 000 000 000 or 10^9

Note: In many European countries a billion means a million millions (10^{12}).

bimodal

See also **frequency, mode, statistics**

A data set that has two modes.

Example

30 students were asked how many hours they spent a week playing sport. The following data was collected and ordered.
0, 1, 1, 2, 2, 2, 3, 3, 3, 3, 3, 3, 3, 3, 4, 4, 4, 4, 4, 4, 4, 4, 5, 5, 5, 5, 6, 6, 6, 7
Two of the values in the set have the highest frequency of 8. As the data has two modes, 3 and 4, the data is bimodal.

binary

See also **bit, byte**

A base-2 number system that uses only 0 and 1 to represent numbers. All numbers can be represented in a binary system. All data is stored on a computer as binary numbers known as 'bits'. Eight bits make up a 'byte'. Electrical circuits are used in computer chips for binary calculations by switching the circuits off for zero and on for one.

Example

Binary (Base-2) system

Place value	a^7	a^6	a^5	a^4	a^3	a^2	a^1	a^0	
Binary	27	2^6	2^5	2^4	2^3	2^2	2^1	2^0	
Value	128	64	32	16	8	4	2	1	Number
								0	0
							0	1	1
							1	0	2
						0	1	1	3
					0	1	0	0	4
				0	1	0	1	0	10
				0	1	1	1	1	15
			0	1	1	0	0	0	25
0	1	0	0	0	1	1	0	0	140

In the binary system, the digits '11' represent the number 'three'. In the base 10 system, '11' represents the number eleven.

binomial

See also **algebra, algebraic expression**

An algebraic expression consisting of two terms that are added or subtracted. The terms are called monomials.

Examples

$2 + a$ $\quad 3a - b$ $\quad 2x^2 + y^2$

binomial expansion

See also **algebra, binomial, binomial product, expression**

The result of multiplying two binomial expressions.

Example

$$(a + b)(c + d) = a(c + d) + b(c + d)$$
$$= ac + ad + bc + bd$$

This can be shown by the area model.

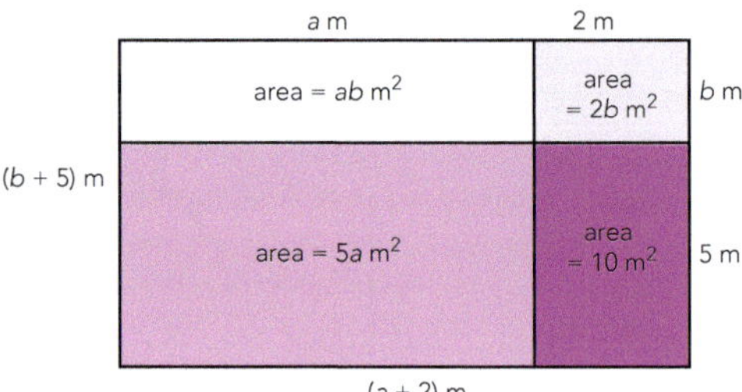

The total area is found by multiplying the total length $(a + b)$ by the total width $(c + d)$ or by finding each separate area and adding them together.

binomial product

See also **algebra, binomial, binomial expansion, expression**

The product of two binomial expressions.

Example

$(a + b)(c + d)$

bisect

See also **bisector, midpoint**

To cut or divide into two equal parts.

Example

This angle has been bisected.

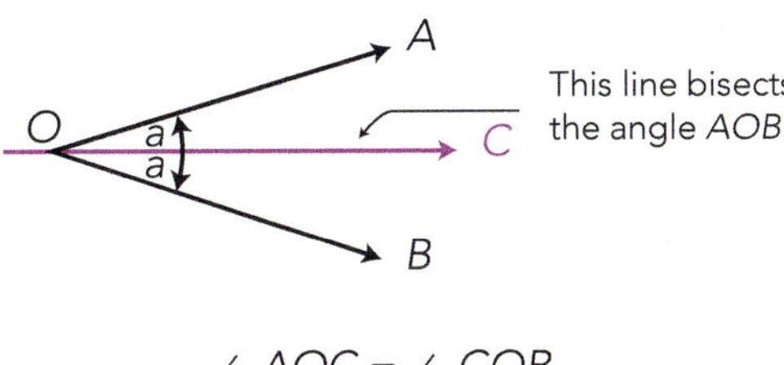

$\angle AOC = \angle COB$

bisector

See also **bisect, interval, line, midpoint, perpendicular**

A straight line which divides an angle, a line or an interval into two equal parts.

Examples

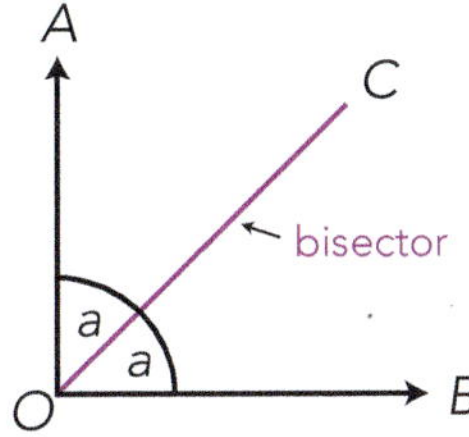

OC is the bisector of angle *AOB*.

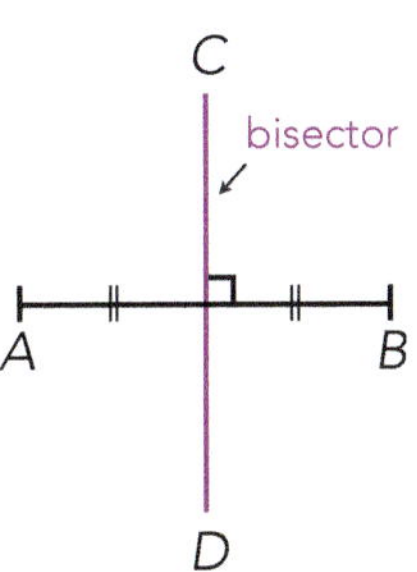

Because the bisector *CD* of the interval *AB* intersects *AB* at right angles, it is a perpendicular bisector of *AB*.

bit

An abbreviation for the words 'binary digit'. Bits are used in calculators, computers and other electronic devices. 0 and 1 are the two binary digits.

bivariate numerical data

See also **independent variable, numerical data, scatter plot, statistics, variable**

A set of data where values for two numerical variables have been collected.

Examples

i The height and weight of members of an athletics team

ii The resting pulse rate of each athlete and the number of hours they spent training

This type of data is often represented on a scatter plot.

Time is often one of the two recorded variables. Time is always the independent variable.

Example

Recording the growth of a small child every month

Boolean function

Mathematical logic used for searching computer databases. Common Boolean functions include AND, OR and NOT.

Example

Database Search: first name = 'John' AND age = '20'

This will only return all people with the first name of John who are aged 20.

Database Search: first name = 'John' OR age = '20'

This will return all people with the first name of John and all people who are aged 20.

Database Search: first name = 'John' NOT age = '20'

This will return all people with the first name of John who are not 20 years old.

boundary

See also **perimeter, region**

A line around the edge of a region.

Examples

i The boundary around a soccer field

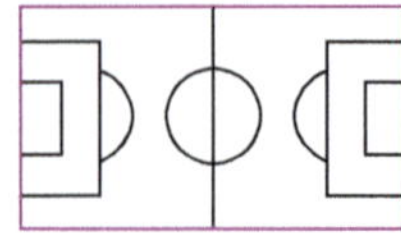

ii The boundary of Queensland

iii The boundary of a hexagon is its perimeter.

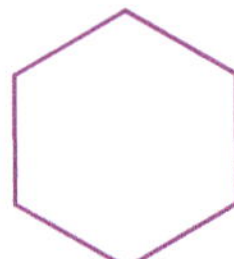

box plot (box-and-whisker plot)

See also **five-number summary, interquartile range (IQR), median, quartile, parallel box plots**

A graphical display used in statistics, constructed using the five-number summary of a data set. The five numbers are: the minimum value, the lower quartile (Q_L), the median, the upper quartile (Q_U) and the maximum value.

Example

This box plot shows the distribution of the weights of each of the players in a rugby squad.

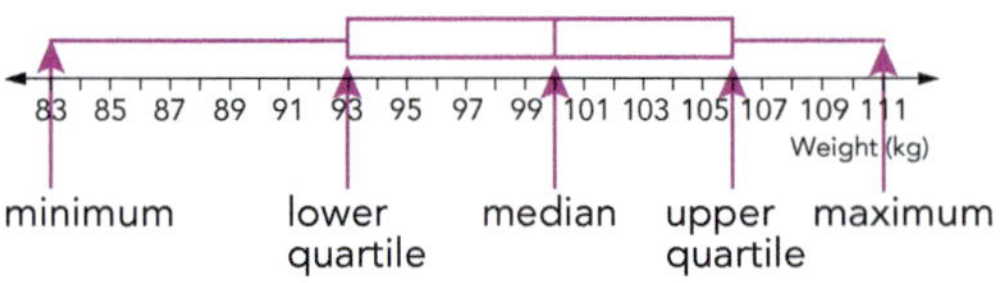

The ends of the box are the upper and lower quartiles. (In the example, $Q_L = 93$ and $Q_U = 106$.)

The length of the box covers the interquartile range, or IQR. (In the example, IQR = 106 − 93 = 13.)

The lines extending from the ends of the box are known as 'whiskers'. On the left the whisker reaches down to the minimum value (83 in the example) and on the right it reaches up to the maximum value (111 in the example).

The difference between the minimum and maximum values is the range. (Range = 111 − 83 = 28.)

The line inside the box indicates the position of the median (100). The median will not necessarily be in the middle of the box. It depends on how symmetrical the distribution of the data is.

braces

See **brackets**

brackets

See also **order of operations, parentheses**

The signs ( ) [ ] { } are used for grouping things or numbers together. Curly brackets are known as braces.

( )	[ ]	{ }
ordinary brackets (parentheses)	square brackets	braces

1 Order of operations
Brackets are used to indicate which part(s) of the calculation are to be done first. Ordinary brackets are used, then square brackets, then finally braces if more sets of brackets are required.

Example

$$5\{2[4(3 + 10) - 35 \div 5]\}$$

$$= 5\{2[(4 \times 13 - 7]\}$$ 1 remove ordinary brackets

$$= 5\{2[52 - 7]\}$$ 2 remove square brackets

$$= 5\{2 \times 45\}$$ 3 remove braces

$$= 5 \times 90$$

$$= 450$$

2 Sample space or set
The sample space of a probability experiment is written inside braces.

Example
Outcomes of rolling a fair die:
{1, 2, 3, 4, 5, 6}

Braces { } are used to stand for the word 'set'. The members of the set are written inside these braces.

Example
The set of counting numbers
{1, 2, 3, 4, 5, 6, 7...}

breadth

See also **height, length, width**

Measurement from side to side, also called width.

Example

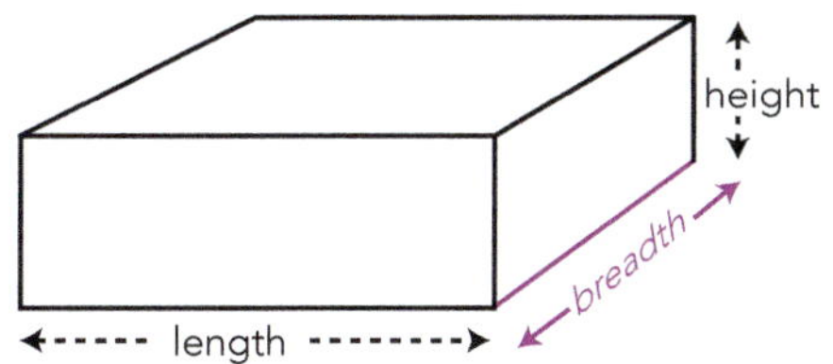

budget

A plan for using money.

Example
Jessica earns $560 a fortnight. Her budget is:

Rent and food	$340
Bus fares	$45
Clothes	$50
Entertainment	$60
Savings	$65
Total	$560

buying on terms

See also **interest**

A way of buying goods by paying for them in instalments instead of in full so they can be taken home and used straight away. This often involves additional charges such as interest and monthly account fees. This method of payment can sometimes be advertised as 'buy now, pay later', or 'interest-free'. The interest-free payment period is usually between 12 and 48 months. If the goods are not paid off in full at the end of the interest-free period, then a high rate of interest is charged.

Example
A TV is on sale for $480 or may be paid off in 24 interest-free monthly instalments of $20, plus a monthly account fee of $2.50. This makes the total cost:

$$\$(24 \times 20) + (24 \times 2.5) = \$540$$

Note that if interest was to be paid on the amount, the monthly repayments could be $24, making the total cost:

$$\$(24 \times 24) + (24 \times 2.5) = \$636$$

C

See also **circumference**

1 The symbol for the Celsius temperature scale. It is used with the symbol for degrees, °.

Examples

0 °C	water freezes
100 °C	water boils

2 A symbol for circumference in formulas.

Examples

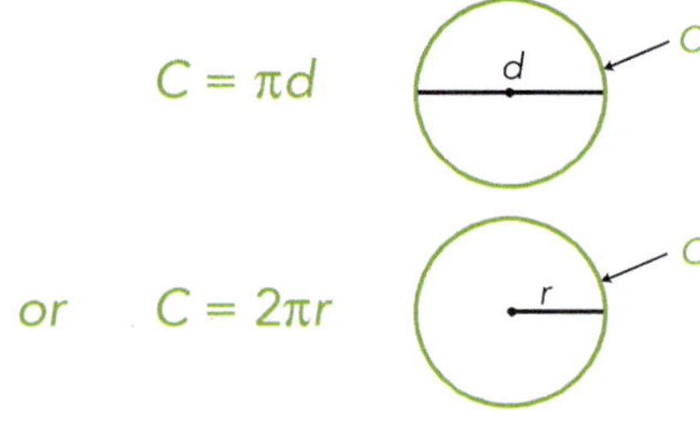

3 In Roman numerals, C stands for one hundred.

Example

CCCXXII = 322

calculate

See also **arithmetic**

Work out the answer. Use one or more mathematical procedures to determine a number, quantity or value.

calculator

See also **abacus**

Calculating aid. Calculators are electronic. They are battery or solar powered.

calendar

See also **day, leap year, month, year**

A calendar represents the way in which a year is broken up into months, weeks and days.

February 2014

Mo	Tu	We	Th	Fr	Sa	Su
					1	2
3	4	5	6	7	8	9
10	11	12	13	14	15	16
17	18	19	20	21	22	23
24	25	26	27	28		

Example

The third Thursday in February 2014 is the 20th.

calliper

See also **compasses, concave, convex**

A measuring instrument similar to compasses with curved legs for measuring the thickness (diameter) of round or curved objects or, turned outwards, for measuring cavities.

Example

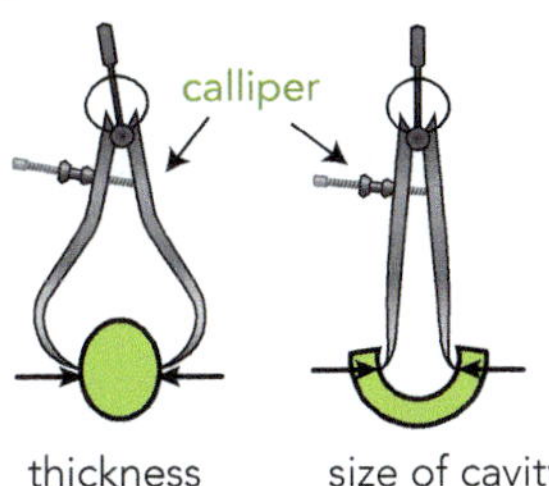

cancelling

See **simplify**

capacity

See also **Metric relationships** on page 188, **volume**

How much a container or hollow solid can hold. Capacity is calculated in the same way as volume, but is usually used when referring to liquid or gas volumes, and uses different units.

Units of capacity are:

millilitre	mL
litre	L
kilolitre	kL
megalitre	ML

$1\text{ mL} = 1\text{ cm}^3$

$1000\text{ mL} = 1\text{ L} = 1000\text{ cm}^3$

$1000\text{ L} = 1\text{ kL} = 1\text{ m}^3$

Example

This water bottle has a capacity of 600 mL.

cardinal number

See also **counting, sequence, set**

The number of elements (members) in a set. The members of the set are counted and the total is the cardinal number of the set.

Example

How many balloons?

The cardinal number of this set of balloons is 5.

carrying

See also **regroup**

Another word for regrouping.

Example

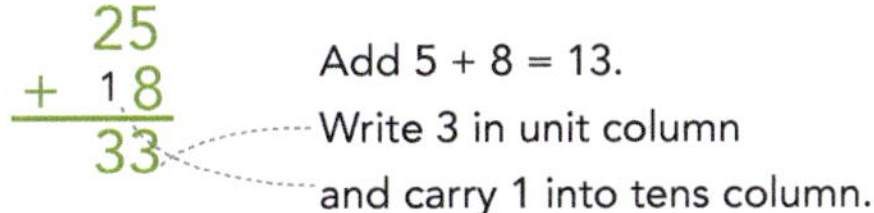

Cartesian coordinates

See **coordinates**

Cartesian plane

See also **coordinates, origin, *x*-coordinate, *y*-coordinate**

A flat surface that is divided into four quadrants by two axes, one horizontal and one vertical. Points can be plotted on this plane using two coordinates to specify their position: an *x*-coordinate (the distance left or right of the origin (0, 0)) and a *y*-coordinate (the distance up or down from the origin).

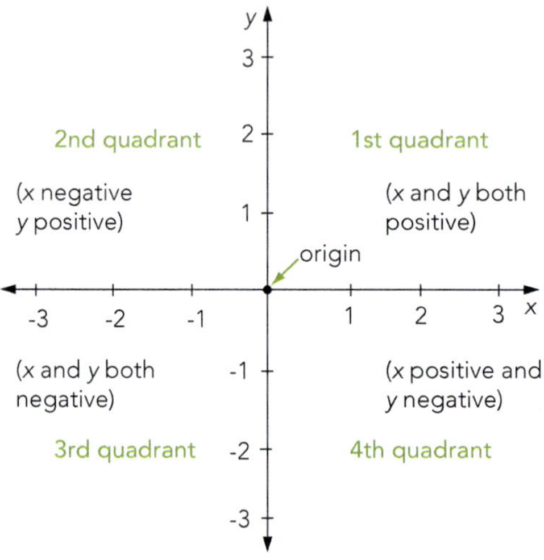

categorical variable

See also **data, numerical data**

In statistics, a type of data where the individual pieces of data are sorted into categories, or groups. This type of data is non-numerical.

Example

The hair colour of each of the students in the class, or the suburb that each student lives in.

Sometimes, these categories may have numbers as their labels, such as the street number of the students' houses. However, this is not true numerical data, as it makes no sense to perform calculations with them (such as finding an 'average' house number).

cc

See also **cubic centimetre**

A symbol sometimes used to show cubic centimetre. The correct symbol is cm^3.

CE (Common Era)

See also **AD, BC**

Indicates the same period as AD.

CE can be used in place of AD.

Celsius scale

See **C, degree Celsius, temperature**

census

See also **data, population, sample, statistics**

The process of collecting data from an entire population.

Example

In Australia, a census is conducted every 5 years to collect information about the Australian way of life so that governments and others can plan for the future.

cent (Symbol: c)

See also **dollar**

One cent is one hundredth of a dollar.

1c = $0.01
$1 = 100c

One cent used to be the smallest coin in Australian currency. Now the five-cent coin is the smallest.

centi

See also **centimetre, Decimal system prefixes** on page 192

A prefix meaning one hundredth.

Example

One centimetre is one hundredth of a metre.

1 cm = 0.01 m

Centigrade

See also **degree Celsius, temperature**

Former name for the Celsius temperature scale.

centimetre (Symbol: cm)

See also **centi, length, unit of measurement**

A unit of length.

1 cm = 0.01 m
100 cm = 1 m

Example

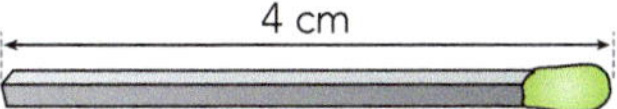

This match is 4 centimetres long.

centre

See also **circle, circumference, radius**

A point that is the same distance from all points of a circle or a sphere. Often represented in geometrical diagrams by the letter *O*.

Example

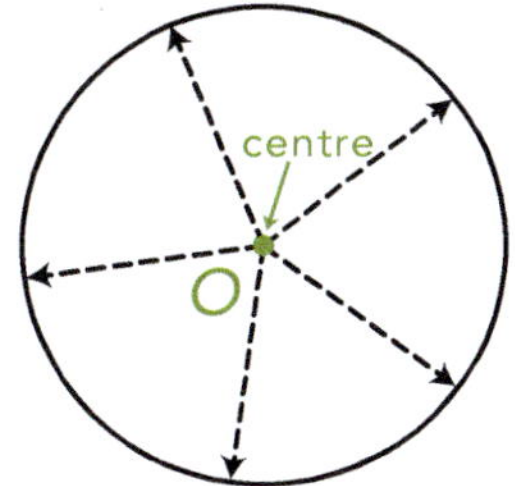

centre of rotation

See also **order of symmetry, rotation, rotational symmetry, turn**

A point about which a shape is rotated.

century

See also **centi**

One hundred.

Examples

- i 100 years
  100 runs in cricket
- ii The twentieth century began on 1 January 1901 and ended on 31 December 2000.
- iii The 21st century began on 1 January 2001.

chance

See also **probability**

The likelihood or probability of an event happening.

chance event

See also **probability**

An event for which the outcome is uncertain.

For some events the chance of possible outcomes can be predicted. However, the outcomes can never be predicted with 100% confidence.

Examples

Tossing a coin, rolling a die, drawing a winning raffle ticket from a hat.

checking

See also **inverse, inverse operations**

A way of making sure that an answer is correct. One way of checking is by using the inverse operation.

Examples

i Addition is checked by subtraction.

The answer 43 is correct.

ii Division is checked by multiplication.

$$4\,\overline{)\,56}\ \ 14,\quad 56,\quad 0 \qquad 14 \times 4 = 56$$

The answer 14 is correct.

Another method is checking by substitution.

Substituting the answer obtained for the unknown into the equation. If the left hand side (LHS) equals the right hand side (RHS), the answer obtained is the solution.

Example

$$2x + 1 = 9$$

Solution: $x = 4$

Check: $\text{LHS} = 2 \times 4 + 1$
$= 8 + 1$
$= 9$
$= \text{RHS}$

So $x = 4$ is the solution.

chord

See also **circumference, diameter**

A line joining two points on a circle.

Examples

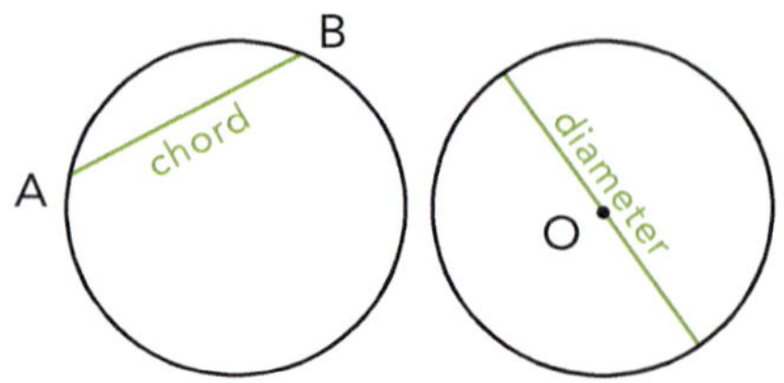

The diameter is the longest chord in a circle.

chronological order

See also **pi, time line**

Events arranged by the date or time when they happened.

Example

The history of π

Time	Who/Where	Value of Π
2000 BC	Babylonia	$3\frac{1}{8}$
300 BC	Archimedes	$3\frac{10}{71}$ to $3\frac{1}{7}$
1220 AD	Fibonacci	3.141 818
1665	Newton	3.141 592 653 589 7932
1705		π sign was first used
1949	ENIAC computer	π correct to 2035 decimal places
1984	Tokyo	π computed to 16 million decimal places

circle

See also **centre, circumference, diameter, plane, radius**

The set of all points in a plane which are at the same distance (radius r) from a given point O (centre).

Example

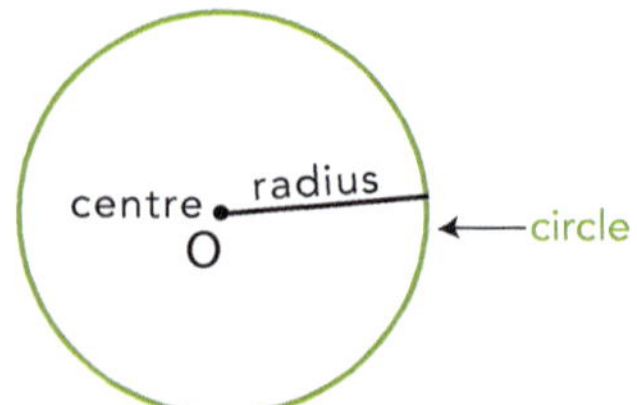

circle graph

See **pie graph**

circular

See also **circle**

In the form of a circle; round.

Example

A merry-go-round is circular.

circumference

See also **circle, diameter, perimeter, pi**

The perimeter of a circle. The distance around the edge of a circle.

If the radius is r units, then the circumference $C = 2\pi r$.

Example

$C = 2\pi r$

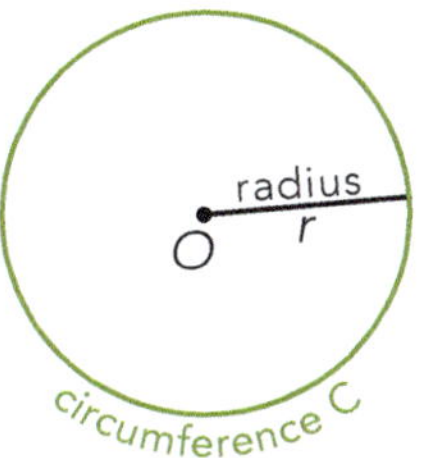

When the diameter d is measured, then the circumference $C = \pi d$.

Example

$C = \pi d$

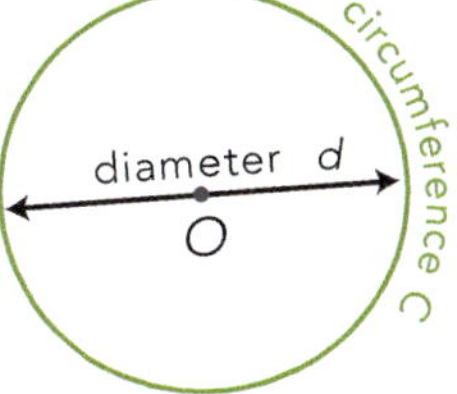

class

See also **classification, classify**

A group, set, or collection of things that have some property or attribute in common.

Example

Triangles, squares, rectangles and kites belong to the class of polygons (closed shapes with three or more straight sides).

class centre

See also **class, class interval, continuous data, cumulative frequency curve, data, discrete data, grouped data, histogram, mean, median, range, statistics**

The centre (middle) of a class interval. It is found by calculating the average of the highest and lowest value in the class interval.

The centre will depend on whether the data is discrete or continuous.

Example

For a class interval 10–<15, the centre is 12 for discrete data but it is 12.5 for continuous data. (This is because the highest value in the class interval in a discrete data set is 14, but as any value up to 15 might be in a continuous data set, 15 is used as the highest value).

classification

See also **attribute, property**

Arrangement into classes, sets or groups, according to attributes or properties.

Examples

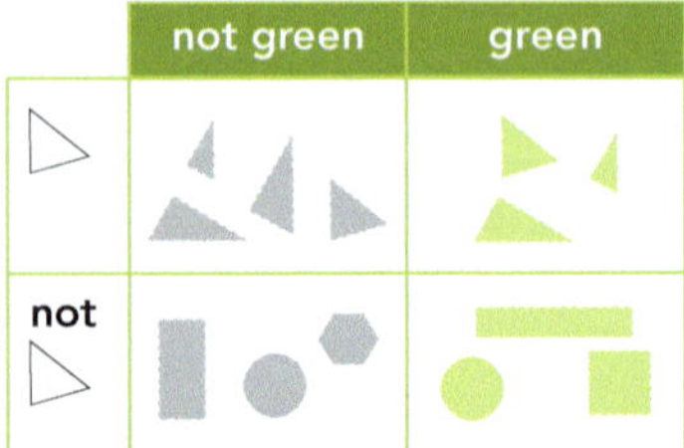

Have pets	Don't have pets
Quong	Halima
Kelly	Nick
Grant	Dean
Toula	Anna
Ali	Scott
Claire	Sachiko

classify

See also **attribute, property, sorting**

Sort objects, ideas or events into groups, classes or hierarchies according to one or more properties or attributes.

class interval

See also **class, class centre, continuous data, cumulative frequency curve, data, discrete data, grouped data, histogram, mean, median, range, statistics**

The range of each group of data when large amounts of raw data are converted into grouped data. This is usually done to construct graphs such as histograms and cumulative frequency curves, and to find approximate values for statistics such as mean and median quickly.

Example

10–<15 is a class interval of 5. It includes 10, 11, 12, 13 and 14 for discrete (counted) data, and all numbers from 10 to <15 for continuous (measured) data.

clockwise

See also **anticlockwise**

The direction in which the hands of a clock normally travel.

Example

The hands on this clock have moved in a clockwise direction.
Screws and bottle tops are tightened clockwise.

closed curve

See also **circle, closed shape, curve, ellipse, open curve**

A curve which starts at a point and comes back to that point.

Examples

i Simple closed curves

ii Closed curves that are not simple

iii Regular closed curves

closed shape

See also **closed curve, polygon, shape**

A shape whose sides begin and end at the same point. A closed shape with straight sides is called a polygon.

Examples

closed shapes

These are not closed shapes.

cm

See also **centimetre, symbol**

The symbol for centimetre.

code

A system of words, letters or symbols which represent other letters, words or sentences. Codes are used for secret writing or signalling.

Example

Morse code

M O T H E R

/– –/– – –/ –/• • • •/•/• – •/

coefficient

See also **algebra, pronumeral**

The number in front of a variable (pronumeral) in an algebraic term. The number is multiplied by the variable.

Examples

i $3y = 3 \times y$
3 is the coefficient of y

ii $7(a + b) = 7 \times (a + b)$
$= 7 \times a + 7 \times b$
7 is the coefficient of $(a + b)$

iii $xy = 1 \times x \times y$
The coefficient of xy is 1.

cointerior angles (allied angles)

See also **alternate angles, angles, corresponding angles, parallel lines, supplementary angles, transversal**

When two or more lines are crossed by a transversal (another line), pairs of cointerior angles are formed. There is one pair on each side of the transversal, in the space between the other two lines.

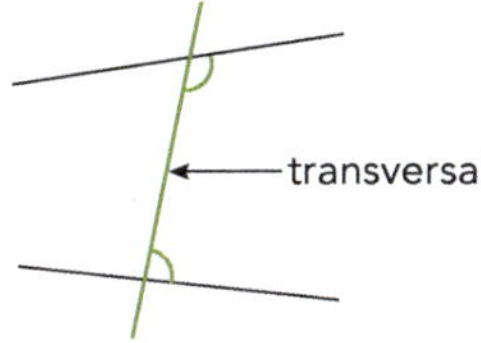

When these two lines are parallel, cointerior angles are supplementary angles (their sum is 180°).

Cointerior angles can be easily remembered as 'C' angles because of the shape they make. Cointerior angles are sometimes called allied angles.

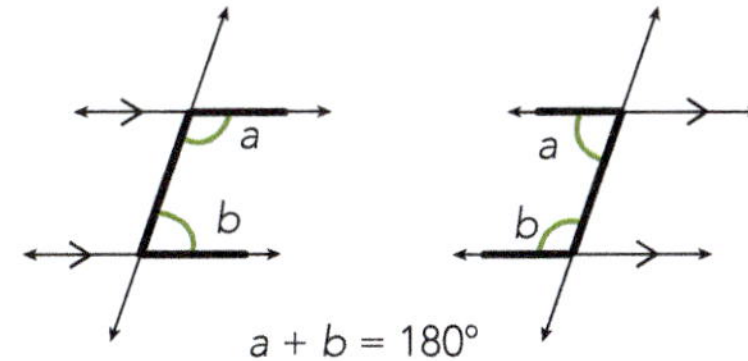

collinear

See also **line, point**

Three or more points that lie on the same straight line.

Example

A, ***B***, ***C*** and ***D*** are collinear points.

column

See also **column graph**

A vertical arrangement, or 'stack' of objects or numbers, one underneath the other.

Examples

13
5
18
27
9

column of numbers

column of books

column graph

See also **bar graph, categorical data, column**

A graph that uses columns of different lengths to represent categorical data.

Example

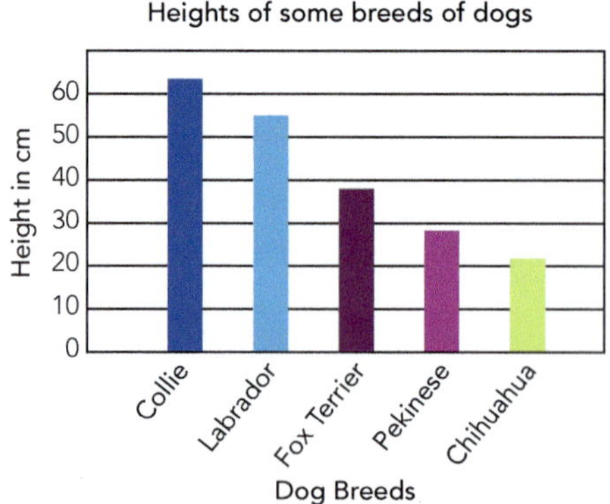

combination

See also **permutation, set, subset**

A way of arranging the objects in a group.

Example

There are four shapes in this group.

The possible pairings are:

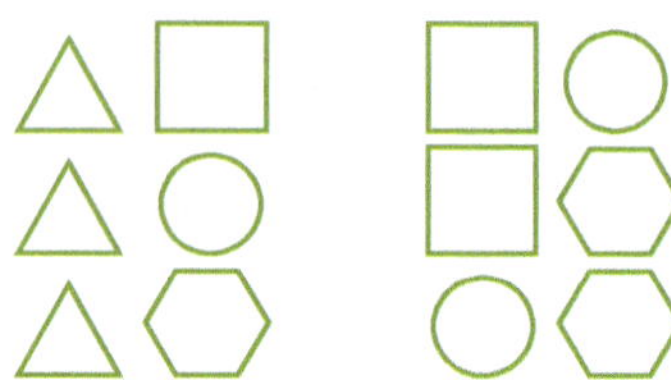

Each pairing is called a combination.

The order in which the shapes are placed in a combination is not important.

commission

See also **percentage, retainer**

A fee or percentage of sales paid to a sales person. Usually, a fixed amount called a retainer is added to the commission to ensure that some income is earned even if there are no sales.

Examples

i A car sales person receives $500 for every new car sold. The sales person receives a commission of $500 each time they sell a car.

ii A real estate agent receives 2.4% of the sale price of each house they sell. They receive 2.4% commission on the selling price of each house they sell.

common denominator

See also **denominator, fraction, lowest common denominator**

A number into which all the denominators of two or more fractions divide exactly.

Example

For the fractions $\frac{1}{2}$ and $\frac{1}{3}$, common denominators are 6, 12, 18, 24, etc.

6 is the lowest common denominator (LCD).

common factor

See also **factor, factor tree, highest common factor**

A number that divides exactly into each of the two or more numbers being considered. Common factors can be found by listing the factors of each number, then looking for numbers that appear in both lists.

Example

12 and 15

Factors of 12: 1, 2, 3, 4, 6, 12

Factors of 15: 1, 3, 5, 15

1 and 3 are common factors of 12 and 15.

(1 is a common factor to any pair of numbers).

common fraction

See **proper fraction**

commutative laws

See also **associative laws, product, sum**

1 The commutative law of addition
The order in which two or more numbers are added does not affect the answer (sum).

Examples

i $6 + 4 = 10$ or $4 + 6 = 10$

ii $(3 + 5) + 7 = 8 + 7 = 15$ or $3 + (5 + 7) = 3 + 12 = 15$

2 The commutative law of multiplication
The order in which two or more numbers are multiplied does not affect the answer (product).

Examples

i $3 \times 8 = 24$ or $8 \times 3 = 24$

ii $(4 \times 5) \times 2 = 20 \times 2 = 40$ or $4 \times (5 \times 2) = 4 \times 10 = 40$

compare

See also **ratio**

To examine two objects, quantities or situations and identify which aspects are the same and which are different.

Examples

same objects

different objects

same heights

different heights

compass

See also **bearing, direction**

An instrument which shows direction. Used in ships and aeroplanes, by bushwalkers and military personnel to navigate (find their way) to a destination.

Example

compasses (pair of)

An instrument used to draw a circle and to mark off equal lengths. Often called a compass, for short.

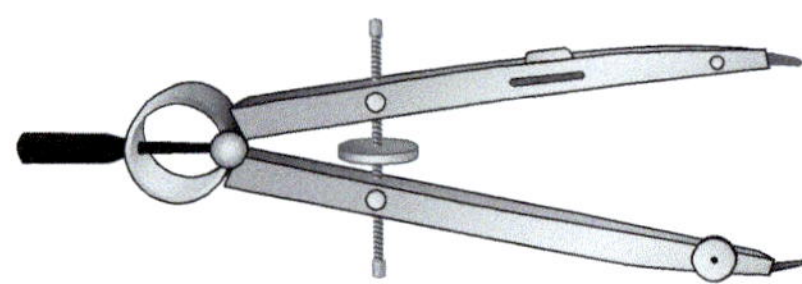

complement

See also **complementary addition, complementary angles, complementary events**

Something that completes or makes a whole.

complementary addition

See also **addition, counting on, subtraction, sum**

1 Finding the amount required to complete a sum.

Example

What has to be added to seven to make ten?

7 + □ = 10

7 + 3 = 10

Answer: Three has to be added.

2 Counting on to a higher total (as change is given after a purchase).

Example

A bag of shopping costing $17.50 was paid for with a $20 note. To calculate the change 'count on' from $17.50 to $20:

$17.50 + 50c → $18.00

$18.00 + $2 → $20.00

Change: $2.50

3 The method of 'subtracting' which converts the subtraction question to an addition question.

Example

21 – 19 = □

19 + □ = 21

Instead of taking nineteen away from twenty-one we think how much must be added to nineteen to make twenty-one.

complementary angles

See also **supplementary angles**

Two angles that together total 90°.

Example

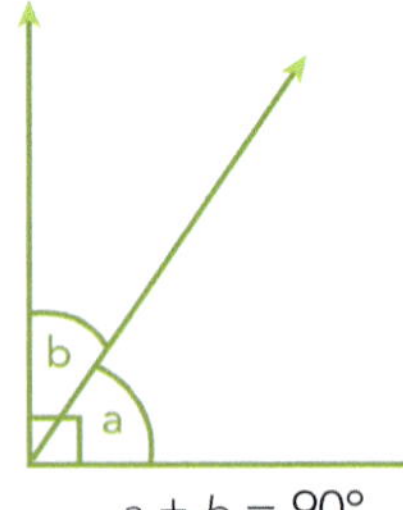

$\angle a$ and $\angle b$ are complementary.

$\angle a$ is the complement of $\angle b$ and $\angle b$ is the complement of $\angle a$.

complementary events

See also **complement, event, outcome, probability**

An event can occur or not occur. These two possible situations are called complementary events and contain all possible outcomes.

Examples

- i Rolling a 6 on a die, and not rolling a 6
- ii Drawing an ace from a pack of cards, and not drawing an ace
- iii Winning a game of table tennis, and not winning the game

Two complementary events can be written as A and A′ (called 'A dash' or 'A prime'). We say that A′ is the complement of A.

The sum of the probabilities of complementary events is 1.

$Pr(A) + Pr(A') = 1$

complex fraction

See also **numerator, denominator**

A fraction whose numerator, denominator, or both, are fractions.

Examples

$\dfrac{\frac{1}{2}}{5}$ $\quad \dfrac{3}{\frac{4}{7}}$ $\quad \dfrac{\frac{1}{2}}{\frac{3}{4}}$ $\quad \dfrac{\frac{a}{b}}{\frac{c}{d}}$

Note: Because the fraction bar '—' means 'divide', we simplify a complex fraction by dividing the fractions.

Example

$\dfrac{\frac{1}{2}}{\frac{2}{3}}$

Divide $\frac{1}{2}$ by $\frac{2}{3}$.

$$\frac{1}{2} \div \frac{2}{3}$$
$$= \frac{1}{2} \times \frac{3}{2}$$
$$= \frac{3}{4}$$

composite number

See also **factors, prime number**

A number with factors other than itself and one. A number that is *not* a prime number.

Examples

i $12 = 3 \times 4$
$\quad = 3 \times 2 \times 2$
$33 = 3 \times 11$

Both twelve and thirty-three are composite numbers.

ii $17 = 17 \times 1 \qquad 23 = 23 \times 1$

Seventeen and twenty-three are not composite numbers.

Numbers which have no other factors except themselves and one, such as seventeen and twenty-three, are called prime numbers.

Every whole number greater than one is either:

- a prime number

  2, 3, 5, 7, 11 …

  or

- a composite number

  4, 6, 8, 9, 10, 12, 14 ….

composite shapes

See also **shapes, area**

Plane shapes that are made of two or more shapes.

composite shapes continued ▶

Example

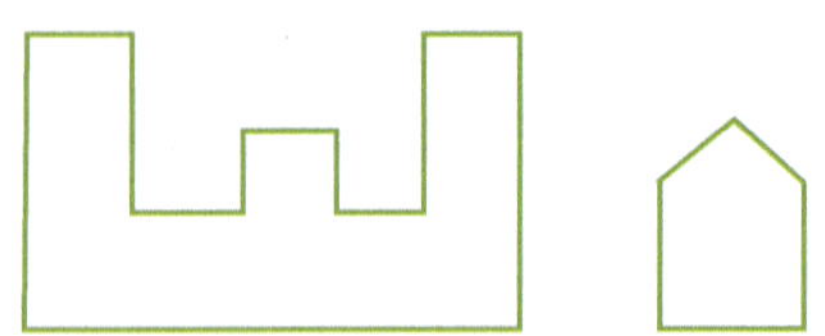

To calculate the area of a composite shape, divide it into simple shapes. Find the area of each shape, then add those to find the area of the composite shape.

Example

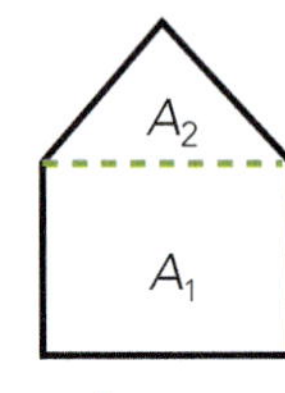

Area = $A_1 + A_2$

compound interest

See also **interest, period, principal**

Interest that is added on a regular basis (such as yearly, monthly or daily) to the principal amount of an investment or loan. This increased amount is then used as the principal for the next interest calculation.

The compound interest is calculated by finding the difference between the amount owed or accrued at the end of the time period and the principal amount.

$$I = A - P$$

The formula for calculating the value of an investment or loan at the end of a set time period is:

$$A = P(1 + r)^n$$

where A is the amount owing or earned at the end of the period, P is the principal (original amount borrowed or loaned), r is the interest rate for the period, expressed as a decimal, and n is the number of compounding periods (e.g. number of years, months or days).

The interest rate, r, is usually expressed as an annual rate. It needs to be converted to the equivalent rate for the compounding period, e.g. an annual rate of 6% gives a monthly rate of $\frac{6}{12} = 0.5\%$.

Example

$1000 invested at 5% for 4 years compounding annually = $1215.51

$1000 invested at 5% for 4 years compounding monthly = $1220.90

$1000 invested at 5% for 4 years compounding daily = $1221.39 (assume 365 days in a year)

computation

See also **abacus, basic operations, calculator, table**

Using the four basic operations of addition, subtraction, multiplication and division to find an answer to a problem. These operations can be performed mentally, using written methods (pen and paper), or with the help of calculating aids such as an abacus, tables, calculators or computers.

compute

See **calculate**

concave

See also **convex**

A shape that is hollowed or rounded inward like the inside of a cave.

Examples

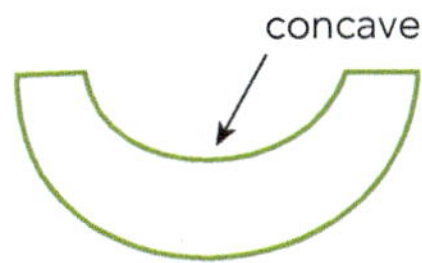

concentric circles

See also **annulus, circle, plane**

Circles that are in the same plane and have the same centre are concentric.

Example

concurrent lines

See also **intersect, parallel lines**

Lines that intersect at the same point.

Example

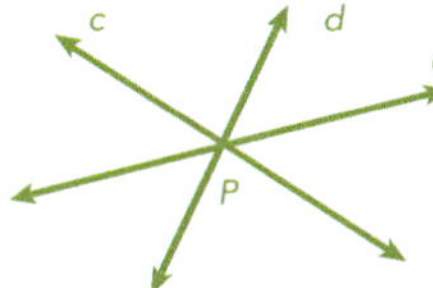

Lines *c*, *d* and *e* are concurrent. They intersect at point *P*.

cone

See also **right 3D shape, solid**

A solid which has a circular base and comes to a point (vertex) at the top (apex), similar in shape to an ice-cream cone. Cones that have the vertex directly above the centre of the circular base are called 'right cones'.

Examples

congruent (Symbol: ≡)

See also **matching angles, matching sides, similar, transformation**

Exactly equal. Matching exactly. Two figures are congruent if they have exactly the same shape and are exactly the same size. One figure can undergo one or more transformations (reflection, rotation or translation) and end up positioned exactly on top of the other.

Examples

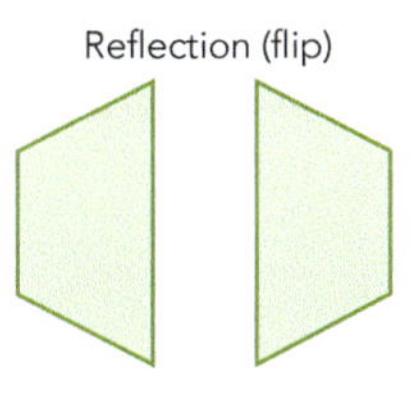

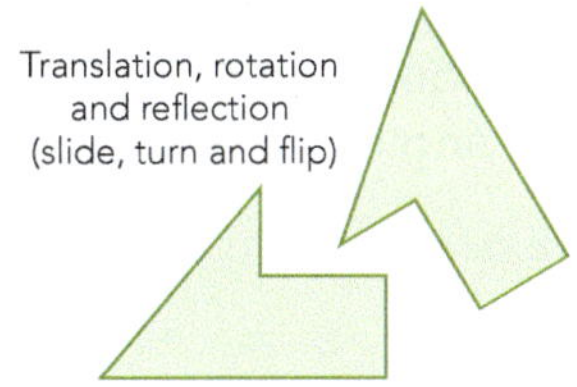

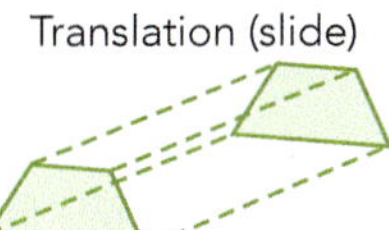

congruent triangles

See also **congruent, hypotenuse, matching angles, matching sides**

Two triangles are congruent if they are exactly the same shape and size, regardless of their position or orientation. All matching angles and side lengths are equal.

Four tests can be applied to determine whether two triangles are congruent.

1 Side, Side, Side (SSS)
All pairs of corresponding sides are the same length.

Example

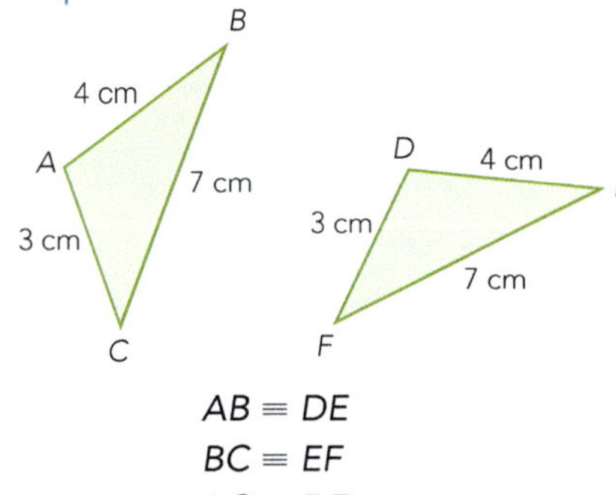

$AB \equiv DE$
$BC \equiv EF$
$AC \equiv DF$
Therefore, $\Delta ABC \equiv \Delta DEF$ (SSS)

2 Side, Angle, Side (SAS)
Two sides of equal length and the angle formed by the two sides is equal (we call this the included angle).

Example

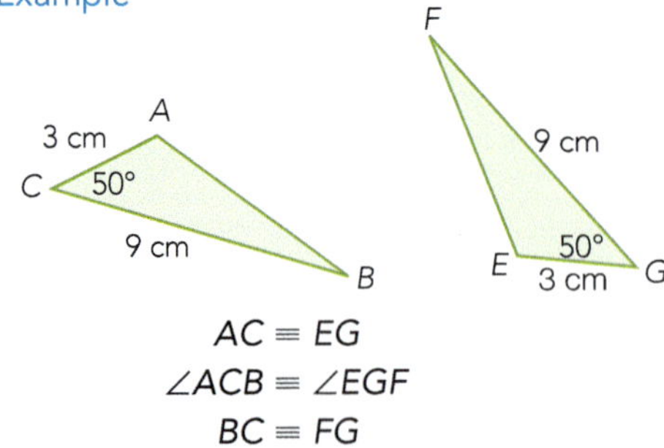

$AC \equiv EG$
$\angle ACB \equiv \angle EGF$
$BC \equiv FG$
Therefore, $\Delta ABC \equiv \Delta EFG$ (SAS)

3 Angle, Angle, Side (AAS)
Two matching angles are the same size and one pair of matching sides are the same length.

Example

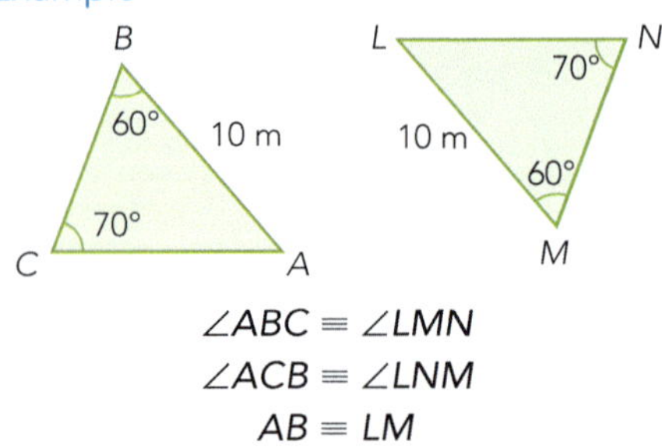

$\angle ABC \equiv \angle LMN$
$\angle ACB \equiv \angle LNM$
$AB \equiv LM$
Therefore, $\Delta ABC \equiv \Delta LMN$ (AAS)

4 Right angle, Hypotenuse, Side (RHS)
In a pair of right angled triangles, matching hypotenuses are equal in length as well as a second pair of matching sides.

Example

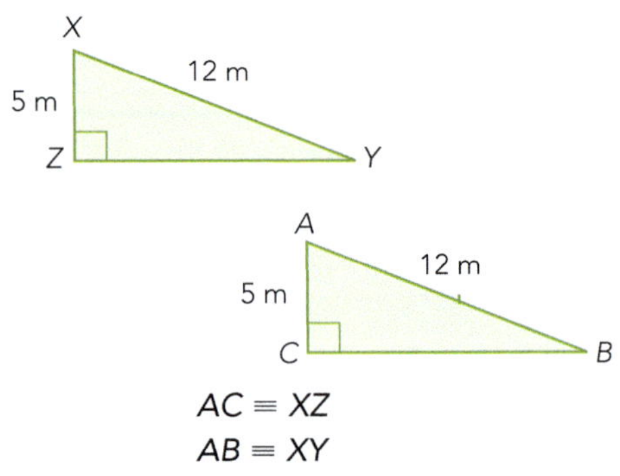

$AC \equiv XZ$
$AB \equiv XY$
Therefore, $\Delta ABC \equiv \Delta XYZ$ (RHS)

conic section

See also **circle, ellipse, parabola**

A figure (circle, ellipse or parabola) formed when a right cone is cut by a plane.

Example

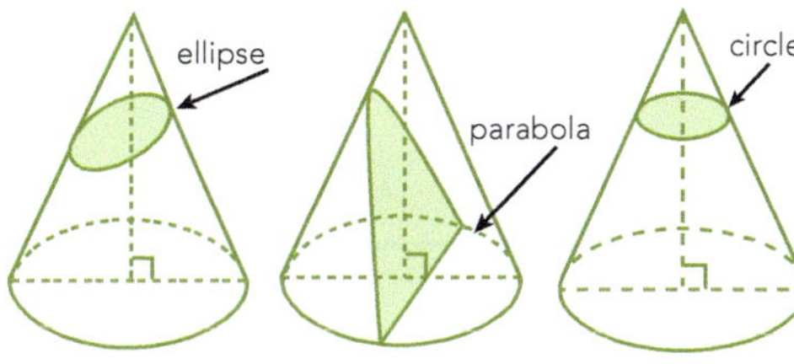

conjecture

See also **natural number, prime number**

A theory that has not been proved but seems to be correct as no contradictions have been found.

Example

Goldbach's conjecture states: 'Every even, natural number is equal to the sum of two prime numbers'.

$2 = 1 + 1$ $\quad 10 = 3 + 7$
$4 = 2 + 2$ $\quad 12 = 5 + 7$ or $1 + 11$
$6 = 3 + 3$ $\quad 24 = 11 + 13$
$8 = 1 + 7$ $\quad 42 = 19 + 23$

consecutive numbers

See also **sequence**

Numbers that follow each other in a sequence.

Example

1 2 3 4 5 6 7 8

conservation of area

See also **area**

Retaining the same area.

Examples

i The three triangles have the same area.

$$A = \tfrac{1}{2} \times 2\text{ cm} \times 2.5\text{ cm}$$
$$= 2.5\text{ cm}^2$$

Even though their shapes are different, they still have the same base length and the same height.

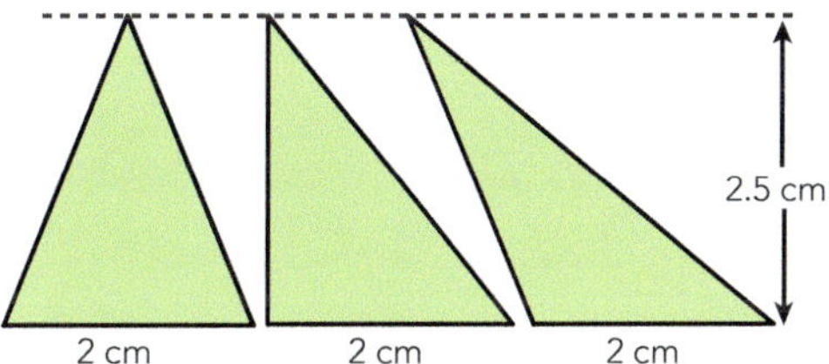

ii The three shapes have the same area of 3 cm^2.

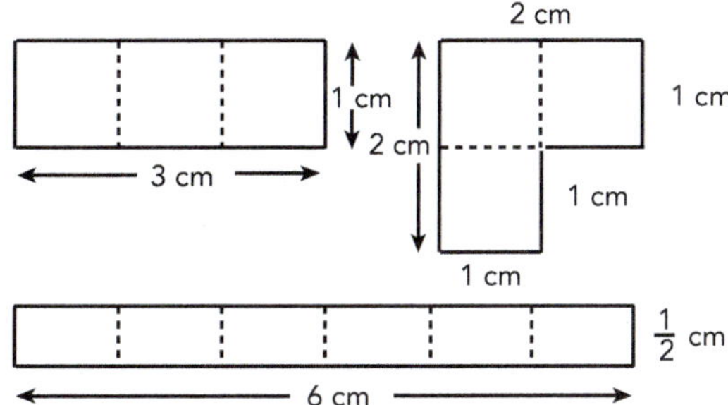

constant

See also **variable**

A term that always has the same value, unlike a variable.

Example

6 is the constant in the algebraic expression $2c + 6$.

continuous data

See also **data, discrete data**

Data that consists of measurements that can take on any decimal value along a continuous scale.

Example

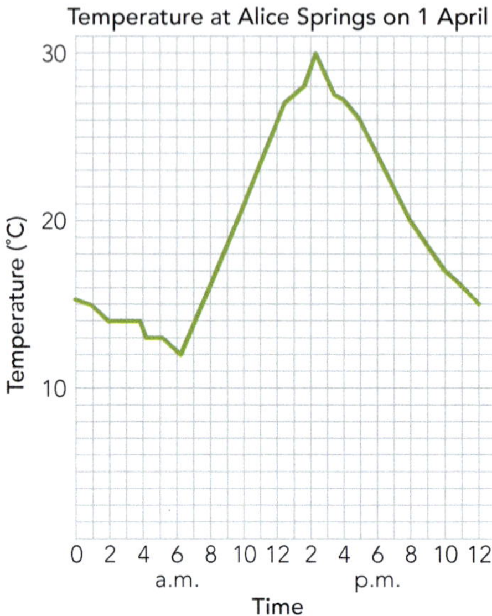

Here the data being measured is temperature. Other examples of continuous data are mass and distance. Whilst the data value may be any decimal value on the scale, the accuracy of the data recorded depends on the accuracy of the equipment used to measure it.

continuous variable

See also **continuous data, discrete data, discrete numerical variable**

A numerical variable in statistics that can take any value within a given range. Data associated with this variable is measured not counted.

Examples

The heights of students in a class.
The time taken by each student to run 100 m.

converging lines

See also **perspective**

Two or more lines that meet at the same point.

Example

converse

See also **number sentence, proof, prove**

A statement that is the reverse of another statement. Some converses are true while others are not.

Example

'All monkeys are mammals' is true but its converse, 'All mammals are monkeys', is not true.

However, 'In a triangle with sides *a*, *b* and *c*, if the angle opposite side *c* is a right angle, then $a^2 + b^2 = c^2$' is true and its converse 'In a triangle with sides *a*, *b* and *c*, if $a^2 + b^2 = c^2$ then the angle opposite side *c* is a right angle' is also true.

convex

See also **concave**

Shaped like the outside of a circle or a sphere. The opposite of concave.

Example

coordinates

See also **axis, Cartesian plane, intersection, ordered pair, origin**

A pair of numbers or letters that show the position of a point on the Cartesian plane. The first number is always the *x*-coordinate (the distance along the *x*-axis, to the left or right), the second is the *y*-coordinate (the distance along the *y*-axis, up or down).

Examples

i Each point on the plane is given an ordered pair of numbers, written in brackets.

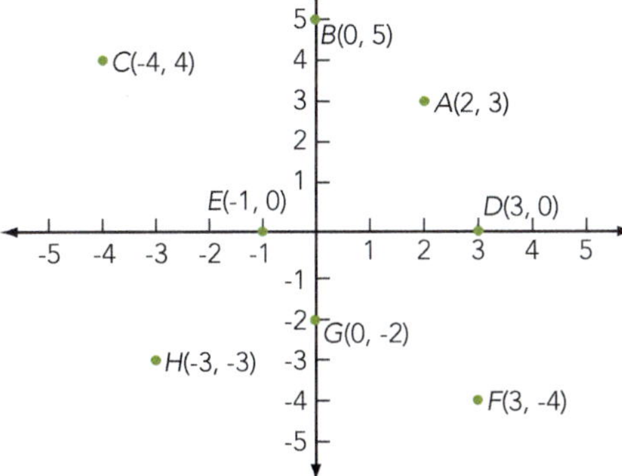

ii Many types of maps use a slightly different coordinate system, known as an 'alphanumeric grid'. Letters are used instead of numbers along the horizontal axis. The coordinate consists of a letter and a number, and refers to a grid square rather than a specific point.

The position of Judith Avenue is B3.

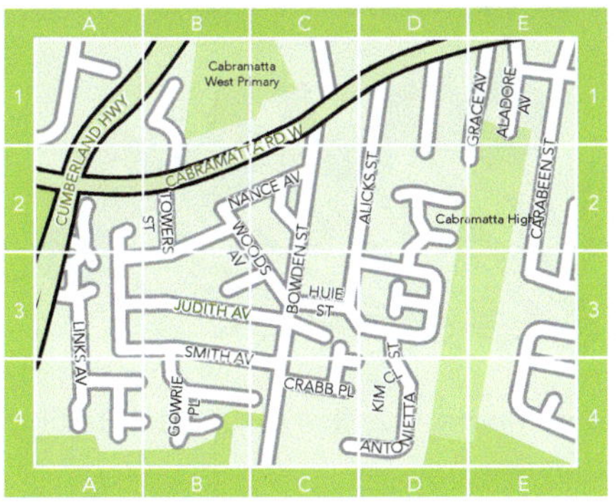

coplanar

Points, lines or intervals that lie in the same plane.

Example

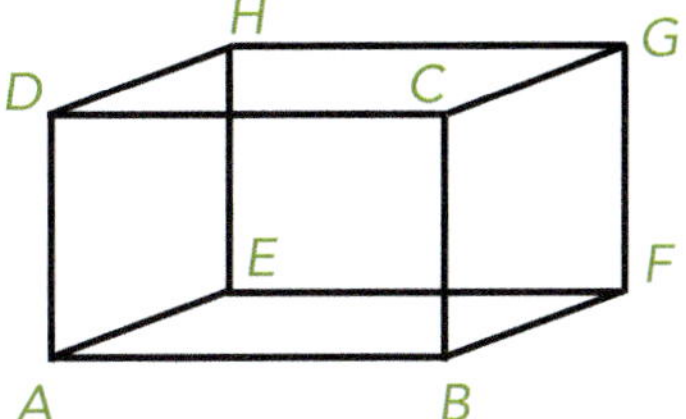

C, *D*, *G* and *H* are coplanar points.

AB and *CG* are not coplanar.

coprime

See also **composite number, factor, factor tree, highest common factor (HCF), prime factor, prime number**

Numbers that have one as the highest common factor (HCF). They therefore have no other common factors.

Example

2 and 3 are coprime.

correspondence

See **many-to-one correspondence, many-to-many correspondence, one-to-many correspondence, one-to-one correspondence**

corresponding angles

See also **angles, parallel lines, transversal**

When two or more lines are crossed by a transversal (another line), pairs of corresponding angles are formed. The angles in each pair lie on the same side of the transversal, and both lie either above or below the other two lines.

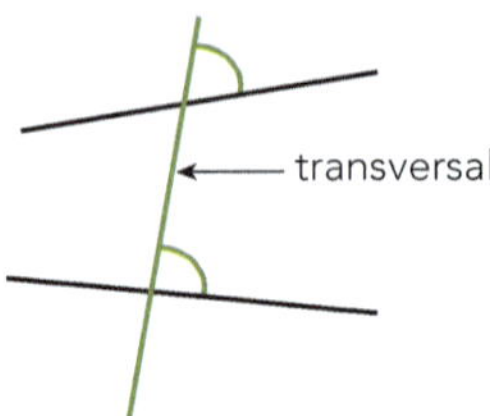

When these two lines are parallel, corresponding angles are equal. They can be easily remembered as 'F' angles because of the shape they make.

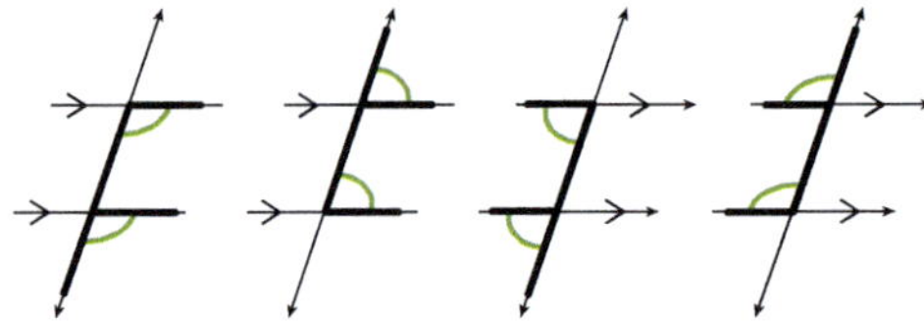

cosine

See also **sine, tangent, trigonometric ratios, unit circle**

One of the three basic trigonometric ratios. In a right-angled triangle, the cosine of an angle θ (the Greek letter 'theta') is the ratio of the side adjacent to the angle and the hypotenuse.

Cosine is usually abbreviated to 'cos' and the ratio written as $\cos\theta = \frac{\text{adjacent}}{\text{hypotenuse}}, \frac{\text{adj}}{\text{hyp}}$ or simply $\frac{A}{H}$.

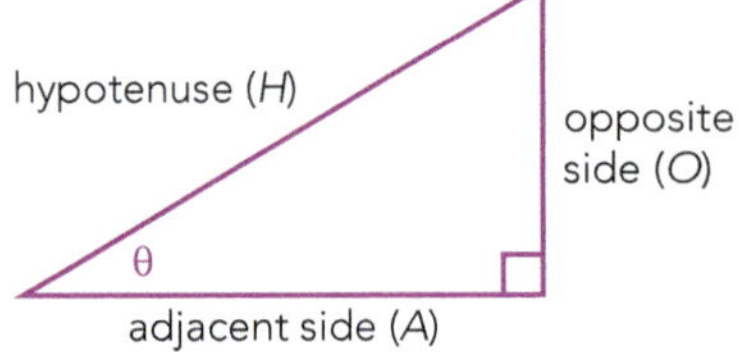

In unit circle trigonometry, cos θ is the *x*-coordinate of a point *P* on the unit circle, where the position of *P* is determined by the angle θ.

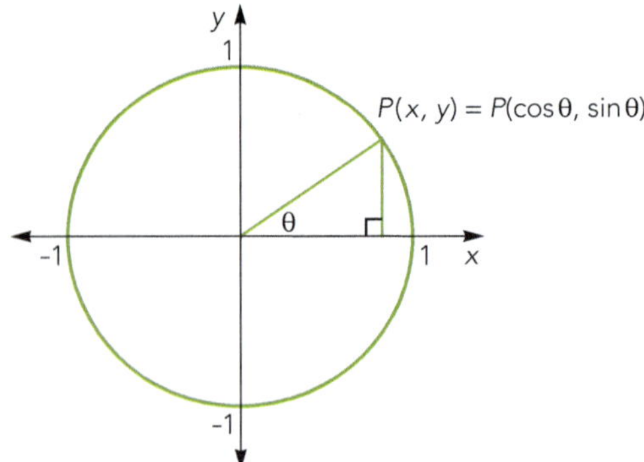

cost price

See also **selling price**

Price at which something is produced or bought.

Example

A car dealer buys a car for $10 000. The cost price of the car is $10 000.

Julia makes jam to sell at her market stall. It costs her $18 to make 12 jars of jam. The cost price of each jar is $1.50 (18 ÷ 12).

counting

See also **cardinal number, sequence, set**

Giving one number to every item in a set. These numbers are in a sequence.

Example

The numbers 1, 2, 3, 4, 5 … are counting numbers.

counting number

See also **cardinal number, number**

A member of the set of numbers used in counting: {1, 2, 3, 4 ...}.

Note: zero is not a counting number.

counting on

Determining the total number of objects in a collection without needing to always begin counting at the number '1'.

Example

A child has counted from 1 to 4 to determine there are four pieces of fruit in a bowl. After five more pieces are added, she then 'counts on' from 4: '5, 6, 7, 8, 9', to determine that there are now nine pieces of fruit in total.

counting system

See also **decimal place-value system**

A way of finding out how many objects there are.

credit card

See also **debit card, interest**

A card issued by a bank or other financial institution that allows the user to obtain credit from the institution in order to get a cash advance or pay for goods or services. This means that the bank or institution loans you the money, or pays the seller on your behalf. You then must pay back the bank. If a repayment is not made within a certain period, interest is charged. (A certain number of days interest free is usually applied to purchases.)

A limit on the amount of credit available is applied by the bank or financial institution.

Example

cross-section

See also **face, front view, plan, plane, section, side view, uniform cross-section**

The face that is created when a solid is cut through by a plane.

Example

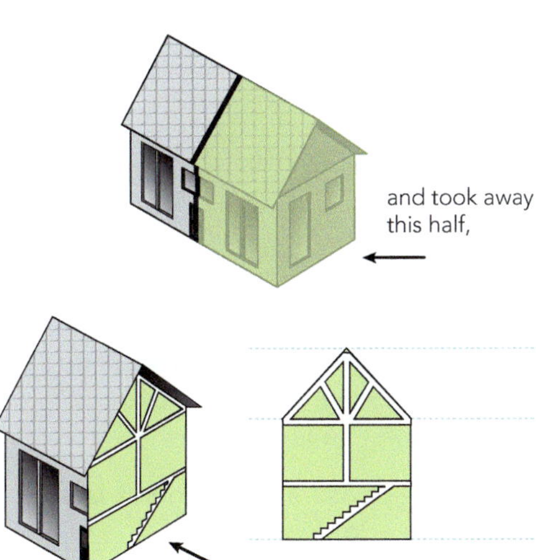

cube

See also **cuboid, face, hexahedron, solid**

A solid, shaped like a box, with twelve edges equal in length, six square faces equal in area and eight vertices (corners). A cube is a type of cuboid. It is one of only five regular polyhedrons, known as the Platonic solids. Another name for a cube is a hexahedron.

Examples

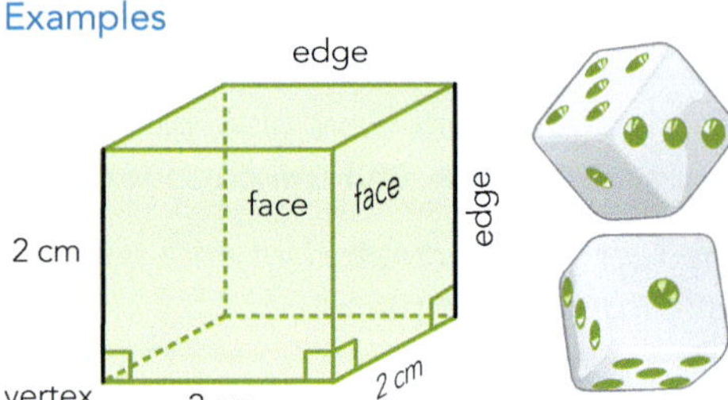

This is a diagram of a 2 cm cube.

cube root

See also **square root**

The cube root of a number is a number that, when multiplied by itself and itself again, produces the original number. A cube root is written using a cube root sign: $\sqrt[3]{\ }$

Example

3 is the cube root of 27.

$$3 \times 3 \times 3 = 27$$

so $\sqrt[3]{27} = 3$

cubic centimetre (Symbol: cm^3)

See also **capacity, cube, unit of measurement, volume**

A unit for measuring volume. It is a cube with edges of 1 cm.

Example

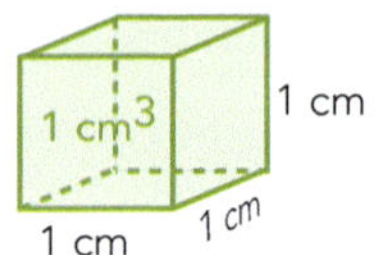

1 cm^3 has a capacity of 1 millilitre.

cubic metre (Symbol: m^3)

See also **capacity, unit of measurement, volume**

A unit for measuring volume. A cube whose edges are 1 metre long has a volume of 1 cubic metre.

Example

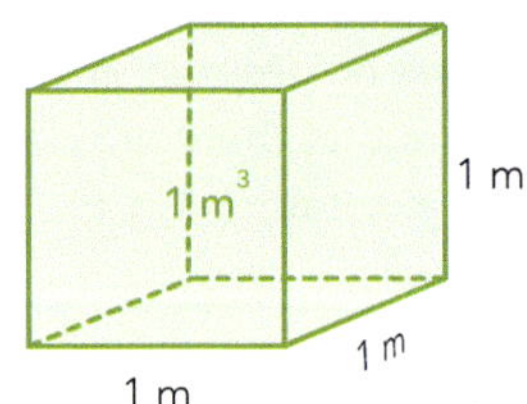

$$\begin{aligned} 1\ m^3 &= 1\ m \times 1\ m \times 1\ m \\ &= 100\ cm \times 100\ cm \times 100\ cm \\ &= 1\ 000\ 000\ cm^3 \end{aligned}$$

1 m^3 has a capacity of 1 kilolitre.

cubic number

See also **index, index notation, power of a number, square number**

A number that has been multiplied by itself, then multiplied by itself again. A number raised to the power of three.

Example

4^3 ← index

↑ base

$$\begin{aligned} 4^3 &= 4 \times 4 \times 4 \\ &= 64 \end{aligned}$$

We read it as '4 cubed' or '4 to the third power'.

cubic unit

See also **cubic centimetre, cubic metre, volume**

A measure of volume.

cuboid

See also **cube, face, hexahedron, prism**

A rectangular solid such as a shoe box. A prism with rectangular and/or square faces. It has twelve edges, six faces and eight corners. The opposite faces are the same shape and size.

Examples

These objects are cuboids.

cumulative frequency

See also **cumulative frequency curve, frequency**

The running total of frequencies; the sum of a particular frequency and any of the frequencies below it. This is often represented in a cumulative frequency histogram, where each column represents a frequency added to the total of the frequencies before it.

cumulative frequency curve

See also **data, histogram, statistics**

A graph created when the end points of a cumulative frequency histogram are joined.

Example

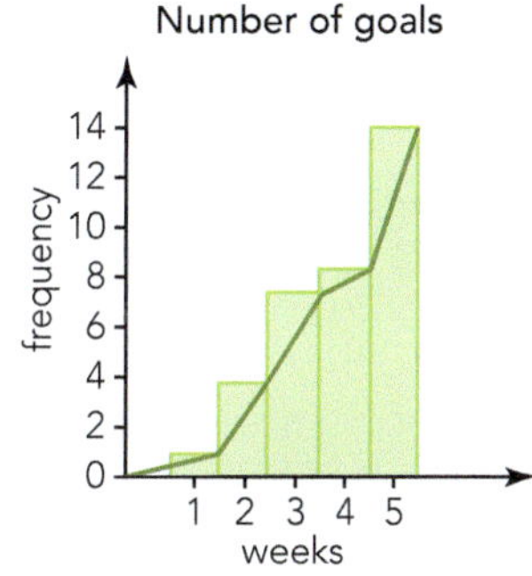

curve

See also **closed curve, open curve**

A line of which no part is straight. There are open curves and closed curves.

Examples

open curves

closed curves

cycle

A system that repeats itself in regular time periods.

Example

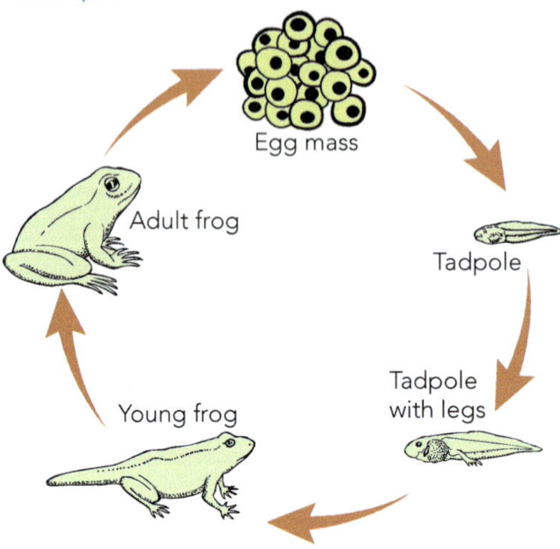

cylinder

See also **capacity, right 3D shape, uniform cross-section**

A solid with two circular faces equal in area at right angles to a curved surface that joins them. A cylinder is similar to a prism in that it has a uniform cross-section.

Examples

Cans are common examples of cylinders.

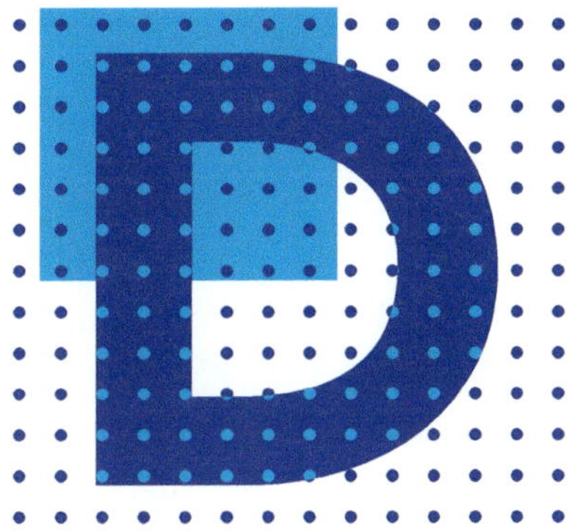

data

A general term used to describe a collection of facts, observations, measurements or symbols.

Example

Students' scores in a maths test were 15, 16, 18, 19, 19, 20, 21, 21, 22 marks.

data display

See also **box plot, column graph, dot plot, frequency table, graph, line graph, sector graph, stem plot**

A visual way of organising or presenting data. This might be in the form of a graph, such as a column, bar, sector or line graph, or a table, such as a frequency table. Other forms of data display include dot plots, stem plots and box plots.

Examples

Column graph

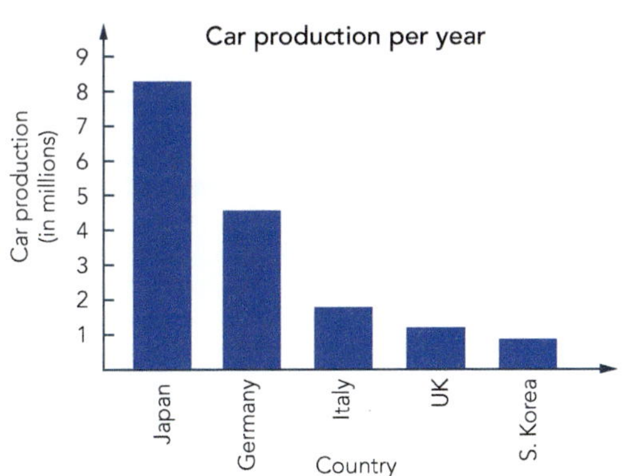

Bar graph

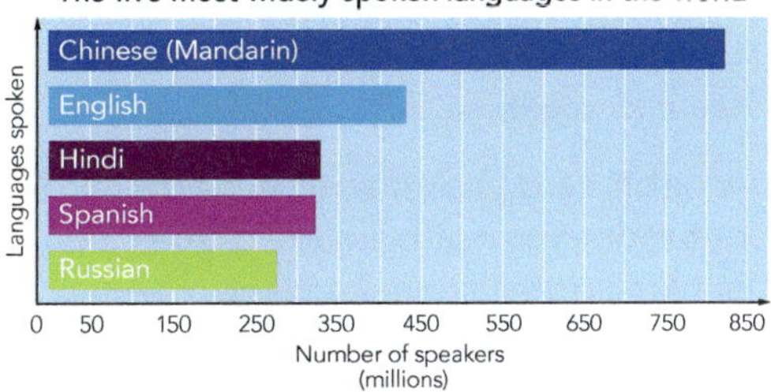

Sector (pie) graph

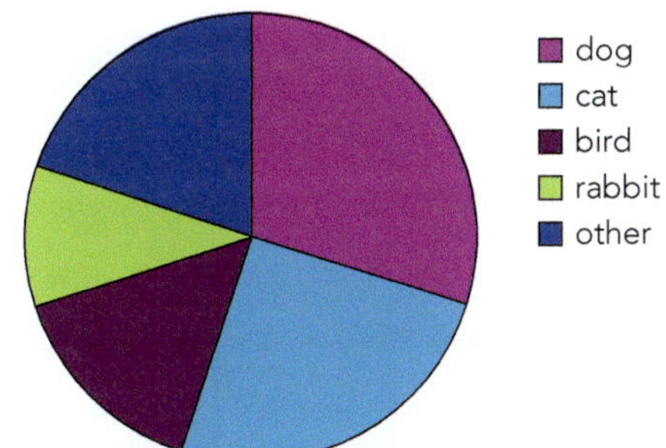

Favourite pets of Year 7 students

Line graph

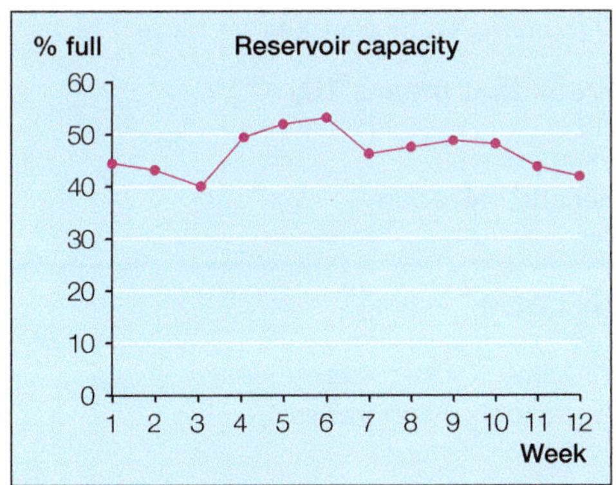

date

Specified time: day, month or year, at which something takes place.

Example
1 January 1901 was the date that the Commonwealth of Australia was formed.

day

The 24-hour period it takes the Earth to turn once on its axis.

debit card

See also **credit card**

A debit card is similar to a credit card but money is not borrowed from a bank or other financial institution. Instead it is deducted from an account into which the cardholder has already deposited money.

deca

See also **decade, decagon, decahedron, Decimal system prefixes** on page 192

Prefix that means 10.

Examples
decade, decagon

decade

See also **deca**

A period of ten years.

decagon

See also **deca, polygon**

A polygon with ten sides.

Example

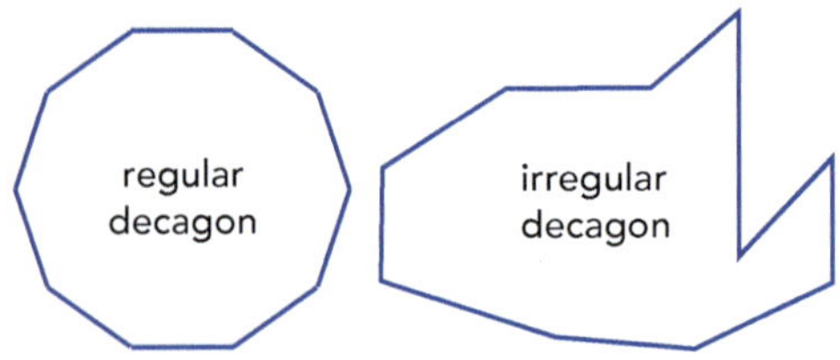

decahedron

See also **frustum, polyhedron**

A polyhedron with ten faces.

Example
This decahedron has been made by joining two pyramids and cutting their tops off.

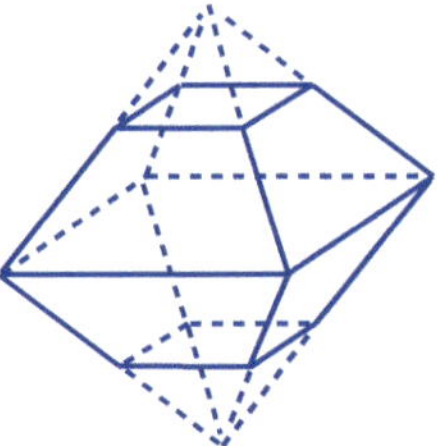

deci

See also **decimal, decimal fraction, decimal place, decimal place-value system, Decimal system prefixes** on page 192

Prefix that means one-tenth.

decimal

See also **decimal place-value system**

Containing ten parts.

decimal fraction

See also **decimal place-value system**

A fraction written as a decimal. Before it can be converted to a decimal fraction, a fraction must be rewritten as a fraction with a denominator that is a power of 10 (10, 100, 1000, etc.).

Examples

$\frac{1}{10} = 0.1$

simple fraction — decimal fraction

$\frac{11}{25} = \frac{44}{100} = 0.44$

simple fraction — decimal fraction

decimal places

See also **decimal**

The number of digits after the decimal point of a number.

Example

8.456 has three decimal places.
8.4567 has four decimal places.

decimal place-value system

See also **base, decimal point, place value**

A numeration system with ten as a base for grouping. Commonly called the 'base ten' system.

10^6	10^5	10^4	10^3	10^2	10^1	10^0		10^{-1}	10^{-2}	10^{-3}
1000000	100000	10000	1000	100	10	1	.	$\frac{1}{10}$	$\frac{1}{100}$	$\frac{1}{1000}$
millions	hundred thousands	ten thousands	thousands	hundreds	tens	units		tenths	hundredths	thousandths

decimal point

See also **point**

A point that separates a decimal fraction from the whole number. A comma is used in Europe.

Example

32.4

decimal point

7,62

decimal system

See **decimal place-value system**

decrease

See also **increase, progression**

Make smaller. A positive number can be decreased by:

- subtracting a positive number
- adding a negative number
- dividing by a number greater than 1
- multiplying by a number less than 1.

Examples

i Decrease this length by 2 cm.

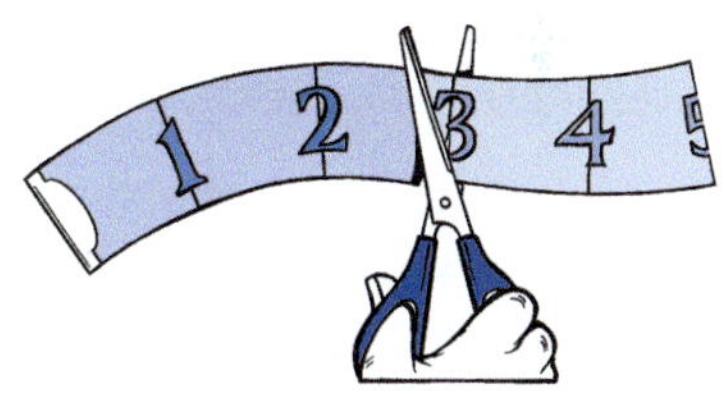

5 cm – 2 cm = 3 cm

ii Decrease $100 by a factor of five.

$100 ÷ 5 = $20

define

See also **pronumeral, variable**

To identify the variable in a given situation and represent it with a symbol or a pronumeral.

Example

A rectangle has two variables, length and width. The length can be defined by the pronumeral *l* and the width can be defined by the pronumeral *w*.
This is usually written as 'let l = length' and 'let w = width'.

degree (Symbol: °)

See also **angle, degree Celsius, geometry, temperature, unit of measurement**

1 In geometry, a degree is a unit for measuring angles.

Examples

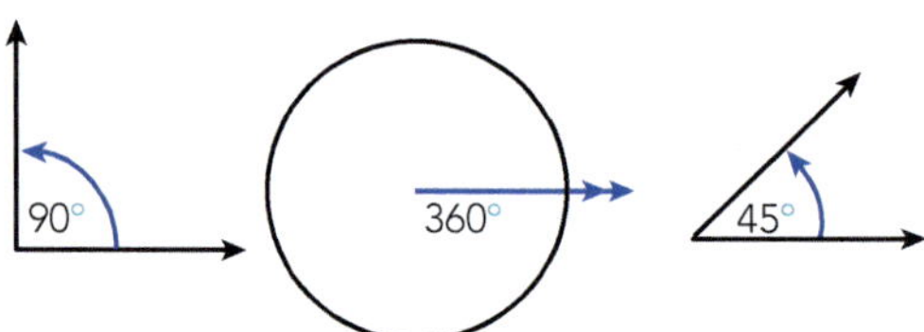

1 degree is divided into 60 minutes
1° (degree) = 60′ (minutes)
1 minute is divided into 60 seconds
1′ (minute) = 60″ (seconds)

(Don't confuse these with the symbols for feet and inches used in the imperial system of measurement.)

2 The unit for measuring temperature.

degree Celsius (Symbol: °C)

See also **temperature, thermometer**

The common unit for measuring temperature (formerly degree Centigrade).

Example

The boiling point of water is 100 °C. The freezing point of water is 0 °C.

degree of a polynomial

See also **algebraic expression, polynomial, power**

The degree of a polynomial is the value of the highest power in the expression.

Example

The degree of $3x^5 - 2x^3 + 4x - 8$ is 5.

denominator

See also **fraction, numerator**

The number written below the line in a fraction; it tells how many parts there are in the whole.

Example

This circle has been divided into 6 equal parts.

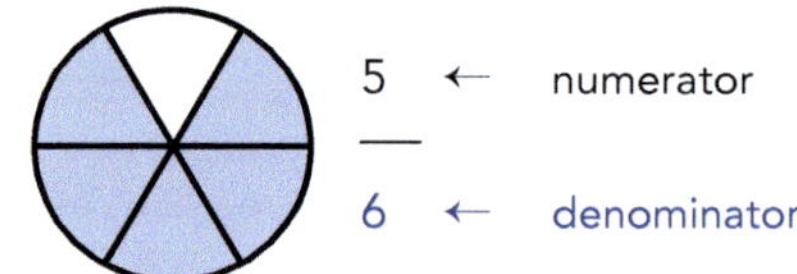

In $\frac{5}{6}$ the denominator is 6.

density

See also **mass, volume**

The ratio of mass to volume. Usually expressed as g/cm^3 or kg/m^3.

A dense material feels heavy for its size. Lead and gold are dense metals.

Example

The density of water at 4 °C is 1 g/cm^3 (1 gram per cubic centimetre).

dependent variable

See also **bivariate data, formula, independent variable, variable (statistics)**

In algebra and in statistics, the dependent variable is the value that changes as a result of changes in the independent variable. A scatter plot or a formula can show the relationship between the variables. The *x*-axis is used to plot the independent variable. The *y*-axis is used to plot the dependent variable.

Example

The number of litres in the petrol tank of a car as the car travels is the dependent variable, and the distance travelled is the independent variable. The decrease in the amount of fuel is a result of travelling further and further.

deposit

See also **withdrawal**

An amount of money paid into an account held at a bank or other financial institution.

Example

An account has $200 in it. A deposit of $50 is made. The account now has $250 in it.

depreciation

See also **appreciation, interest, principal**

A decrease in the value of an object over time.

Example

A car bought for $24 000 was sold a year later for $19 500. The depreciation in 12 months was $4500.

depth

How deep something is. Measurement from the top down, from the front to the back or from the surface inwards.

Examples

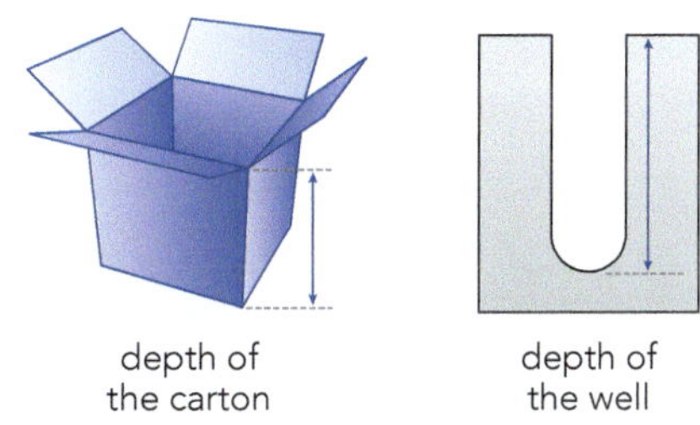

depth of the carton

depth of the well

descending order

See also **ascending order, decrease**

Going down or decreasing in value.

Example

The following lengths have been arranged in descending order:

5.7 m 4.9 m 3.8 m 1.25 m

↑ longest ↑ shortest

diagonal

See also **polygon**

A line segment joining two corners that are not next to each other in any polygon.

Examples

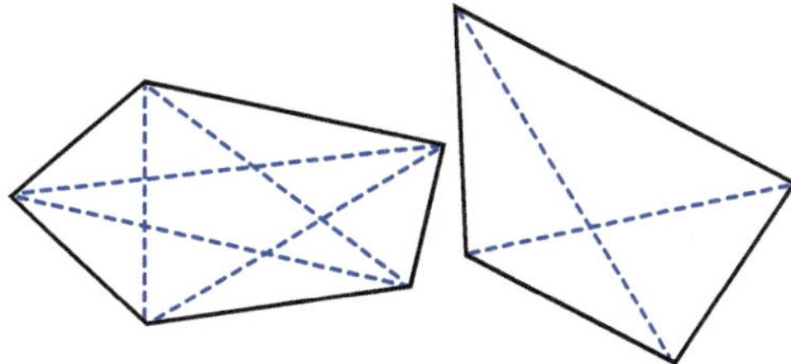

The dotted lines are diagonals.

diagram
See also **figure**

A name given to pictures or sketches of geometric figures. It is also used for simplified drawings which explain or describe other things.

Examples

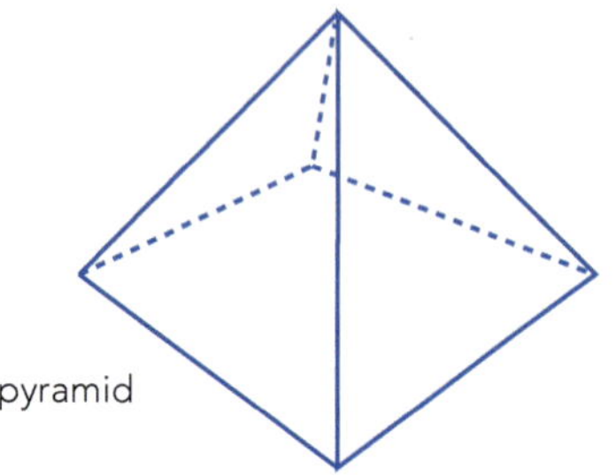

diameter
See also **chord, circle, circumference, line segment, radius**

A line segment joining two points of a circle and passing through the centre of the circle. The diameter is the same length as two radii (*r*).

Example

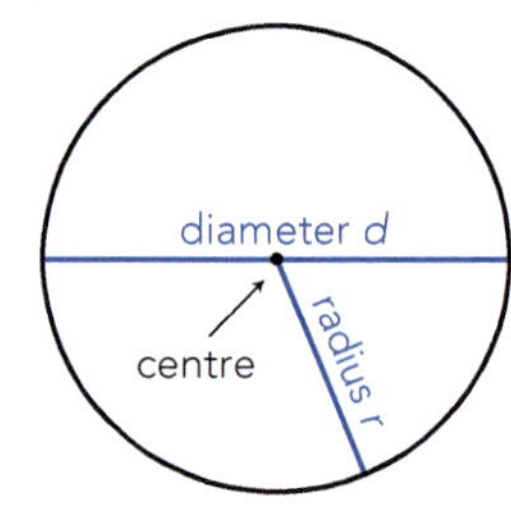

$d = 2r$

die (Plural: dice)

A regular polyhedron, usually a cube, marked with a certain number of spots or numerals. Used in games.

Examples

Some dice have more than six faces.

difference
See also **minuend, subtract, subtraction, subtrahend**

The amount by which two numbers differ.

Example

$10 - 3 = 7$

minuend ↑ subtrahend ↑ difference ↑

The difference between ten and three is seven.

digit
See also **place value**

The individual numerals 0, 1, 2, 3, … 9 that are used to form numbers.

Examples
4 is a one-digit number.
56 is a two-digit number.
813 is a three-digit number.

digital clock

See also **a.m., analogue clock, p.m., time interval**

A clock or a watch that shows time by displaying first a number to represent the hour then the number of minutes past the hour. It has no clock hands.

Example

This clock shows nine forty or twenty to ten.

dimension

See also **one-dimensional, plane, space, three-dimensional, two-dimensional**

A property that can be measured, related to plane and space.

1 One-dimensional (1D) objects have only length.

Examples
lines, curves

line
curve
one dimension

2 Two-dimensional (2D) objects have length and width. They are plane figures (flat shapes).

Examples
plane figures, such as polygons, circles

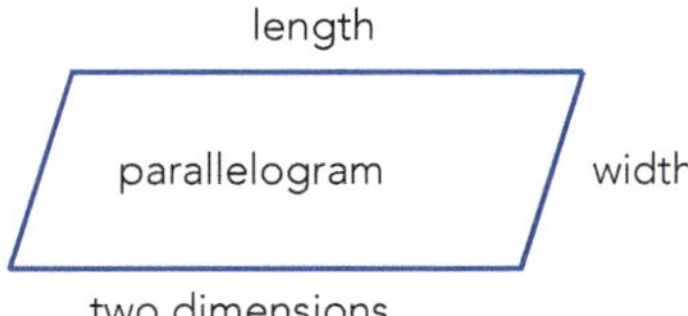

3 Three-dimensional (3D) objects have length, width and height. They are solid objects.

Examples
solids, such as cubes, pyramids

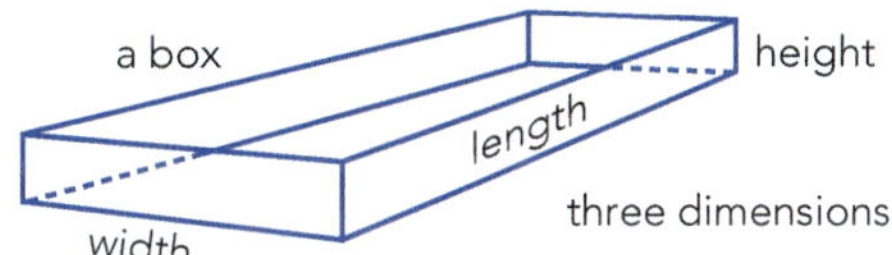

Note: A point (dot) has no dimensions.

direct proportion

See **proportion**

directed numbers

See also **integers**

Numbers that are positive or negative, or zero. Directed numbers that are positive or negative whole numbers, and zero, are called integers. Directed numbers can be shown on a number line or axis.

Example
Show -7, -2, 0, 3 and 6 on a number line.

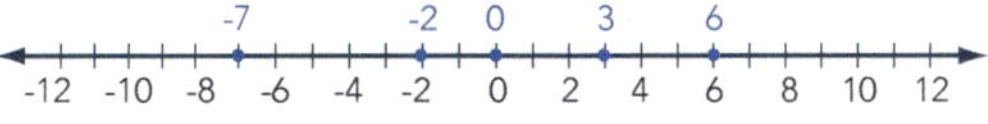

direction

See also **anticlockwise, clockwise, compass**

1 The way to move.

Examples

Left, right, up, down, above, below, inside, outside, near, from behind, forwards, backwards, etc.

2 Compass directions.

Examples

north	(N)
east	(E)
south	(S)
west	(W)
north-east	(NE)
south-east	(SE)
south-west	(SW)
north-west	(NW)

discount

See also **percentage, selling price**

If the price of something is reduced, it is sold at a discount.

Note: Discounts are often offered as a percentage of the selling price.

Example

A coat normally sold for $60 is sold for $48 after a discount of $12 is given.

discrete data

See also **continuous data, data**

A set of data that can be counted. They are exact values.

Example

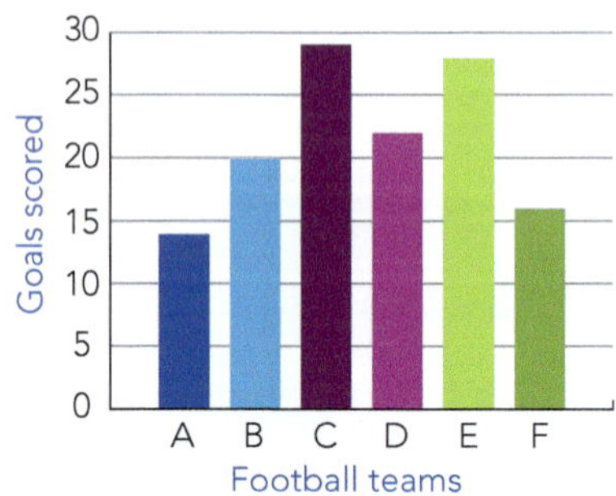

discrete variable

See also **continuous data, continuous variable, discrete data**

In statistics, a discrete variable is a numerical variable that can take only exact values within a given range. Data associated with this variable is counted, not measured. It does not include numbers that represent categories, such as PIN numbers, house numbers or phone numbers.

Examples

The number of children in a family, the number of spoons in a drawer, the number of houses in a street.

displacement

See also **volume**

1 A change in the position of an object or of a quantity of material.

Example

The school bus leaves the bus depot, picks up students along its route and arrives at the local school 5 km from the depot. The displacement of the bus is 5 km, although it has travelled a distance of 20 km.

2 The pushing of a liquid out of the way by an object immersed in it.

Example

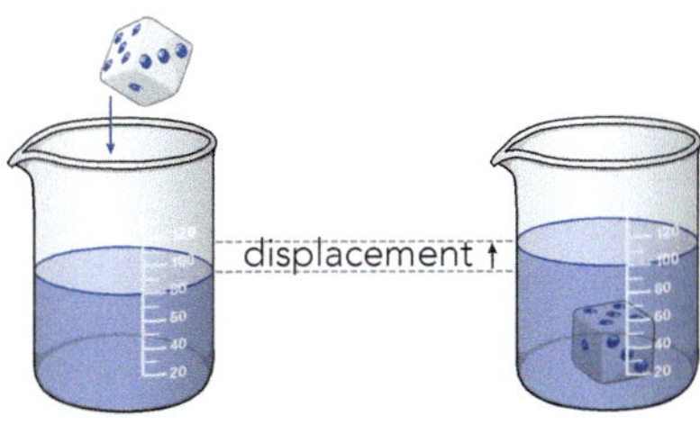

The quantity of water displaced by an immersed object.

The water displacement method is used to measure the volume of objects. The volume of displaced water is equal to the volume of the object if it is fully submerged.

distance

The length between one point and another.

Example

Distance between the points of the compasses is 5 centimetres.

3 km

Distance from my house to town is 3 kilometres.

distribute

See also **division**

To deal out or give a share of something to each individual. If a quantity is distributed evenly, an equal amount has been given to each.

Example

The teacher distributes the school newsletter to the class.

distribution

See **frequency distribution**

distributive law

See also **brackets, expand, expanded notation**

Every term inside the brackets is multiplied by the term that is immediately outside. This process is called 'expanding the brackets'.

$$a(b \pm c) = ab \pm ac$$

Examples

$$\begin{aligned} 2(c + 6) &= 2c + 2 \times 6 \\ &= 2c + 12 \end{aligned}$$

$$\begin{aligned} 3(n - 5) &= 3n - 3 \times 5 \\ &= 3n - 15 \end{aligned}$$

dividend

See also **divisor, quotient**

A number which is to be divided by another number.

Example

$$24 \div 6 = 4$$

↑ dividend ↑ divisor ↑ quotient

24 is the dividend.

divisible

See also **factors, remainder**

A number is divisible by another number if, after dividing, there is no remainder.

Example

$72 \div 9 = 8 \quad 72 \div 8 = 9$

Seventy-two is divisible by nine and also by eight.

Nine and eight are factors of seventy-two.

divisibility tests

See also **divisible, factors, remainder**

Tests that can be applied to see if one number is divisible by another.

A number is …

divisible by	if	Examples
2	the last digit is even	2, 4, 6, … 122 … 358 … 1000
3	the sum of all digits can be divided by 3	261: 2 + 6 + 1 = 9 3672: 3 + 6 +7 + 2 = 18 18: 1 + 8 = 9
4	the last two digits are divisible by 4	1024: 24 ÷ 4 = 6
5	the last digit is 5 or 0	15, 70 …
6	the last digit is even and the sum of its digits is divisible by 3	7446: 7 + 4 + 4 + 6 = 21
7	there is no divisibility test	
8	the last 3 digits are divisible by 8	75384: 384 ÷ 8 = 48
9	the sum of its digits is divisible by 9	3123: 3 + 1 + 2 + 3 = 9
10	the number ends in 0	10, 20, 30 …

Important: No number can be divided by 0.

division

Division is a mathematical operation which can be interpreted in several different ways:

1 Grouping (quotition).

Example

How many groups of three can be made with fifteen apples?

The apples are to be placed into groups of equal size, three to a group. The problem is to find out how many groups there will be.

$15 \div 3 = 5$

There are five groups of three apples.

2 Repeated subtraction is a form of grouping.

Example

Share fifteen apples among five children. How many apples will each child get?

Give one apple to each child. Continue this process until there are no apples left. Count how many apples each child gets.

If each child gets one apple
$15 - 5 = 10$

If each child gets another apple
$10 - 5 = 5$

If each child gets a third apple
$5 - 5 = 0$

Each child gets three apples.

$15 \div 5 = 3$

divisor

See also **dividend, quotient**

A number which is to be divided into another number.

Example

$$\underset{\text{dividend}}{\underset{\uparrow}{24}} \div \underset{\text{divisor}}{\underset{\uparrow}{6}} = \underset{\text{quotient}}{\underset{\uparrow}{4}}$$

6 is the divisor.

dodecagon

See also **polygon**

A polygon with twelve sides.

Examples

dodecahedron

See also **pentagon, polyhedron, regular polyhedron**

A solid (polyhedron) with twelve faces. A regular dodecahedron is made by joining together twelve congruent regular pentagons. It is one of the five Platonic solids.

Example

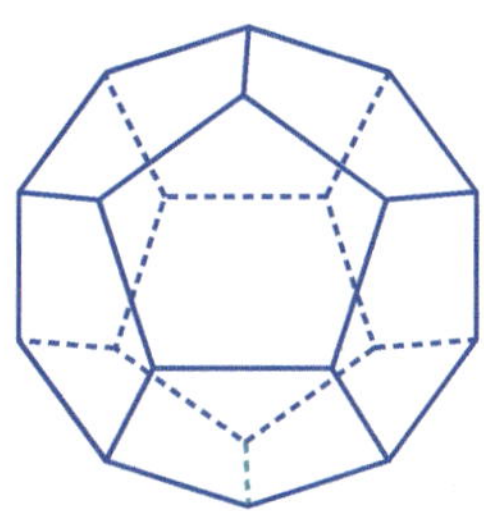

regular dodecahedron

dollar (Symbol: $)

See also **cent**

A unit of money, worth 100 cents.

dot plot

See also **data, discrete numerical data**

A simple statistical graph where each data value is represented as a dot on a section of a number line. Where two or more data values are the same, the dots are stacked vertically, giving an indication of the distribution, or spread, of the data. This type of graph is often used for discrete numerical data. It can also be used for categorical data.

Example

Number of pets owned by members of class 7A.

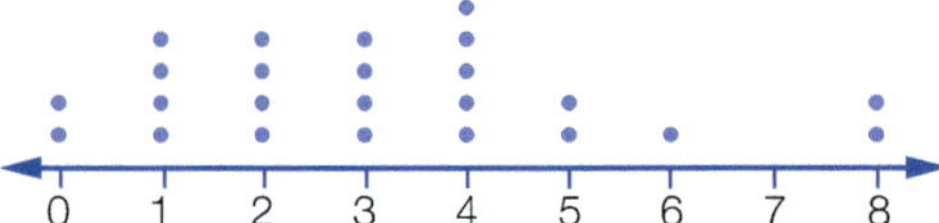

double

See also **multiplication**

Twice as many, or the same again.

Examples

is double

Double 8 is 16.
10 is double 5.

dozen

Twelve items.

Example

one dozen eggs = twelve eggs

edge

See also **face, intersection, plane**

In geometry, the line that is the intersection of two plane faces.

Examples

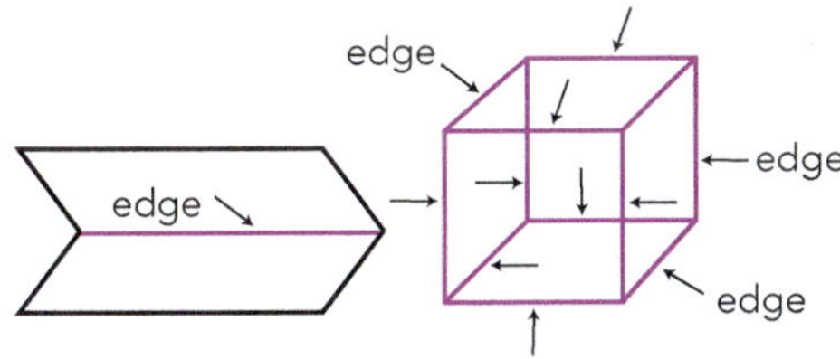

element of a set

See also **cardinal number, set**

One of the individual objects that belong in (are members of) a set.

Example

 is an element of the set of shapes above.

elevation, angle of

See **angle of elevation**

ellipse

See also **closed curve, parabola**

A closed curve that looks like an elongated circle (a circle stretched in one direction).

Examples

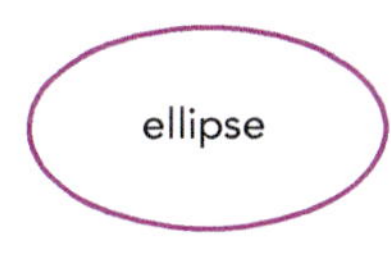

A football is elliptical in shape.

enlargement

See also **reduce, scale drawing, similar, transformation**

Making bigger. Enlargement is a commonly used transformation. An enlargement produces two similar figures. It can be made in many ways: using a grid, using rays and a centre of enlargement, using a photocopier or computer.

Example

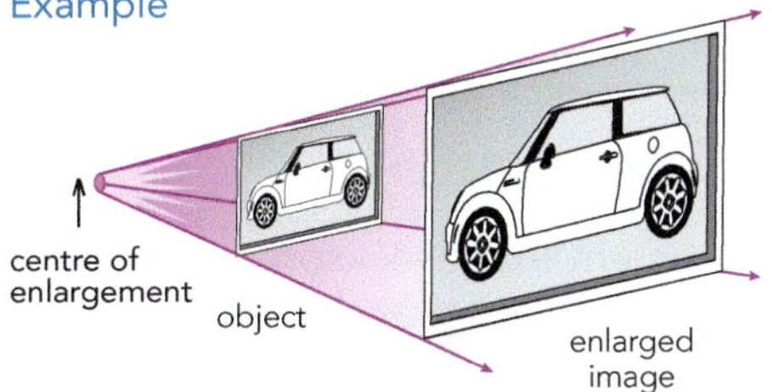

equal (Symbol: =)

See also **equality, equal sign, number sentence**

1 Identical in quantity.

Example

These two packets of coffee have equal mass (1 kilogram).

2 Of the same value.

Examples

One $5 note equals five $1 coins.

3 Indicate equivalent expressions.

Examples

$1 + 8 = 3 + 6$
$7 \times 2 + 1 = 3 \times 5$

The left hand side (LHS) and the right hand side (RHS) are equal because the expression on the LHS of the '=' symbol has the same value as the RHS.

The LHS is equal to the RHS.

equality

See also **equal, equation, inequality**

The state of being equal.

A statement that two expressions are equal, usually expressed as an equation.

Examples

$2 + 4 = 6$
$2x + 1 = 9$
$3x + 1 = x + 7$

equally likely

See also **chance event, probability**

Events which have the same chance of occurring are said to be equally likely.

Example

When a die is rolled fairly, the six numbers, 1, 2, 3, 4, 5 and 6, are equally likely to occur.

equal sign (Symbol: =)

See also **equal, symbol**

The name of the symbol which means 'is equal to' or 'equals'.

It is often placed between two expressions. It shows that:

3 + 5	=	8
↑	↑	↑
this	is equal to	this

equation

See also **equality, inequality, place holder, pronumeral, variable**

A statement that two expressions are equal. An equation has a left hand side (LHS) and a right hand side (RHS) which are equal or balanced. The equal sign is written in between them.

Example

$x + 4 = 7$

This equation is true only if x has the value of three.

The x and other symbols or letters used in equations to stand for a quantity are called variables.

equidistant
See also **parallel lines**

The same distance apart at every point.

Example
The distance between parallel lines is equal (the same) at every point so parallel lines are equidistant.

equilateral
See also **equilateral triangle**

Having sides of equal length.

A square, regular pentagon, hexagon and other regular polygons have sides of equal length and angles of equal size.

Examples

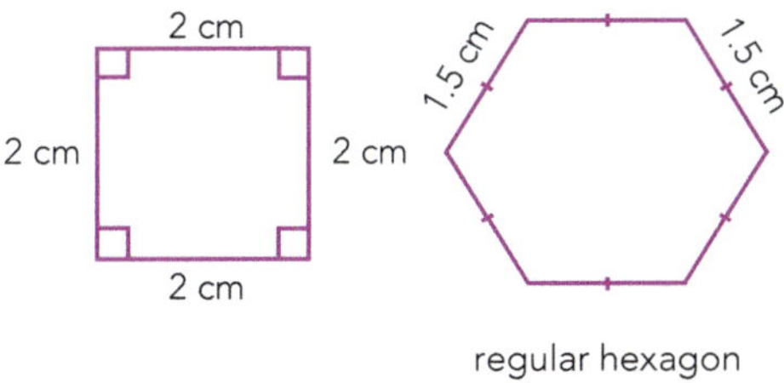

regular hexagon

equilateral triangle
See also **equilateral, triangle**

A triangle that has three sides of equal length and three equal angles.

Examples

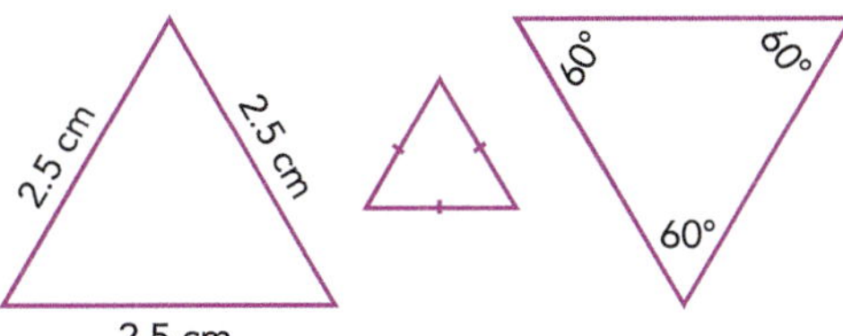

The angles of any equilateral triangle are always 60°. Equal sides can be marked with a dash.

equivalent
See also **amount, value**

Having the same value.

The same amount.

Example

A \$2 coin is equivalent to two \$1 coins.

equivalent angle
See also **cosine, quadrant, sine, tangent, trigonometry**

In trigonometry, an angle in the first quadrant that has the same trigonometric magnitude as an angle in another quadrant.

Examples

$$\sin 120° = \sin 60°$$
$$\cos 280° = \cos 80°$$
$$\tan 130° = \tan 50°$$

equivalent equations
See also **equation, operation, solution, solve**

Equations that have the same solution. Performing the same operation on each side of an equation produces an equivalent equation.

Example

$$4x + 3 = 27$$
$$4x = 24 \text{ (subtract 3 from both sides)}$$
$$x = 6 \text{ (divide both sides by 4)}$$

These are all equivalent equations.

equivalent fractions

See also **equivalent, fraction**

Fractions that represent the same number or amount.

Example

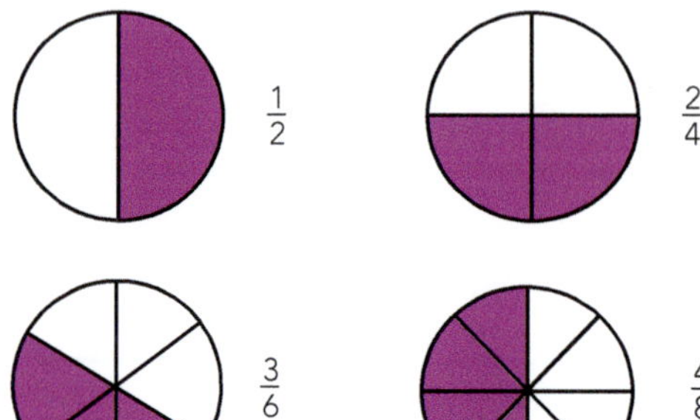

Fractions $\frac{1}{2} = \frac{2}{4} = \frac{3}{6} = \frac{4}{8}$ are equivalent.

equivalent ratio

See also **proportion, ratio**

Multiplying or dividing each of the parts in a ratio by the same number gives an equivalent ratio. The proportion of the parts remains the same.

Example

$$\begin{array}{rcccc} & 2 : & 3 : & 5 & \\ & \downarrow & \downarrow & \downarrow & \times 4 \\ = & 8 : & 12 : & 20 & \end{array}$$

estimate

See also **accurate, approximately, calculate, rounding**

1 A rough or approximate calculation.

2 A number that has not been calculated accurately. An estimate of the answer is often useful to check that a calculated answer is reasonable.

Example

An estimate of 1.9×3 is

$$2 \times 3 = 6$$
$$\therefore 1.9 \times 3 \approx 6$$

3 Trying to judge or guess what a measure or result will be.

Example

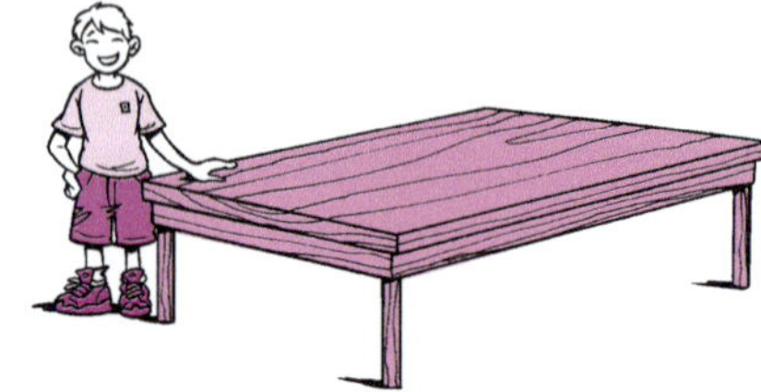

The table is 13 handspans long, that is, roughly 2 metres.

evaluate

See also **arithmetic, calculate**

To find the value of.

Examples

i Evaluate 21×3

$$\begin{array}{r} 21 \\ \times 3 \\ \hline 63 \end{array}$$

The value of 21×3 is 63.

ii Evaluate $p + 3q$, if $p = 2.5$ and $q = 7$

$$\begin{aligned} p + 3q &= 2.5 + (3 \times 7) \\ &= 2.5 + 21 \\ &= 23.5 \end{aligned}$$

even number

See also **digit, divisible**

A number that is divisible by two. All even numbers finish with one of the digits: 0, 2, 4, 6 or 8.

event

In probability, a situation or experiment where there can be at least two different outcomes.

Examples

i Drawing a card from a pack is an event with fifty-two different possible outcomes.
ii Tossing a coin is an event with only two possible outcomes.
iii Rolling a die is an event with six possible outcomes.
iv A cricket match is an event with three possible outcomes (win, lose, draw).

exact

See also **approximately**

Precise, accurate, correct in every way, not approximate.

exact answer

See also **decimal, irrational number, pi, rational number, surd**

A number that is in exact decimal, fraction or surd form. Rational numbers must be shown with the exact number of decimal places, repeating decimal notation or as a fraction. Irrational numbers such as π, e and all surds must be left in the answer.

Examples

The exact answers for

$3 \times \pi = 3\pi$

$\sqrt{2} \times \sqrt{3} = \sqrt{6}$

exchange

See also **equivalent, multibase arithmetic blocks, rate**

1 When we go shopping, we exchange money for goods. Money is the medium of exchange.

Example

$2.30 is the price of the toy car.

2 Money can also be exchanged for money of equivalent value.

Example

is the same amount as

3 Multibase arithmetic blocks (MAB) can be exchanged.

Example

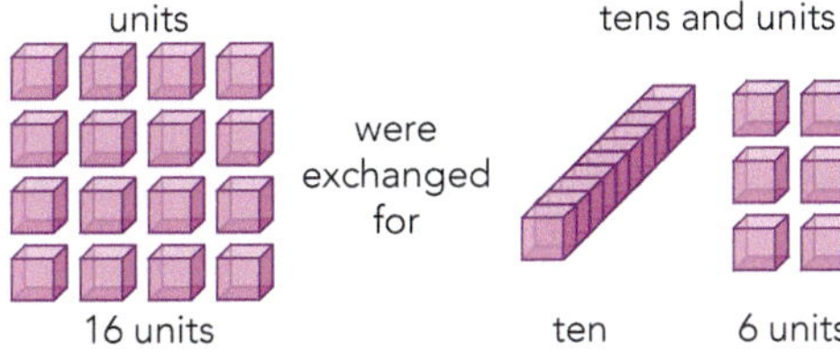

expanded notation

See also **index notation, scientific notation**

A way of writing numerals or algebraic expressions in full or without brackets.

Examples

i Numerals

$$249 = 200 + 40 + 9$$
$$\text{or} = (2 \times 100) + (4 \times 10) + (9 \times 1)$$
$$\text{or} = 2 \times 10^2 + 4 \times 10^1 + 9 \times 10^0$$

ii Index numbers

$$4^3 = 4 \times 4 \times 4$$
$$y^5 = y \times y \times y \times y \times y$$
$$a^2b^4 = a \times a \times b \times b \times b \times b$$

iii In algebra

$$2(a + 2b) = (2 \times a) + (2 \times 2b)$$
$$= 2a + 4b$$

expanding the brackets

See also **brackets, distributive law, factorise**

Using the distributive law to remove the brackets in a factorised expression. It changes a product into a sum or difference.

Example

$$3(a + 4) = 3 \times a + 3 \times 4$$
$$= 3a + 12$$

exponent

See **index**

exponential

See also **exponent, index**

A relationship between variables where one of the variables is an exponent or index.

Examples

$y = 2^x$
$N = 0.5^t$

expression

See **algebraic expression**

exterior

See also **interior angles**

The outside of an object or shape.

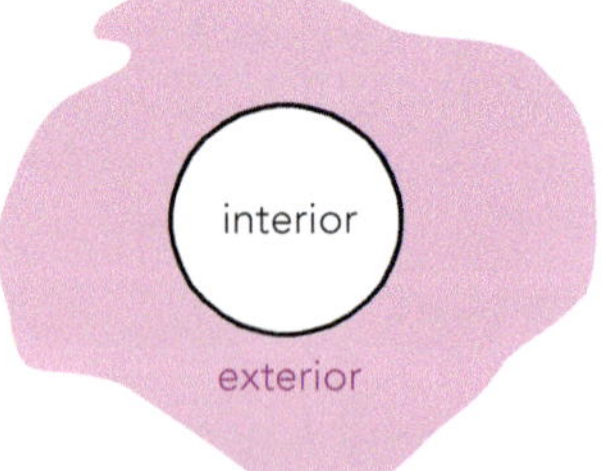

Examples

i Exterior angle

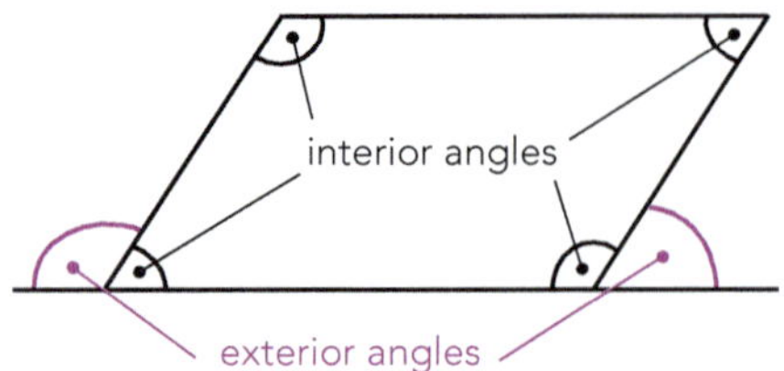

ii Exterior angle of a triangle

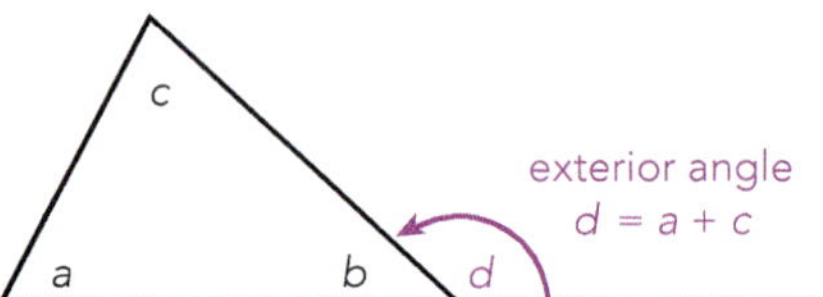

The exterior angle of a triangle is the sum of the two opposite interior angles.

extrapolation

See also **graph, interpolation, line of best fit, scatter plot**

The process of extending the pattern of a graph to make predictions outside the range of known values.

Example

When a line of best fit is fitted to a scatter plot, a prediction can be made for other related points. For instance, if $x = 9$, y is predicted to be 25. This process is called extrapolation.

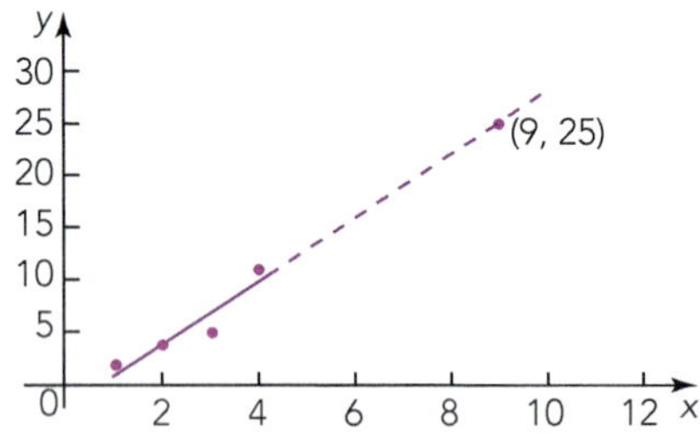

face

See also **edge, surface, three-dimensional**

In a three-dimensional solid, a face is the flat part of the surface that is bounded by the edges.

Examples

i A cube has six faces. All six faces are squares.

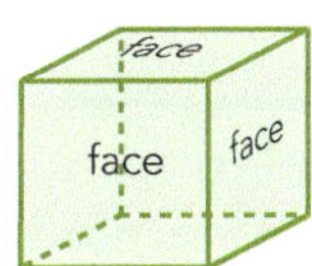

ii A tetrahedron has four faces. All four faces are equilateral triangles.

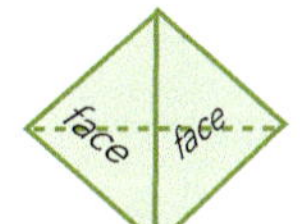

iii A pyramid has five faces. Four of the faces are triangles. One face is a square.

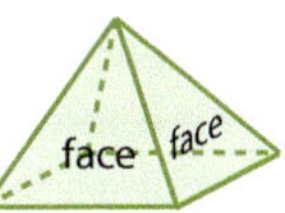

factorisation

See also **algebraic expression, distributive law**

The process of simplifying algebraic expressions by extracting a common factor.

Example

Factorise $3a + 6b$

$$3a + 6b$$
$$= 3 \times a + 2 \times 3 \times b$$
common factor
$$= 3(a + 2b)$$

factorise

See also **distributive law, factor, factor tree, prime factor of a number**

To factorise a number or algebraic expression, first find the factors, the numbers or terms that divide exactly into it. Then write the number or expression as a product of its factors.

Examples

i 21 is factorised by writing it as 3×7.

ii 36 is factorised by writing it as 4×9. It can be factorised further by writing 4×9 as $2 \times 2 \times 3 \times 3$, or $2^2 \times 3^2$. It is now written as a product of prime factors.

iii $4x + 12$ is factorised by writing it as $4 \times x + 4 \times 3$ or $4(x + 3)$.

factorised form

See also **expanded form, factorisation, factor, factor tree**

An expression written as a product of factors.

Example

$4(x - 5)$ is an expression written in factorised form. It can be written in expanded form as $4x - 20$.

factor

See also **composite number, factor tree, prime number, whole numbers**

Any whole number that can be divided exactly into another number ('exactly' means with no remainder).

Examples

		factor
i	$6 \div 1 = 6$	1
	$6 \div 2 = 3$	2
	$6 \div 3 = 2$	3
	$6 \div 6 = 1$	6

1, 2, 3 and 6 are factors of 6.

ii $5 \div 1 = 5$
$5 \div 5 = 1$

5 has only the factors 5 and 1. It is a prime number.

factor theorem

See also **polynomial, remainder theorem**

The factor theorem can be used to find factors of a polynomial, $P(x)$. If dividing a polynomial $P(x)$ by the expression $(x - a)$ gives a remainder of 0, then $(x - a)$ is a factor of $P(x)$.

The theorem states that:

If $P(a) = 0$, then $(x - a)$ is a factor of $P(x)$.

Similarly, if $P(\frac{b}{a}) = 0$, then $(ax - b)$ is a factor of $P(x)$.

Examples

i $x - 2$ is a factor of $P(x) = x^3 - 5x + 2$
because $P(2) = 2^3 - 5 \times 2 + 2$
$= 0$

ii $2x - 1$ is a factor of $2x^3 + x^2 - x$
because $P(\frac{1}{2}) = 2(\frac{1}{2})^3 + (\frac{1}{2})^2 - \frac{1}{2}$
$= 0$

factor tree

See also **prime factor of a number**

A diagram that shows the prime factors of a given number.

Example

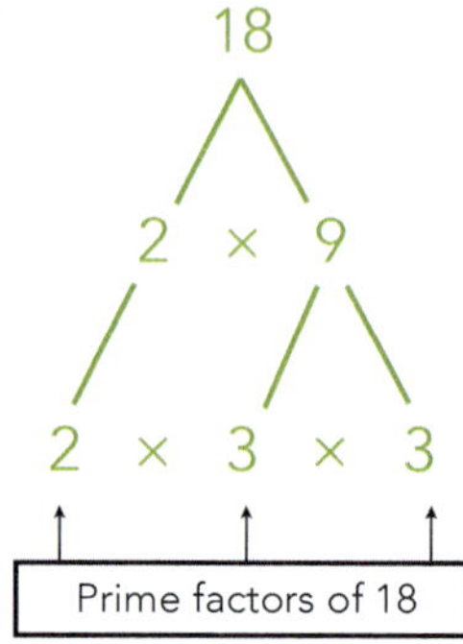

$18 = 2 \times 3 \times 3$
$= 2 \times 3^2$

false number sentence

See also **number sentence, true sentence**

A number sentence that is not true.

Examples

i $5 < 1$ is a false number sentence.
$3 + 7 = 15 - 6$ is a false number sentence.

ii The open number sentence $3 + \square = 10$ becomes false if $\square$ is replaced by any other number than 7.
If $\square$ is replaced by 7, it will become a true number sentence.

figure

See also **diagram**

Another name for a numeral, line, shape or a solid.

Examples

i Write in figures: thirty-six 36

ii Half of this figure has been coloured in.

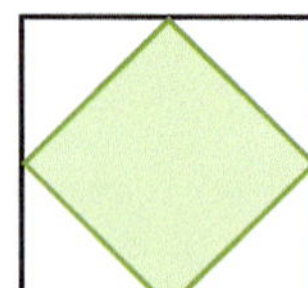

finite

See also **infinite, perimeter, region, set**

Anything that has boundaries or has a definite number of members (although these may be too many to count).

Examples

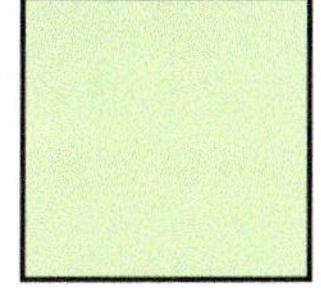

i The region inside a square is finite because it is bounded by a perimeter.

ii The set of months in a year is a finite set because the months can be counted.

iii The number of hairs on a dog is finite but it would be almost impossible to count them.

first

The one at the beginning, before any other.

Example

The first shape from left to right is a square.

flat

See also **cube, face, multibase arithmetic blocks (MAB), plane, surface**

1 Being in one plane only, two dimensional (2D), not solid.

Examples

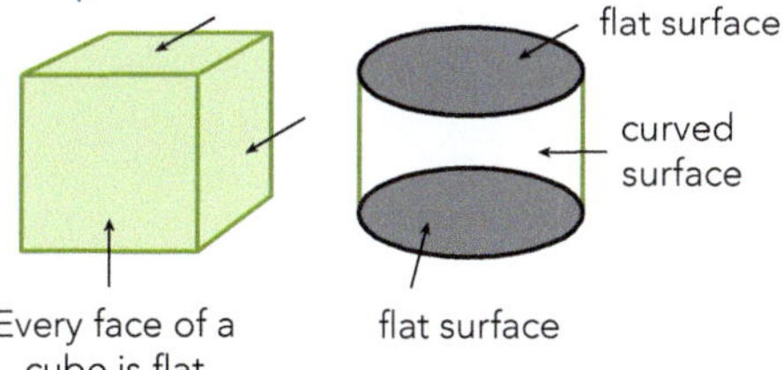

2 The name used for the multibase arithmetic block representing one hundred.

Example

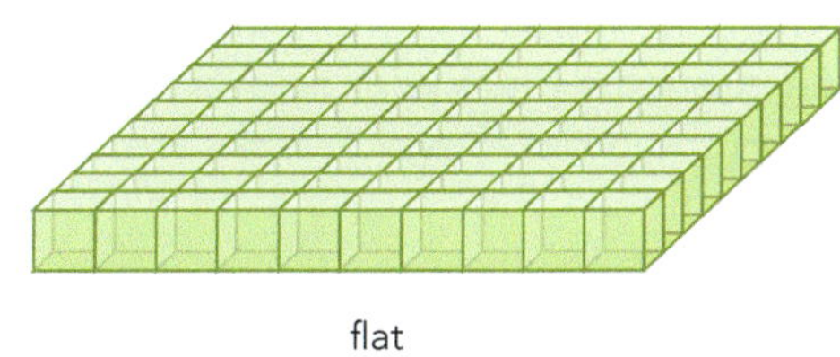

flexible

See also **rigid**

The ability of a jointed structure to change shape by changing the angle sizes but retaining the length and arrangement of the sides.

Example

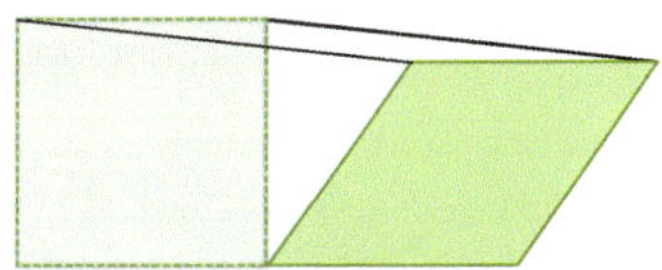

A rectangle is a flexible structure, as it can be turned into a parallelogram.

flip

See also **axis of symmetry, reflection, transformation**

To turn over. Reflection can be thought of as flipping an object over a mirror line (an axis of symmetry).

Example

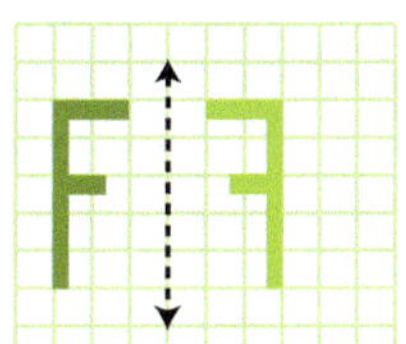

flowchart

See also **order of operations, backtracking**

A type of diagram that represents a process. It shows the steps in boxes and connects them with arrows, and shows the order in which tasks are to be attempted. Flowcharts can be used in equation solving.

Example

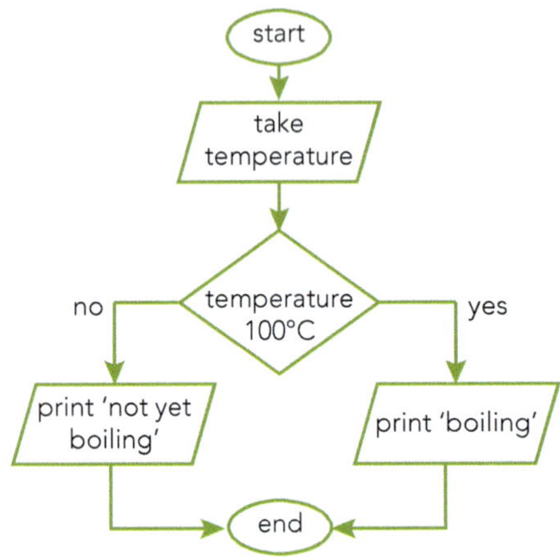

foot (Plural: feet) (Symbols: ′, ft)

See also **inch, mile**

A unit of length in the imperial measurement system.

1 foot ≈ 30 centimetres
1 foot = 12 inches

The altitude of an aeroplane or the depth of a submarine is measured in feet.

Example

A plane flies at an altitude of 20 000 ft.

formula (Plural: formulae, formulas)

See also **area, equation, symbol**

An equation that uses symbols to represent a general rule.

Example

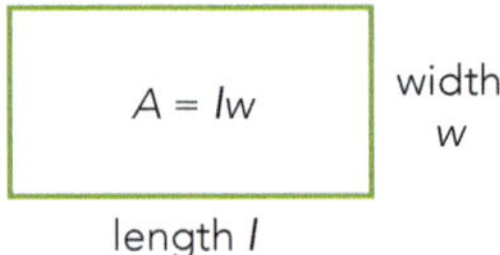

The area of a rectangle is found when its length is multiplied by its width. This is represented by the formula:
$A = lw$.
The width is sometimes called the breadth and the letter b is used to represent it. The formula for the area of a rectangle therefore becomes:
$A = lb$.

fortnight

Fourteen days, two weeks.

fraction

See also **cancelling, common denominator, decimal fraction, equivalent fractions, improper fraction, mixed number, proper fraction, simple fraction**

A number that shows parts of a whole.

Examples

i The fraction $\frac{3}{4}$ means 3 parts out of a total of 4 equal parts.

3 parts out of 4 parts are coloured.

ii 7 parts out of 100 parts are coloured in.

The fraction is $\frac{7}{100}$.

iii Show $\frac{3}{4}$ of 8.

$\frac{6}{8} = \frac{3}{4}$

frequency

See also **data, frequency table, tally**

The frequency of any item in a set of data is the number of times that item occurs in the set.

Example

A die was rolled 50 times and the number was recorded for each roll. A tally of the 50 scores was kept.

Number	Tally	Frequency
1	𝍸 ||	7
2	𝍸 𝍸 ||	12
3	𝍸 ||||	9
4	𝍸 |||	8
5	𝍸 |	6
6	𝍸 |||	8

Number 2 had the highest frequency.

Number 5 had the lowest frequency.

frequency distribution

See **frequency table**

frequency table

See also **frequency, class interval, class centre**

A table that lists the frequency of each data value in a data set.

Example

The number of pets owned by each member of a Year 7 class.

Number of pets	Frequency
0	3
1	6
2	7
3	4
4	2
5	1
6+	1
Total	24

Note: '6+' means 6 pets or more

The total of all of the frequencies is shown in the last row of the table. This is useful as a check to make sure all of the data has been collected.

When there is a lot of data, values are often grouped together. The range of data values in a group is called the class interval.

Example

The masses of parcels delivered by the post office in one week

Parcel Mass (kg)	Frequency
0–< 2	36
2–< 4	29
4–< 6	13
6–< 8	8
8–< 10	4
10–< 12	7
12+	16
Total	113

Note: A class interval written as 4–< 6 means 'all parcels with a mass of 4 kg or greater, but less than 6 kg.'

front view

See also **plan, side view**

A diagram of an object, as seen from directly in front of it.

Example

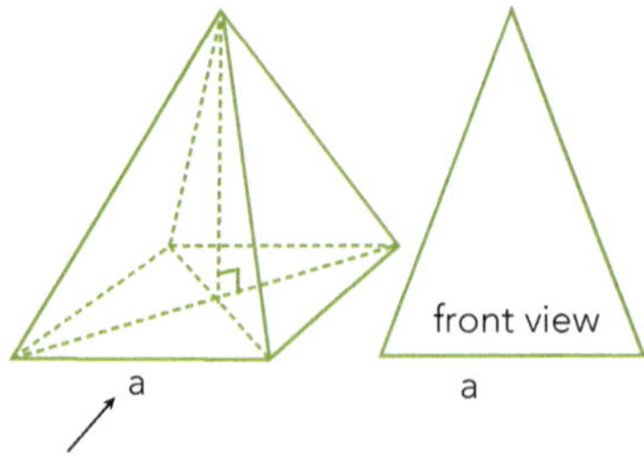

frustum

See also **decahedron, pyramid, section**

The section of a pyramid remaining when it is cut by a plane parallel to the pyramid's base and the top pyramid section is removed.

Example

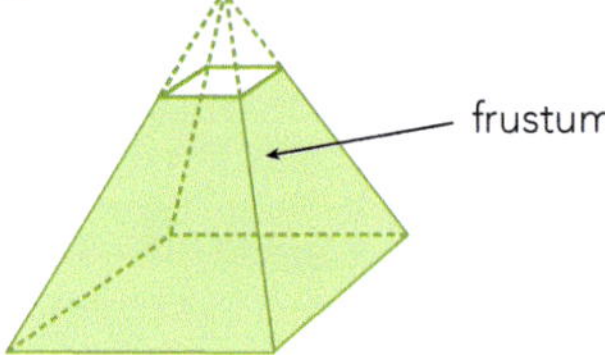

function

See also **dependent variable, graph, independent variable, many-to-one correspondence, one-to-one correspondence, output**

A special type of relationship where each independent variable (input) generates exactly one dependent variable (output). A function can have a one-to-one or many-to-one correspondence. A graph of a function can be identified easily by using the vertical line test. If a vertical line passes through the graph only once for any input value, the relationship is a function. A function is often denoted by *f*.

Example

i The height of water in a glass being filled from a tap over a time period (one-to-one).

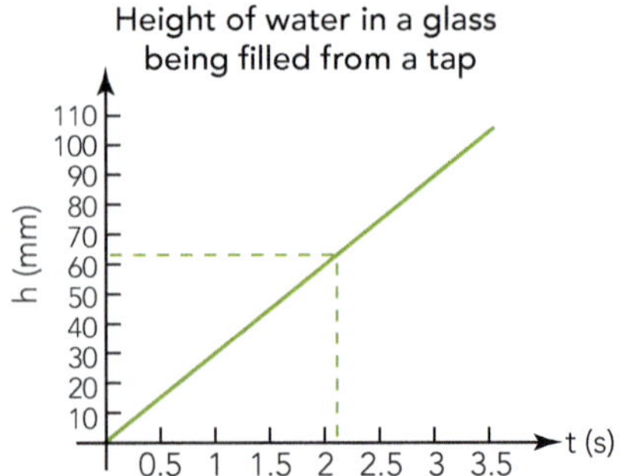

ii The height of a ball being thrown upwards over the time it is in flight (many-to-one).

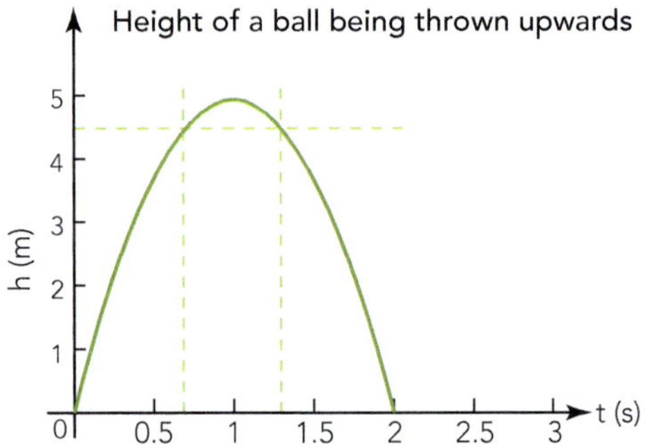

furthest (farthest)

See also **distance**

The longest distance away.

Example

Name	Distance
Kate	5.50 m
Paul	5.89 m
Mattie	5.47 m

Paul jumped the furthest.

g
See also **mass, weight**

1 The symbol for the unit gram.

2 A symbol for gravity. The force of gravity on the Earth's surface is 1 g.

gallon
See also **imperial measurements, litres**

Unit of volume in the imperial measurement system.

1 imperial gallon ≈ 4.5 litres

Example

In the USA petrol is sold by the gallon.

geo-board
See also **equilateral triangle, grid, pattern**

A board studded with nails forming a pattern or grid, usually of squares or equilateral triangles.

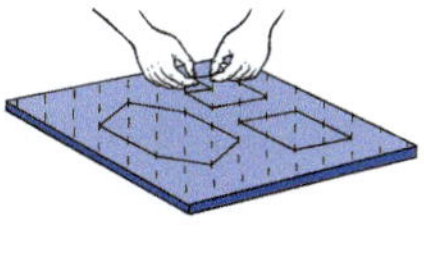

Geo-boards are used for shape and number activities in which elastic bands are arranged around sets of nails.

geometric sequence
See **sequence**

geometry
See also **measure, property, solid, space, surface**

The part of mathematics that is the study of the relationships, properties and measurements of solids, surfaces, lines, angles and space.

geo-strips

Strips of plastic, metal or cardboard with holes equally spaced down the centre of the strips. They are used for making shapes.

Examples

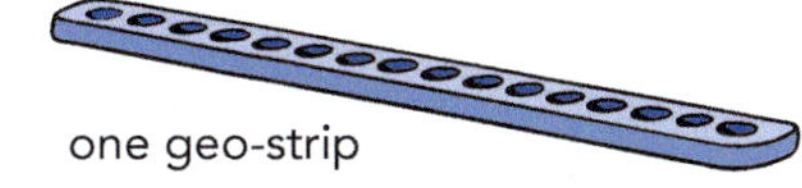

one geo-strip

Shapes made using geo-strips

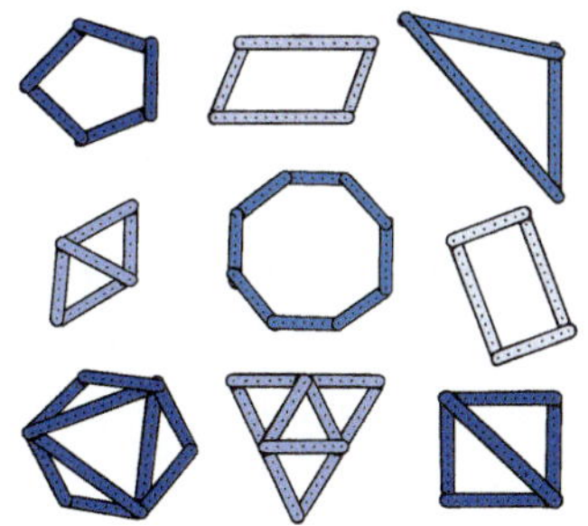

googol

A very large number. It is the numeral 1 with one hundred zeros after it.

1 000 000 000 000 000 000 000 000 000
000 000 000 000 000 000 000 000 000 0...

gradient

See also **coordinates, ratio**

A measure of the slope, or 'steepness' of a line. The gradient is expressed as the ratio (in fraction form) of $\frac{\text{rise}}{\text{run}}$, where the 'rise' is the vertical change in *y*-value between two points on the line, and the 'run' is the horizontal change in *x*-value between the same two points.

If a line slopes upwards from left to right, the gradient is a positive number. If the line slopes downwards from left to right, the gradient is negative. The gradient of a horizontal line is zero. The gradient of a vertical line is undefined.

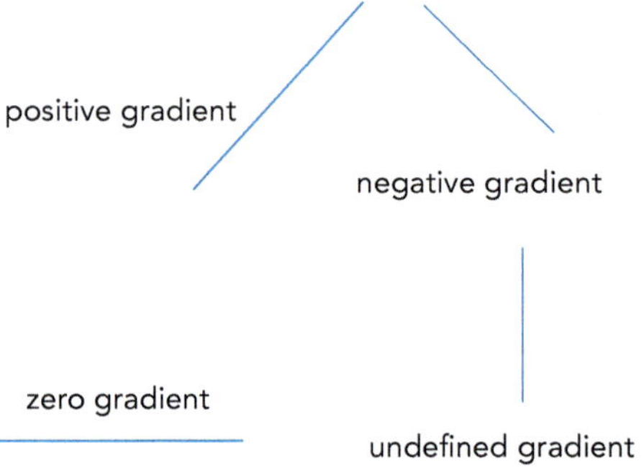

If the two points on the line are written with the coordinates (x_1, y_1) and (x_2, y_2), then the rule gradient = $\frac{\text{rise}}{\text{run}}$ can be written as the formula $m = \frac{y_2 - y_1}{x_2 - x_1}$, where m is the symbol for gradient, $y_2 - y_1$ is the change in the *y*-values and $x_2 - x_1$ is the change in the *x*-values.

Example

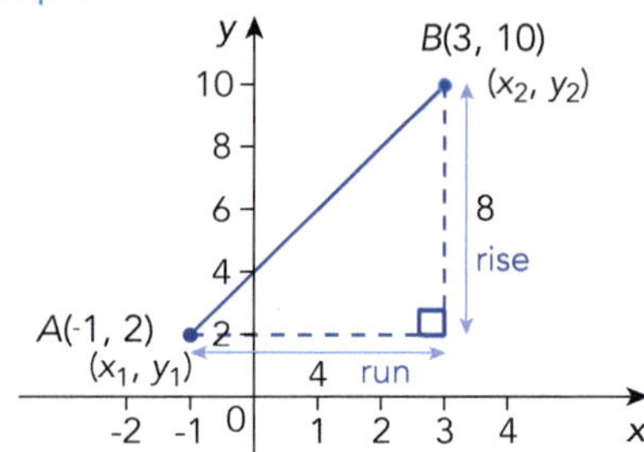

In the above example of the line between the points (-1, 2) and (3, 10), the 'rise' is 8 and the 'run' is 4.

$$\frac{\text{rise}}{\text{run}} = \frac{8}{4} = 2$$

The value of the gradient is 2.

Gradient can also be thought of as the angle of inclination to a horizontal base line, or the 'pitch' of a line. ('Pitch' is often used to describe the angle of the roof of a house).

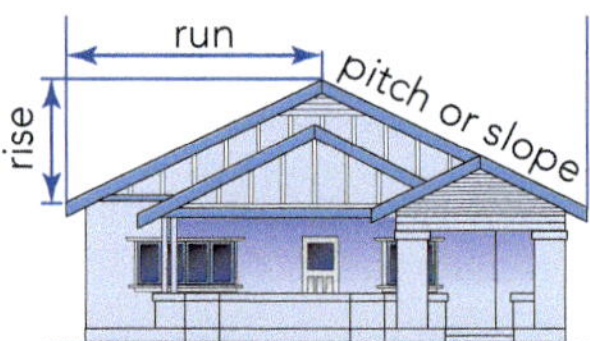

gradient–intercept form

See also **gradient, intercept, linear equation**

The form of a linear equation written as $y = mx + b$, where m is the gradient and b is the *y*-value of the *y*-intercept.

Example

A line with a gradient of 3 and a *y*-intercept of (0, 5) has the equation $y = 3x + 5$.

graduated

Marked off with measurements.

Examples

i A ruler is graduated in centimetres.

ii A thermometer is graduated in degrees.

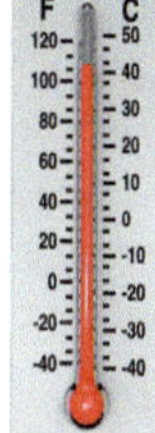

gram (Symbol: g)

See also **mass, unit of measurement**

A unit of mass.

1000 g = 1 kg

Examples

i The mass of this block of chocolate is 200 grams.

ii The mass of ten matches is approximately 1 gram.

graph

See also **axes, bar graph, column graph, data display, line graph, pictograph, sector graph**

A visual display of data, drawn on a set of axes. There are different kinds of graphs.

Examples

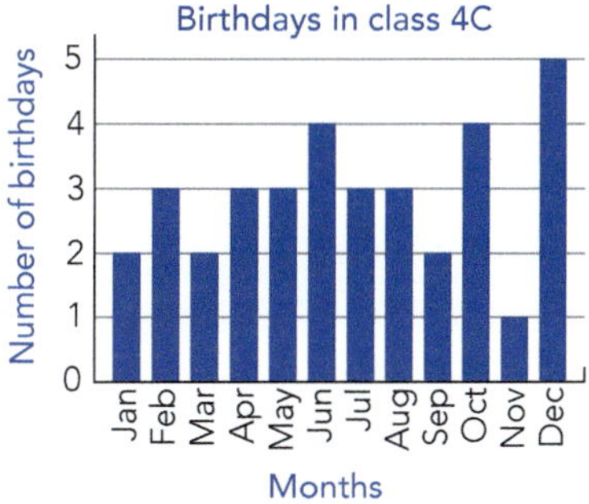

This is a column graph

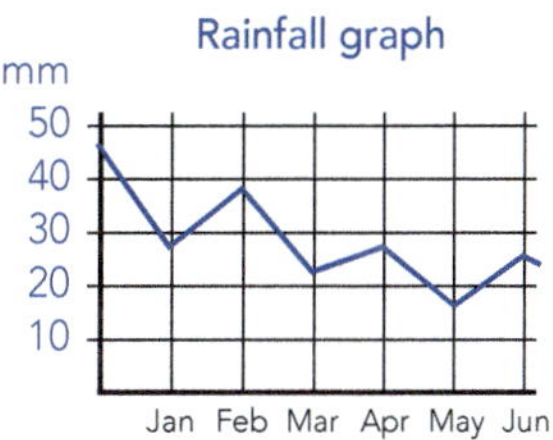

This is a line graph

graph paper

See also **graph, grid, isometric paper, scale drawing**

Paper ruled in squares, used for scale drawing and graphing.

Examples

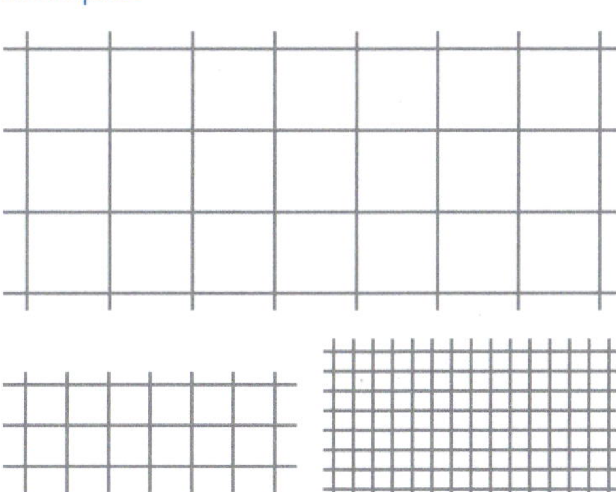

greater than (Symbol: >)

See also **less than**

A relation between a pair of numbers showing which is greater. More than. Larger than.

Example

$7 > 6$

↑ greater than

greatest common divisor (GCD)

See **highest common factor**

grid

See also **graph paper, isometric paper**

Lines that go across, up and down, creating a pattern of identical shapes (usually squares). Often found on maps and graphs.

Example

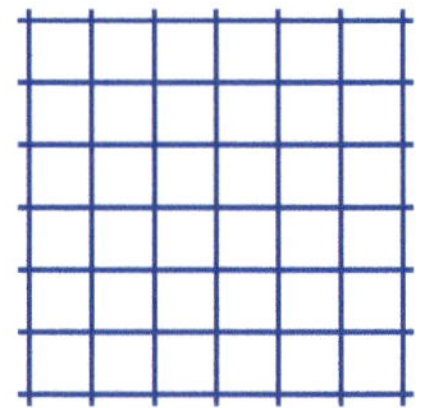

gross

Twelve dozen, 144.

gross income

See also **income, income tax, net income, tax deduction**

Money earned before tax and other deductions. Gross income includes salary or wages, landlord's rental, dividends from shares, bonuses and commissions.

Example

Robert has a job with a gross salary of \$75 000 p.a. He receives \$24 000 a year in rental income and was paid a bonus of \$5000. His gross income is \$104 000.

group

See also **grouping**

1 Putting things together in a set or group, usually based on a common characteristic. In the decimal system, numbers are grouped into powers of tens.

Example

Hundreds	Tens	Units
2	4	3

243 = 2 groups of 100
4 groups of 10
3 groups of 1

2 Two or more objects or people.

Example

a group of boys

grouped data

See also **class centre, class interval, data, statistics**

Data that has been grouped using class intervals. Grouped data is used when there is a large amount of data, to simplify the data and the calculation of statistics from the data. Individual data values are lost but calculated statistics are close approximations to the actual statistics.

Example

The Fantastic Foxes basketball team scored these points in their last 40 games.

72, 80, 63, 45, 58, 47, 45, 52, 63, 40, 43, 50, 53, 47, 72, 76, 42, 57, 83, 61, 81, 50, 56, 73, 64, 83, 46, 66, 76, 75, 68, 61, 62, 79, 58, 71, 68, 80, 68, 76

This information can be shown by constructing a frequency table and grouping the results.

Number of points scored	Tally	Frequency
40–44	|||	3
45–49	~~||||~~	5
50–54	||||	4
55–59	||||	4
60–64	~~||||~~ |	6
65–69	||||	4
70–74	||||	4
75–79	~~||||~~	5
80–84	~~||||~~	5
		Total 40

grouping

See also **division, set**

Putting things together into sets with the same number in each set.

Example

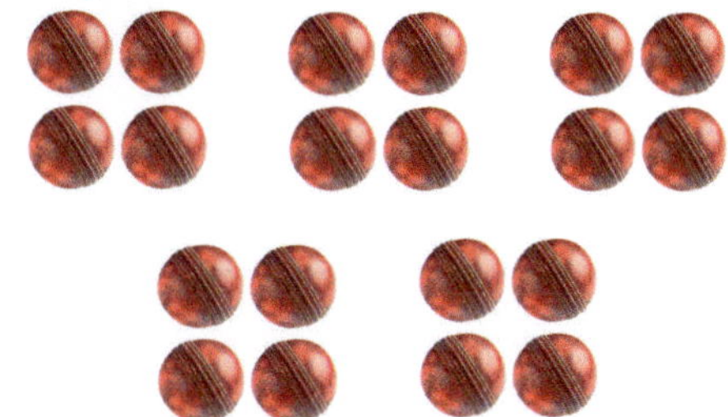

Twenty balls are grouped into five sets of four.

grouping symbols

See **brackets, order of operations, parentheses**

GST (Goods and Services Tax)

See also **selling price, tax**

A tax imposed on goods and services in Australia. It is 10% of the selling price of the goods or service. It excludes fresh food and essential items and services.

Example

The selling price of a shirt is $45.00 before GST. The GST on the shirt is $4.50. Therefore, the shirt is sold for $49.50.

h

Symbol for height, hour, prefix hecto-.

ha

See also **acre, area, hectare**

The symbol for hectare, a measurement of area.

half (Plural: halves)

One part of two equal parts.

Examples

i

ii Half of twenty-four is twelve.

$$\frac{1}{2} \times 24 = 12$$

iii An orange has been cut into two halves.

handspan

See also **estimate, informal unit**

The distance from the top of the thumb to the top of the smallest finger when the hand is fully stretched.

Example

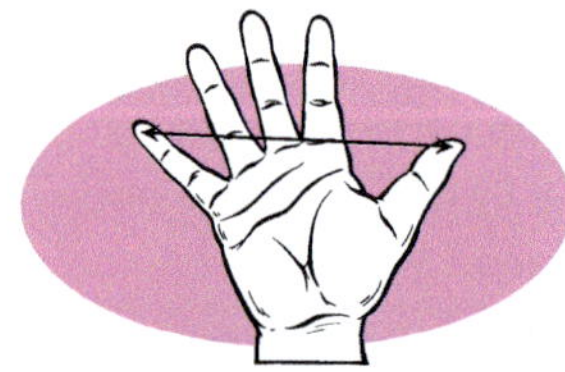

This is a handspan

A handspan is used as an informal unit for estimating the lengths, heights or widths of objects.

hecta, hecto

See also **hectare**

Prefix that means 100.

hectare (Symbol: ha)

See also **area, unit of measurement**

A unit of area.

One hectare is the area of a square with side lengths of 100 metres.

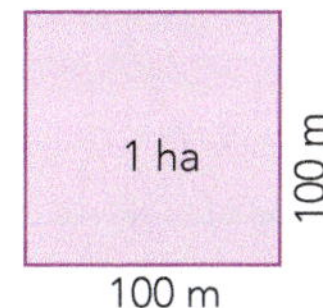

The area of a soccer field is approximately half a hectare.

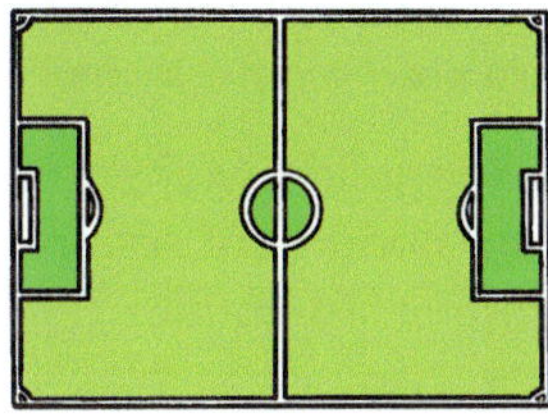

Areas of land, such as farms or parks, are often measured in hectares.

heft

See also **weight**

To judge the weight of objects by lifting them in the hands.

Examples

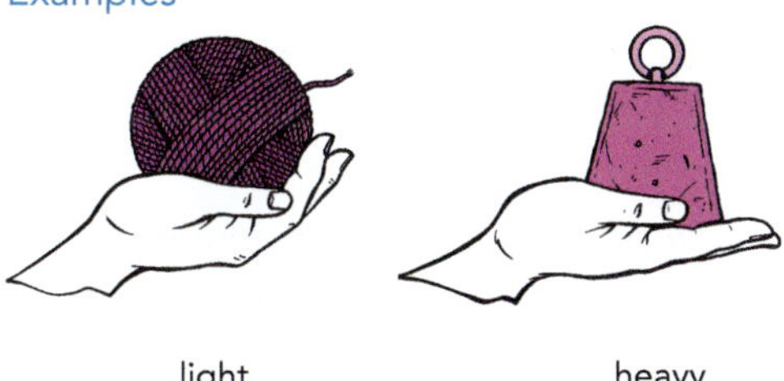

light heavy

height

See also **altitude, vertical**

Measurement from top to bottom, the vertical distance. Height is measured at right angles to the horizontal ground or base.

Examples

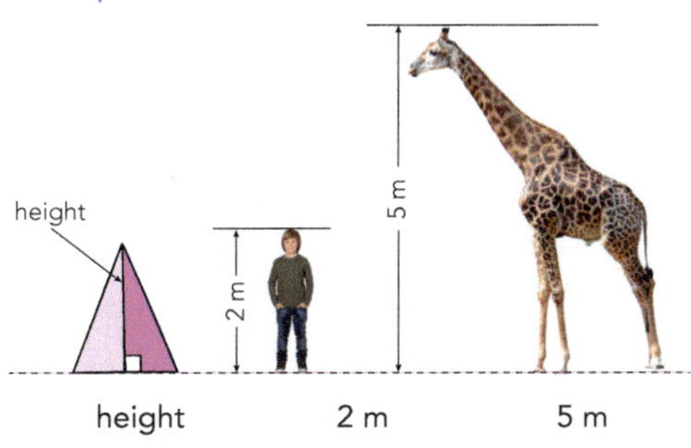

height 2 m 5 m

hemisphere

See also **sphere**

Half of a sphere.

Example

Australia lies in the southern hemisphere.

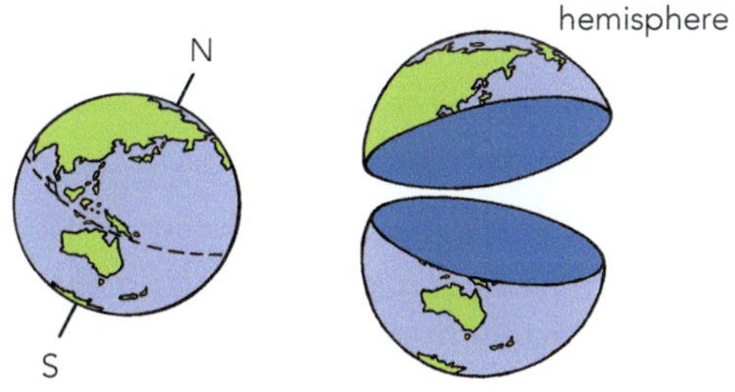

Each part is $\frac{1}{2}$ of a sphere.

heptagon

See also **polygon**

A polygon with seven sides and seven angles. Regular heptagons have all sides equal in length and all angles the same.

Examples

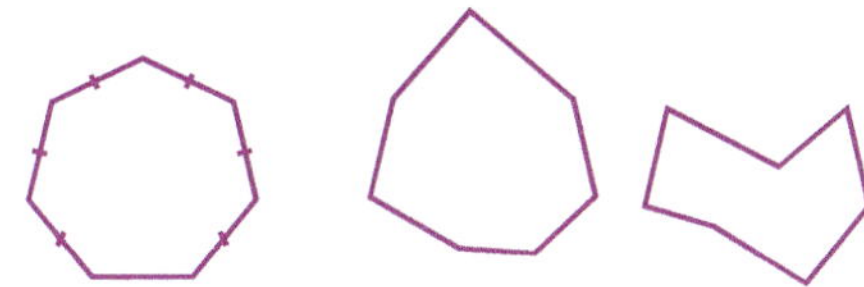

regular heptagon irregular heptagons

hexadecimal

See also **binary, decimal, octal**

Containing sixteen parts or digits. It is a base sixteen number system that is made up of sixteen digits. The digits represented by this number system are 0 to 9 and then A to F. This number system is used primarily by computer systems, particularly by the programming languages that control computer hardware. It is also the number system used to represent colours on web pages.

Example

Digits represented:

0, 1, 2, 3, 4, 5, 6, 7, 8, 9

A = 10	B = 11	C = 12
D = 13	E = 14	F = 15

hexagon

See also **polygon**

A polygon which has six sides and six angles. Regular hexagons have all sides equal in length and all angles the same.

Examples

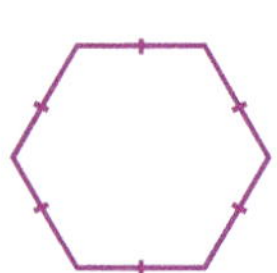

regular hexagon

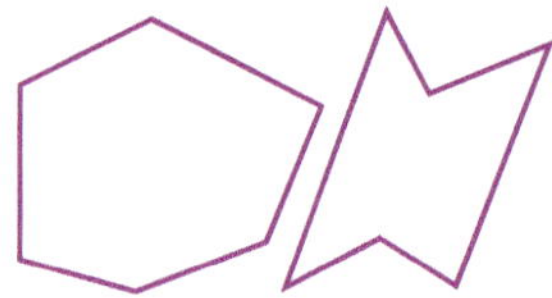

irregular hexagons

Honeycomb is made up of regular hexagons.

hexagram

A shape formed by two intersecting equilateral triangles.

Example

hexahedron

See also **cube, cuboid, polyhedron, prism, regular polyhedron**

A solid (polyhedron) with six faces. All cuboids are hexahedrons.

A cube is a regular hexahedron; all six faces are congruent squares, all internal angles are equal.

Examples

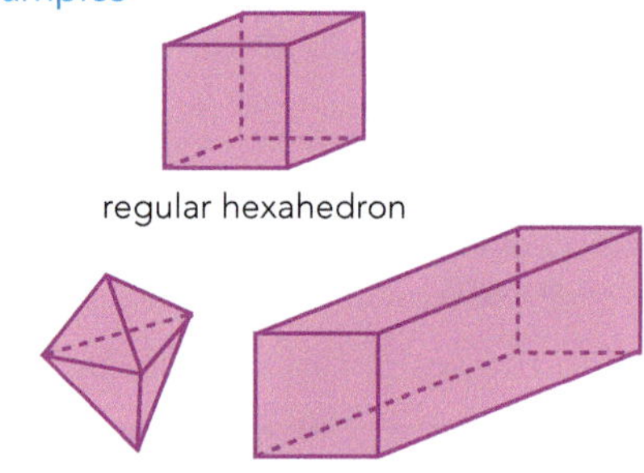

highest common factor (HCF)

See also **divisor, factor, factor tree**

The largest number that is found in each of the lists of factors of the numbers or expressions being considered. Also called the greatest common divisor (GCD) or greatest common factor.

Examples

i 36 and 24

Factors of 36: 1, 2, 3, 4, 6, 9, 12, 18, 36

Factors of 48: 1, 2, 3, 4, 6, 8, 12, 16, 24

The largest number that occurs in both lists is 12. 12 is the HCF of 36 and 24.

ii 4*a* and 10*ab*

$4a = 2 \times 2 \times a$

$10ab = 5 \times 2 \times a \times b$

The HCF is 2*a*.

Hindu–Arabic system

See also **numeral, place value**

Our modern system of numbers is the result of centuries of development.

The symbols for all the digits, except zero, probably originated with the Hindus in India, as early as 200 BC.

Hindu numerals

The Arabs adopted the system.

Arabic numerals (13th century AD)

The numerals, including zero, were standardised after the invention of the printing press in the 15th century.

0 1 2 3 4 5 6 7 8 9

The modern system has very useful characteristics:

- it has only ten digits: 0, 1, 2, 3, 4, 5, 6, 7, 8, 9
- it uses a place-value system: the value of the digit depends on its placement in the numeral:

37	307	13 700
↑	↑	↑
3 × 10	3 × 100	3 × 1000

histogram

See also **column, column graph**

A type of graph that looks similar to a column graph, but has several key differences. Histograms are used to display grouped numerical data.

The data in a frequency table is used to produce a histogram. The class intervals of data are represented as the scale on the *x*-axis, and the frequency of each class on the *y*-axis. Each frequency is represented as a column, but there are no gaps between the columns.

Example

100 students were asked how many hours a week they spent playing computer or console games.

The results are shown in the frequency table below.

Gaming times (h)	Frequency
0–<2	2
2–<4	14
4–<6	16
6–<8	24
8–<10	20
10–<12	16
12–<14	8

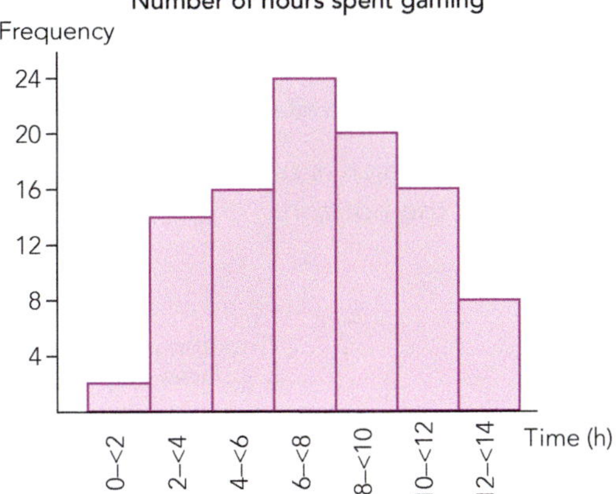

horizon
See also **horizontal line**

Line at which land or water and sky appear to meet.

horizontal
See also **parallel lines, right angle, vertical**

Line parallel to, or on a level with, the horizon.

A vertical line is at right angles to the horizon.

Example

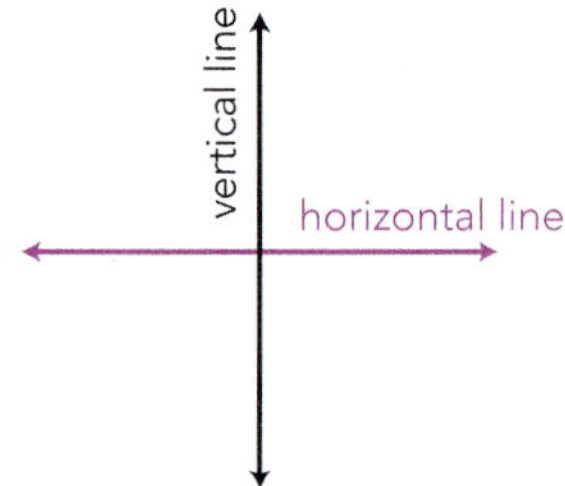

horizontal surface
See also **horizon, parallel lines, surface**

Any surface which is parallel to, or on a level with, the horizon.

Example

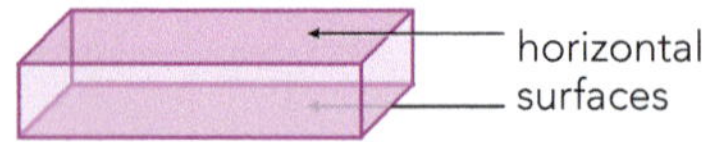

hour (Symbol: h)
See also **unit of measurement**

A unit of time.

Examples

1 hour = 60 minutes
= 3600 seconds
24 hours = 1 day

hundred
See also **decimal place-value system**

$100 = 10 \times 10$ or 10^2

hyperbola
See **rectangular hyperbola**

hypotenuse
See also **Pythagoras' theorem, right-angled triangle**

The longest side of a right-angled triangle, which is always the side opposite the right angle.

Example

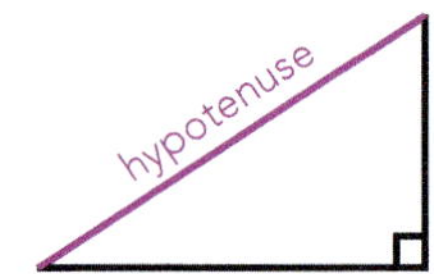

icosahedron

See also **polyhedron, regular polyhedron**

A polyhedron with twenty faces.

A regular icosahedron is formed by joining together twenty congruent equilateral triangles. It is one of the five Platonic solids.

Example

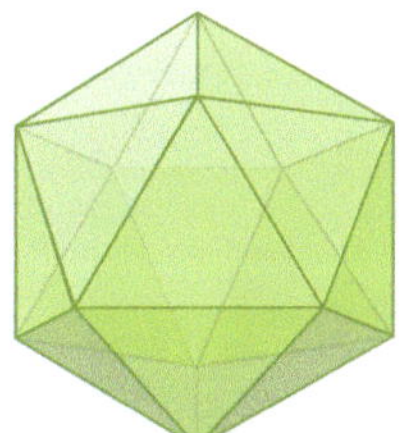

regular icosahedron

identical

Exactly alike.

Example

image

See also **enlargement, reflection, rotation, transformation, translation**

A figure that has undergone a transformation (reflection, rotation, translation or enlargement) produces a second figure called the image. The first figure is called the original.

Examples

i Triangle *ABC* has been reflected across the vertical line to give triangle *A′B′C′* as the image.

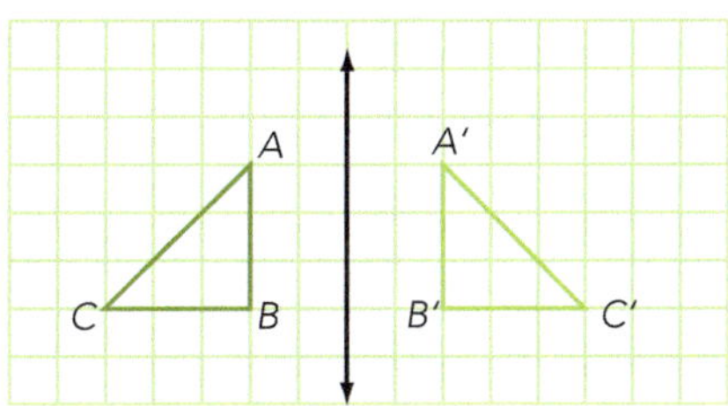

ii Pentagon *ABCDE* has been rotated around the point *O* to give *A′B′C′D′E′* as the image.

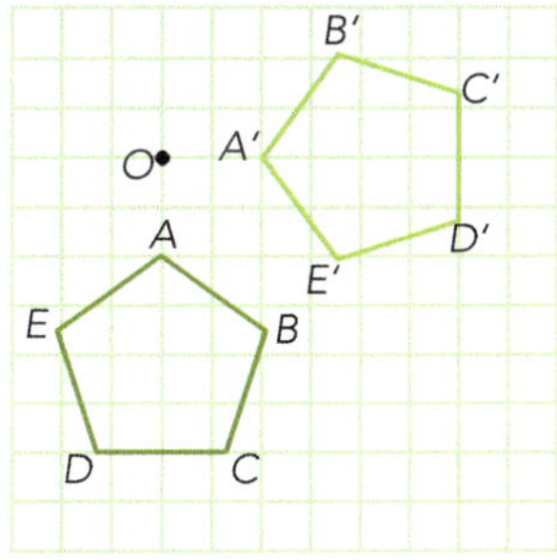

improper fraction

See also **denominator, fraction, mixed number, numerator, proper fraction**

A fraction whose numerator is greater than its denominator. The number represented is greater than 1.

Example

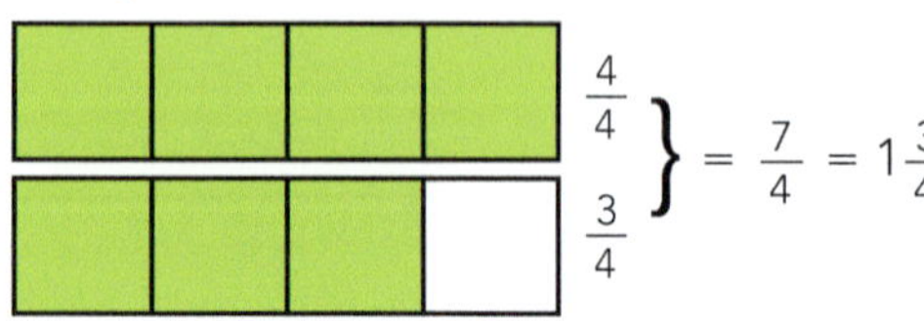

inch (Symbol: ", in)

See also **foot, mile**

A unit of length in the imperial measurement system.

1 inch ≈ 2.54 cm
12 inches = 1 foot

income

See also **gross income, income tax, net income, tax deduction**

Money received for work done and from business activities and investments, such as shares, property or savings. Income before tax and other deductions is called gross income, and income after deductions is called net income.

Example

Robert has a gross income from his employment of $75 000. He has income from interest on his bank account of $270 per year and a rental property that earns him $300 per week.

increase

See also **decrease, progression**

Make larger. A positive number can be increased by

- adding a positive number
- subtracting a negative number
- multiplying by a number greater than one
- dividing by a number between 0 and 1.

Examples

i The price of a three-dollar bus ticket has been increased by fifty cents.

$3 + 50c = $3.50

ii My family of two cats has increased by a factor of three. How many cats do I have now?

$2 \times 3 = 6$

I have six cats.

independent event

See also **die, event, outcome, probability**

In a probability situation, an outcome of one event that has no effect or influence on the outcome of another event.

Example

Drawing a card from a pack, then rolling a die. The type of card that is drawn has no effect on which number is rolled.

independent variable

See also **bivariate numerical data, dependent variable, formula, variable**

In algebra and in a bivariate data set, the value that causes change in the dependent variable.

A scatter plot can be constructed or a formula can be used to show the relationship between the variables. The *x*-axis is used to plot the independent variable.

In a data set where time is one of the variables, time is always the independent variable.

Example

If water is filling a cylindrical tank, time is the independent variable. The volume of water in the tank is a dependent variable. As time changes (increases), it causes a change (increase) in the volume of water. The height of water in the tank is another dependent variable.

index (Plural: indices)

See also **base, cube root, expand, exponent, index notation, power of a number, square root**

A number, reduced in size, written higher and to the right of another number called the base. The index tells you how many times the base will appear when written as a string of repeated multiplications.

Example

In 3^6, 6 is the index and 3 is the base.

$$3^6 = 3 \times 3 \times 3 \times 3 \times 3 \times 3$$

The index is also called the exponent or power.

In $\sqrt[3]{5}$ the index is $\frac{1}{3}$. In $\sqrt{5}$, the index is $\frac{1}{2}$.

index laws

In algebra, when working with indices or algebraic expressions, the following laws apply:

Law	Example
$x^a \times x^b = x^{a+b}$	$5^3 \times 5^2 = 5^{3+2} = 5^5$
$\frac{x^a}{x^b} = x^{a-b}$	$\frac{5^3}{5^2} = 5^{3-2} = 5^1 = 5$
$x^0 = 1$	$5^0 = 1$
$(x^a)^b = x^{a \times b} = x^{ab}$	$(5^3)^2 = 5^{3\times 2} = 5^6$
$(x \times y)^a = x^a y^a$	$(5 \times 4)^3 = 5^3 \times 4^3$
$(\frac{x}{y})^a = \frac{x^a}{y^a}$	$(\frac{5}{4})^3 = \frac{5^3}{4^3}$
$x^{-a} = \frac{1}{x^a}$	$5^{-3} = \frac{1}{5^3}$
$\sqrt[n]{a} = a^{\frac{1}{n}}$	$\sqrt[3]{5} = 5^{\frac{1}{3}}$

index notation

See also **base, cubic number, index, power of a number, scientific notation, square number**

A shorthand way of writing large numbers such as 1 000 000. Also called index form.

Example

Using index notation:

$$1\,000\,000 = 10 \times 10 \times 10 \times 10 \times 10 \times 10 = 10^6$$

10^6

index, power or exponent

base

is read as:
'ten to the power of six' or
'ten to the sixth power'.

inequality

See also **equality, greater than, less than, not equal**

A statement that one quantity is less than or greater than another.

The symbols <, > and ≠ are used to express inequalities.

Examples

$5 \neq 6$	Five is not equal to 6.
$5 < 6$	Five is less than 6.
$6 > 4$	Six is greater than 4.

inequality signs

Sign	Meaning
$<$	less than
$\leq$	less than or equal to
$\neq$	not equal to
$>$	greater than
$\geq$	greater than or equal to

inequation

See also **equality, equation, inequality**

A statement that two quantities are not equal.

Example

$$x + 5 > 7$$
$$-5 \quad -5$$
$$x > 2$$

This inequation is true for any number greater than 2. It has the solution $x > 2$. For example, if $x = 3$, $3 + 5 = 8$, which is greater than 7.

infer

See also **prediction**

Make a predictive statement or conclusion, based on observation or reasoning.

infinite

See also **finite, set, whole numbers**

Without bounds of size or number, unlimited, not finite, endless.

Example

The set of whole numbers is an infinite set.

infinity (Symbol: ∞)

See also **infinite**

Expressing quantity without bounds.

informal unit

See also **handspan, standard unit, unit, unit of measurement**

Also known as a non-standard unit. Any unit used for measurement that is not part of a standardised system.

Example

A handspan is an informal unit of length, where a standard unit of length is a metre (m).

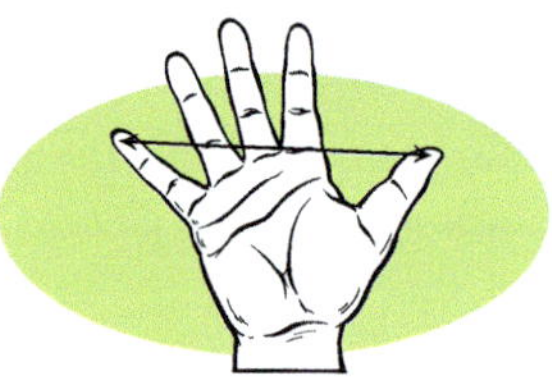

integers

See also **directed numbers, negative numbers, positive numbers, set, whole number**

Positive or negative whole numbers and zero.

Examples

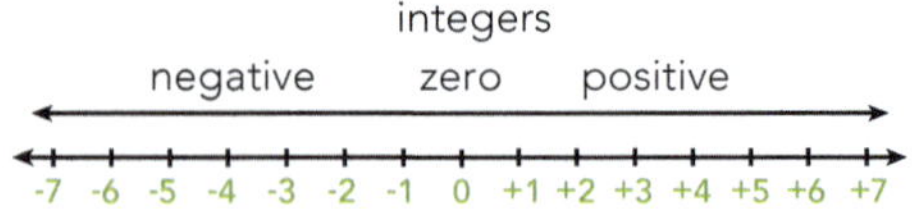

The set of integers:
{-6, -5, -4, -3, -2, -1, 0, 1, 2, 3, 4, 5...}

intercept

See also **coordinates, gradient, *x*-intercept, *y*-intercept**

The point where the graph of an equation crosses an axis.

Example

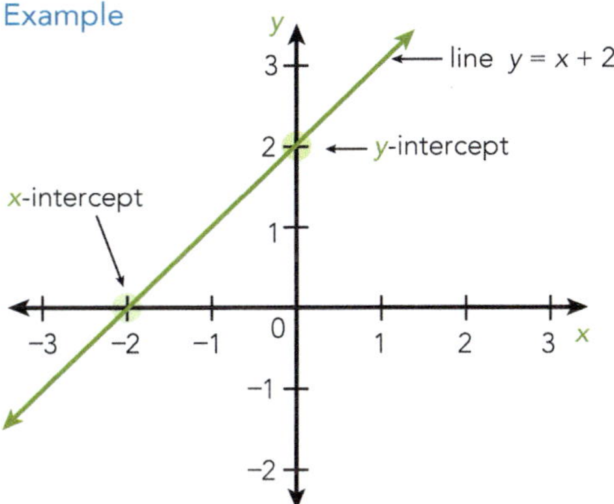

The line $y = x + 2$ crosses the y-axis at point (0, 2). The point (0, 2) is called the y-intercept.

The line also crosses the x-axis at point (–2, 0), which is called the x-intercept.

interest

See also **compound interest, interest rate, principal, simple interest**

An amount of money that is charged or paid for the use of money. There are two types of interest, simple and compound.

1 Simple interest is calculated only on the amount that is borrowed or invested. It is calculated using the formula

$$I = PRT$$

where I is the interest, P is the principal, R is the rate for a time period and T is number of time periods. (N is sometimes used instead of T.)

2 Compound interest is charged on the principal and the interest that has accrued over the time period and is calculated using the formulas

$$I = A - P \text{ and}$$

$$A = P\left(1 + \tfrac{r}{100}\right)^n$$

where A is the amount at the end of the interest period, P is the principal, r is the rate for a time period and n is the number of time periods.

Examples

i The bank pays interest to a person who puts money into a savings account, as the bank can use that money to lend to someone else.

ii People who borrow money from a bank have to pay the bank interest on the amount borrowed, in return for using the bank's money.

interest rate

See also **interest, per annum, principal**

The interest rate is a rate that is charged or paid for the use of money. It is often expressed as an annual percentage of the principal. The interest rate charged for money that is borrowed from a financial institution is always higher than the interest rate offered on savings by that institution.

Examples

i A bank offers a home loan rate of 6.5%.

ii A credit union offers an interest rate of 3.5% on a savings account.

interior

See also **exterior**

The inside of an object or shape.

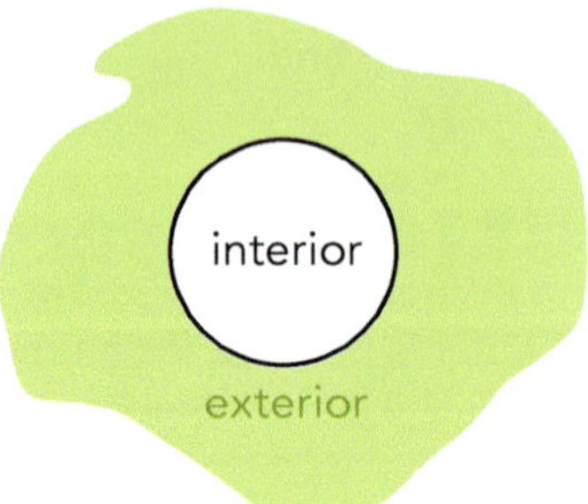

interior angles

See also **exterior**

Angles inside a shape.

Example

The sum of the interior angles inside any triangle is 180°.

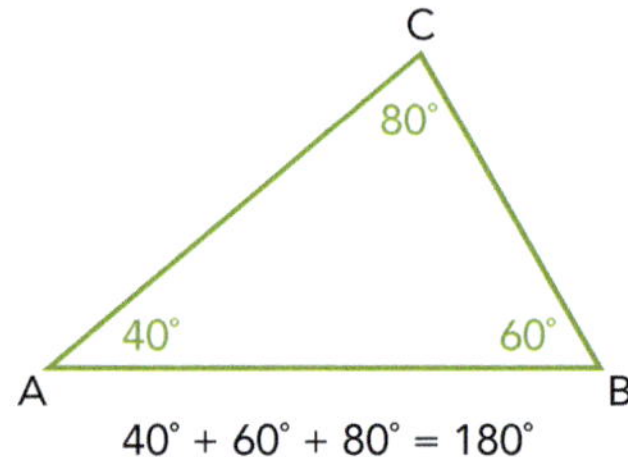

intersect

To cut across. To cross each other.

Example

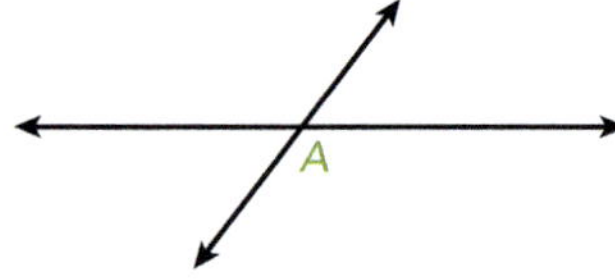

The two lines intersect at point A.

intersection

See also **coordinates, origin, region, set, shape**

1 The place where two or more lines meet, like an intersection of two streets.

Example

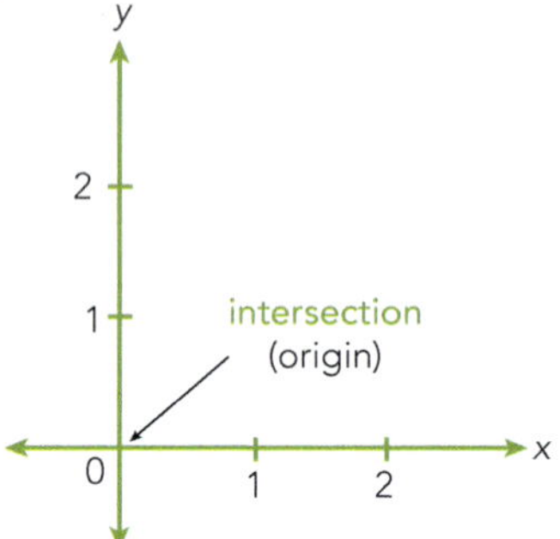

The point of intersection of the x-axis and the y-axis is the origin, (0, 0).

2 The region where shapes overlap.

Example

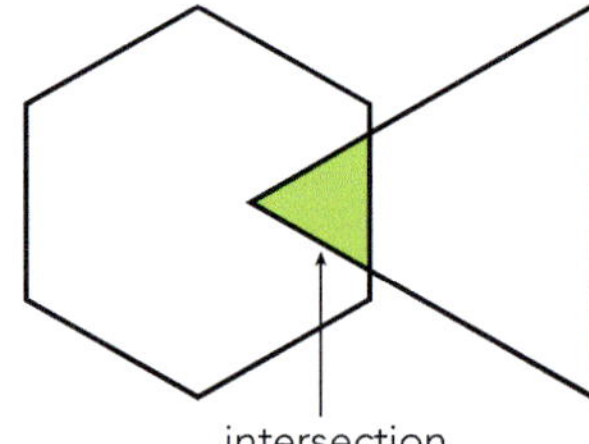

3 (Of sets) The set of elements that are common to both sets.

Example

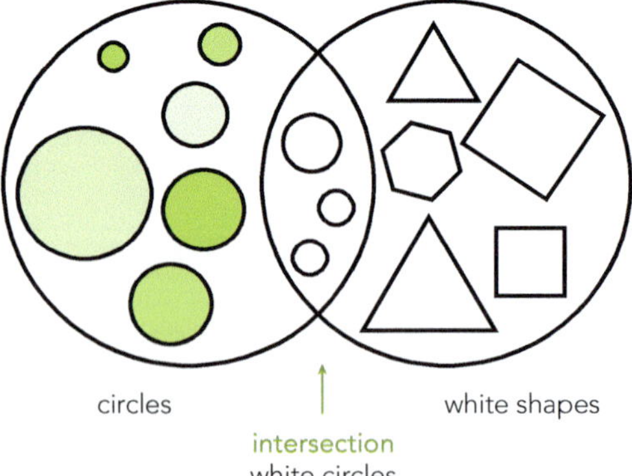

interquartile range (IQR)

See also **data, quartile, statistics**

In statistics, a measure of the spread of the middle 50% of the values of a data set. It is the difference between the lower quartile (Q_L) and the upper quartile (Q_U).

Because it is unaffected by outliers, or the shape of the data distribution, the IQR is a good measure of the consistency of a data set. A small IQR means that the data is closely grouped around the median.

Example

Number of runs scored by two cricket players in 14 innings.

Player 1:
8 11 29 31 33 41 46 52 59 62 70 78 95 102

$Q_L = 31$ (25th percentile) median = 49 (50th percentile) $Q_U = 70$ (75th percentile)

$$\begin{aligned} IQR &= Q_U - Q_L \\ &= 70 - 31 \\ &= 39 \end{aligned}$$

Player 2:
0 2 9 17 23 37 48 52 57 64 73 79 82 97

$Q_L = 17$ (25th percentile) median = 50 (50th percentile) $Q_U = 73$ (75th percentile)

$$\begin{aligned} IQR &= Q_U - Q_L \\ &= 73 - 17 \\ &= 56 \end{aligned}$$

The IQR of Player 2 is much greater than the IQR of Player 1. It could be concluded that Player 1 is the more consistent player.

interval

See also **line, line segment**

The amount of time, or distance, between two events or points.

Examples

i There is a twenty-minute interval between the two films.

ii Line segment

inverse

See also **additive inverse, invert, proportion, ratio**

Inverted in position, order or relation. When one quantity increases, the other decreases at the same rate.

inverse operations

See also **operation, reciprocal**

The operation which reverses the action of the original operation.

Examples

i – (subtraction) is the inverse operation to + (addition)

$4 + 3 = 7$ and
$7 - 3 = 4$
are the inverse of one another.

ii ÷ (division) is the inverse of × (multiplication)

$6 \times 3 = 18$ and
$18 \div 3 = 6$
are the inverse of one another.

invert

See also **flip**

Turn upside down, flip, reverse position.

Examples

$\frac{1}{2}$ inverts to $\frac{2}{1}$ or 2

$\frac{3}{4}$ inverts to $\frac{4}{3}$ or $1\frac{1}{3}$

irrational number

See also **rational number, real number**

Number that cannot be written as an integer or fraction.

Examples

π $\sqrt{2}$ $\sqrt{3}$ $\sqrt[3]{2}$

irregular polygon

See also **polygon, regular polygon**

A shape in which not all sides are equal in length, and/or at least one angle is different in size from the other angles.

Examples

isometric drawing

See also **perspective**

A drawing where the three dimensions are represented by three sets of lines 120° apart, and all measurements are in the same scale (not in perspective).

Example

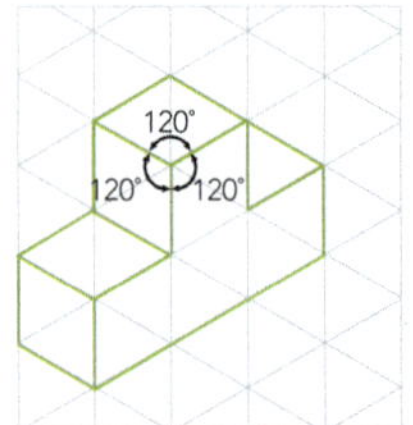

isometric paper

See also **equilateral triangle, isometric drawing**

Paper with dots or lines that make equilateral triangles. Used for isometric drawings.

Example

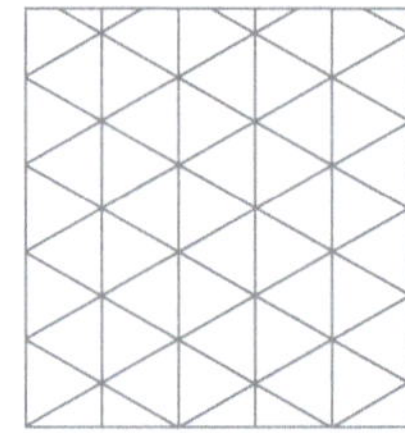

isometric grid paper

isometric dot paper

isosceles triangle

See also **equilateral triangle, scalene triangle**

A triangle in which two sides have the same length and two angles have the same size.

Examples

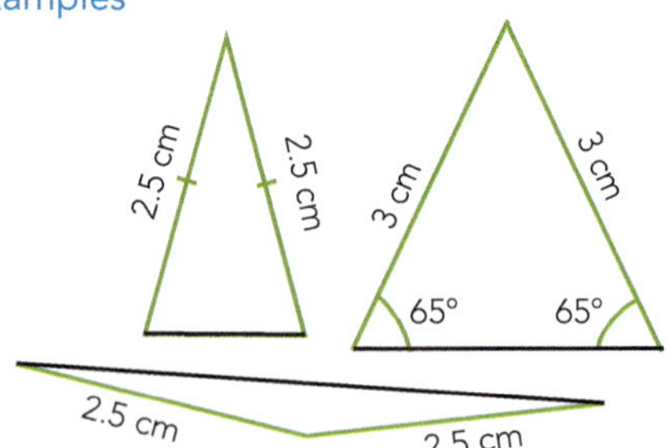

jigsaw

A puzzle in which pieces fit together to form a picture.

Example

joule

See also **kilojoule**

Unit of energy or work. It replaces the former unit, calorie.

kilo

See also **Decimal system prefixes** on page 192, **kilogram, kilojoule, kilolitre, kilometre**

Prefix that means one thousand.

kilogram (Symbol: kg)

See also **gram, mass, unit of measurement**

The base unit of mass.

1 kg = 1000 g

Example

The mass of this packet of sugar is 1 kilogram.

kilojoule (Symbol: kJ)

See also **joule**

Used for measuring energy or work.

1 kilojoule = 1000 joules

Example

This piece of chocolate cake contains about 2000 kilojoules.

kilolitre (Symbol: kL)

See also **capacity, unit of measurement, volume**

A unit of volume (capacity) for measuring liquids.

1 kL = 1000 L

Example

Five 200-litre oil drums hold 1 kilolitre.

kilometre (Symbol: km)

See also **distance, unit of measurement**

A unit of distance. Distances between towns are measured in kilometres.

1 km = 1000 m

Example

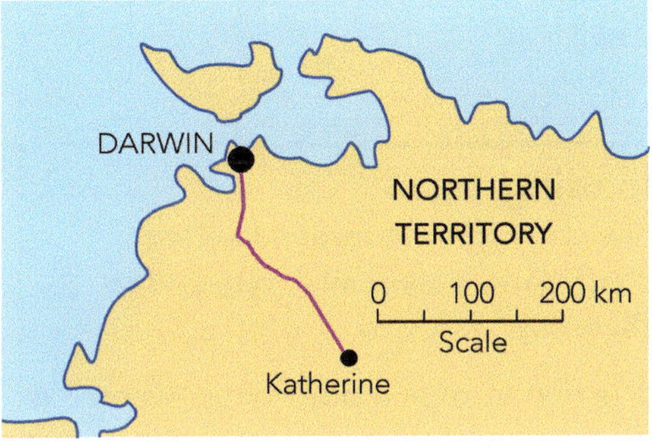

The road distance from Darwin to Katherine is 352 kilometres.

kite

See also **quadrilateral**

A quadrilateral that has pairs of adjacent sides equal in length.

The diagonals are perpendicular to each other. The long diagonal is the perpendicular bisector of the short diagonal. One pair of opposite angles are equal.

$$\angle ADC = \angle ABC$$

knot (Symbol: kn)

See also **speed**

Measure of speed at sea and in aviation, equal to travelling one nautical mile per hour.

1 nautical mile = 1.852 kilometres

Example

A ship moving at 20 knots is travelling as fast as a vehicle on land travelling about 37 kilometres per hour.

L

See **capacity, litre**

1 The symbol for litre.

2 In Roman numerals L stands for fifty.

lateral

See **equilateral, problem solving**

LCD

See **lowest common denominator**

LCM

See **lowest common multiple**

leading coefficient

See also **factor theorem, leading term, polynomial, remainder theorem**

The coefficient of the leading term in a polynomial.

Example

In the polynomial $3x^4 - 5x^3 - 6x^2 + 4x + 7$, 3 is the leading coefficient.

leading term

See also **factor theorem, leading coefficient, polynomial, remainder theorem**

The first term in a polynomial when it is written in polynomial form in descending order of powers of the variable.

Example

In the polynomial $3x^4 - 5x^3 - 6x^2 + 4x + 7$, $3x^4$ is the leading term.

leap year

A year which has 366 days instead of 365 days. It occurs every 4 years.

In a leap year February has 29 days instead of 28 days.

When the year number can be divided by 4 leaving no remainder, then it is a leap year.

Examples

i 1979 ÷ 4 = 494 (r3)
1979 was not a leap year.

ii 2012 ÷ 4 = 503
2012 was leap year.

Century years are not leap years unless they are divisible by 400.

Example

1600, 2000, 2400 are leap years.
1500, 1700, 1800 are not leap years.

least

The smallest thing or amount in a group.

Example

The toy car costs the least amount.

length

See also **centimetre, distance, interval, kilometre, metre, millimetre**

How long something is from end to end.

1 The measure of distance.

Some metric units of length are:

millimetre	mm
centimetre	cm
metre	m
kilometre	km

Examples

i This ruler is 30 centimetres long.

ii The length of this table is 1.8 metres.

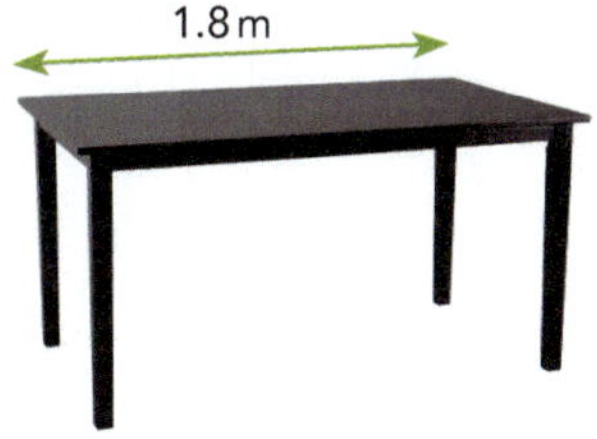

2 An interval of time.
Some intervals of time are: second, minute, hour, day, week, month, year, decade, century.

Example

A lunch break could be 50 minutes or 1 hour.

less than (Symbol: <)

See also **greater than, inequality signs**

A relation between pairs of numbers showing which is smaller.

Example

$$5 < 7$$

↑ less than

like terms

See also **power of a number, unlike terms, variable**

In algebra, terms that have exactly the same variable and power. Like terms can be added and subtracted; unlike terms cannot.

Examples

Like terms	Unlike terms
$4x$, $3x$	a, b
$5x^2y$, x^2y	$3x^2$, 3

line

See also **curve, horizontal line, infinite, interval, line segment, vertical**

A long thin mark drawn on a surface. It can be straight or curved. It has no thickness and has only one dimension. A straight line extends without end in both directions. The arrow heads indicate this.

A straight line is the shortest possible distance between two points.

Example

The interval (line segment) *AB* is the shortest distance between *A* and *B* and has a finite length.

Examples

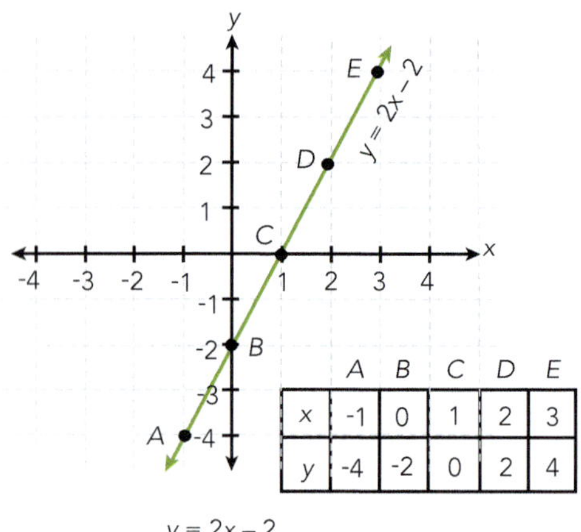

	A	B	C	D	E
x	-1	0	1	2	3
y	-4	-2	0	2	4

$y = 2x - 2$

linear

See also **line, linear equation**

1. Involving measurement in one dimension only.
2. A relationship between two variables that gives a straight line when graphed.

linear equation

See also **equation**

An equation that produces a straight line when graphed. The highest power of both the dependent and independent variables in a linear equation is 1.

line graph

See also **continuous data, graph, independent variable, line, line segment**

A graph consisting of lines used to show data that changes over a period of time. Time is always shown on the *x*-axis as the independent variable. Individual data values are plotted as points, then the points are joined with straight line segments. The data being plotted must be continuous data.

Example

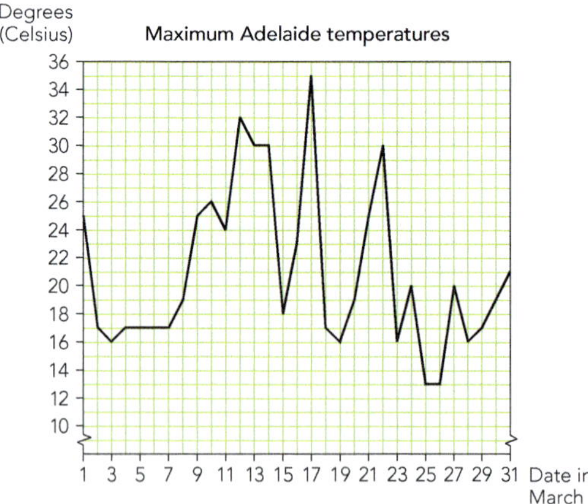

line of best fit

See also **data, scatter plot, variable (statistics)**

A line drawn to show a relationship that may exist between two variables, usually resulting from the collection of experimental or observational data, that have been plotted as a scatter plot. It minimises the sum of the distances from each data point to the line.

Example

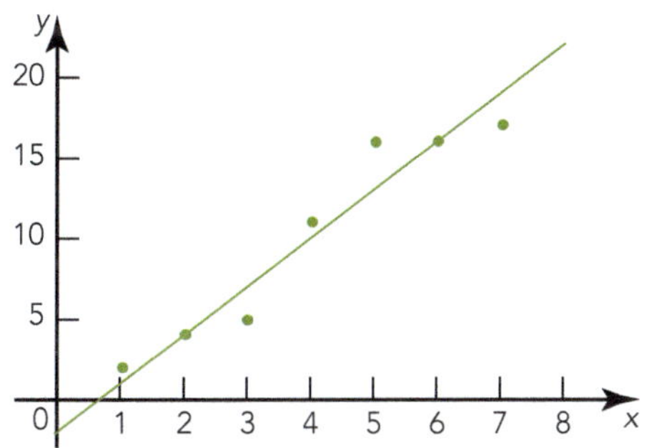

line of symmetry

See **axis of symmetry**

line segment

See also **interval, line**

Part of a straight line. It has a finite length. Also called an interval.

Example

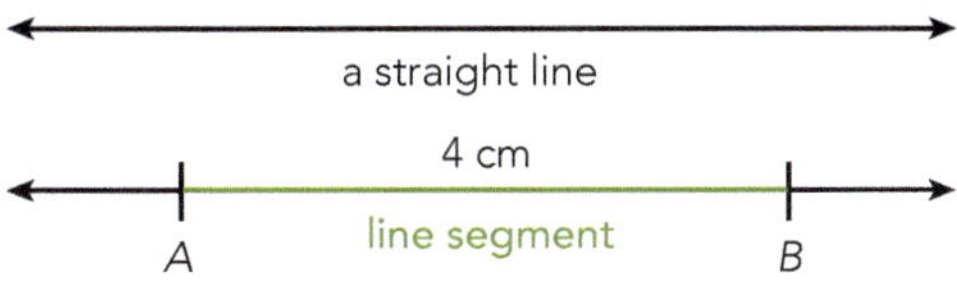

The line segment *AB* is 4 cm long.

litre (Symbol: L)

See also **capacity, unit of measurement, volume**

A unit of capacity used to measure the volume of liquid or gas that a container can hold.

$$1 \text{ L} = 1000 \text{ cm}^3$$
$$= 1000 \text{ mL}$$
$$1000 \text{ L} = 1 \text{ kL}$$

Example

A carton of milk holds 1 litre.

location (statistics)

See also **mean, median, mode, quartile, range, statistics**

A measure of location is a single value that is used to represent a data set. The most commonly used measures of location are the mean and the median. The mode is occasionally used but is not really a measure of location.

logarithm

See also **exponent, index, power of a number**

Another word for power, index or exponent. The logarithm, or 'log' of a number is the power to which a given base must be raised, in order to produce the number.

If we let b = the base (a positive number, $b \neq 1$)
y = the power
x = the number ($x > 0$)

We can write $b^y = x$ and $\log_b x = y$, which we say as 'the log of x to the base b is y'.

Logarithms are often written using base 10; however, other bases can be used.

Example

$100 = 10^2$, so $\log_{10}100 = 2$

$8 = 2^3$, so $\log_2 8 = 3$

Logarithms are not always whole numbers. Logarithms can also be negative numbers.

Example

$\log_{10}45 = 1.6532.....$

The 'log' key on a scientific calculator can be used to find the base 10 log of any positive number.

loss

See also **cost price, profit, selling price**

The difference between the cost price and selling price of an article when the cost price is the larger amount. It is equivalent to a negative profit.

Example

A car dealer buys a car for \$10 000 and sells the same car for \$9000. The dealer suffers a loss of \$1000.

lowest common denominator (LCD)

See also **common denominator, denominator, fraction, lowest common multiple**

The lowest number that is divisible by the denominators of given fractions. The lowest multiple of two or more denominators.

Example

What is the LCD of fractions $\frac{1}{4}$ and $\frac{1}{10}$?

Multiples of 4: 4, 8, 12, 16, (20), 24, 28, 32, 36, (40), 44 …

Multiples of 10: 10, (20), 30, (40), 50, 60, 70 …

The lowest number into which 4 and 10 divide exactly is 20.

Therefore 20 is the LCD.

Lowest common denominators are used in addition and subtraction of fractions. Fractions with different denominators must be converted to equivalent fractions with the same denominator before they can be added.

Example

$$\frac{1}{4} + \frac{1}{10} = \frac{5}{20} + \frac{2}{20}$$
$$= \frac{7}{20}$$

lowest common multiple (LCM)

See also **multiple**

The lowest number that is a multiple of two or more given numbers.

Example

What is the LCM of 2 and 3?

The multiples of 2 are:
2, 4, (6), 8, 10, (12), 14, 16, (18) …

The multiples of 3 are:
3, (6), 9, (12), 15, (18), 21, …

Common multiples are: 6, 12, 18…

The lowest common multiple of 2 and 3 is 6.

m

1 The symbol for metre.

2 The symbol for the prefix milli. Milli means one thousandth ($\frac{1}{1000}$).

M

1 The symbol for the prefix mega. Mega means one million (1 000 000).

2 In Roman numerals M means 1000.

MAB

See **multibase arithmetic blocks**

magic square

A puzzle where the numbers are arranged in a square so that each row, column and diagonal add up to the same total.

Example

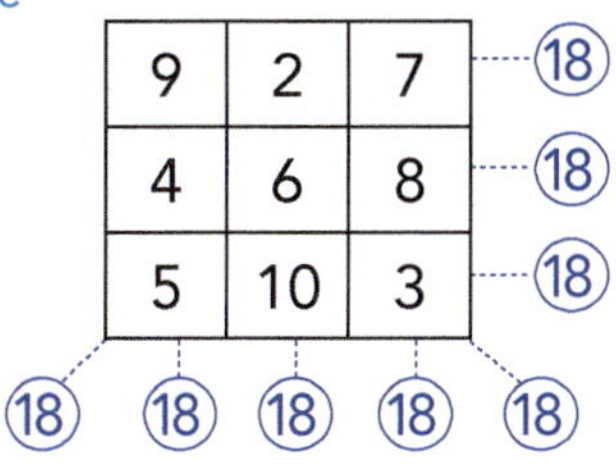

9	2	7
4	6	8
5	10	3

magnitude

See also **directed numbers**

The size of something, or how big it is.

Example

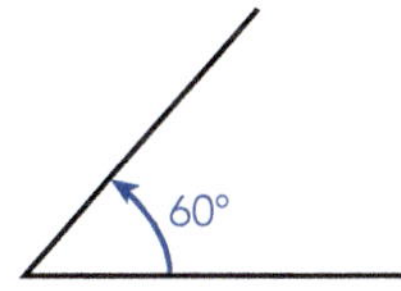

The magnitude of this angle is 60°.

The sign of the number is not considered when finding the magnitude.

The magnitude can be indicated using modulus signs | |.

Example

The magnitude of –463 is 463 or |–463| = 463

many-to-many correspondence

See also **many-to-one correspondence, one-to-many correspondence, one-to-one correspondence**

A matching between members of two sets for which more than one member of the first set is paired with more than one member of the second set.

many-to-many correspondence continued ▶

Example

All the cups and saucers in a matching set of crockery. Any cup can be paired with any saucer and vice versa.

many-to-one correspondence

See also **arrow diagram, one-to-one correspondence**

A matching between members of two sets for which more than one element of the first set is paired with only one element of the second. Arrows are used to show the relationship.

Example

Children and their favourite drink

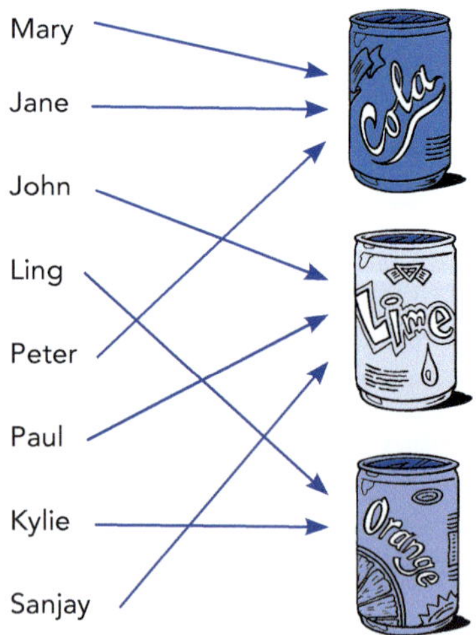

Three elements (Mary, Jane and Peter) of the first set are associated with one element (Cola) of the second set.

mapping

See also **image, many-to-one correspondence, one-to-one correspondence, set**

A matching operation between two sets in which each member of the first set is assigned only one member of the second set as a partner or image.

Example

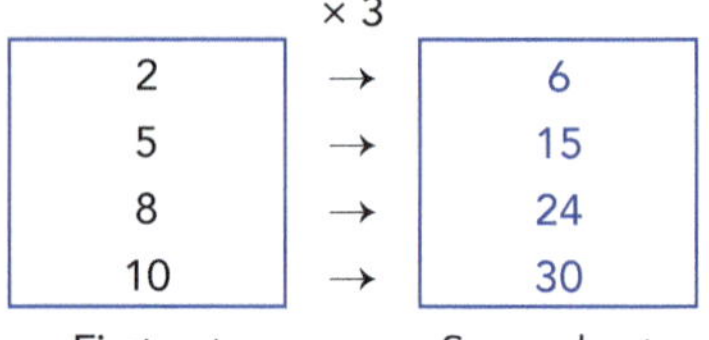

First set	× 3	Second set
2	→	6
5	→	15
8	→	24
10	→	30

In the above example, 2 maps onto 6, so 6 is the image of 2.

markup

See also **cost price, discount, loss, profit, selling price**

The amount added to the cost price of an item to get the selling price.

Example

A lamp that costs a retailer $42 is sold for $79. The markup is $37.

mass

See also **unit of measurement, weight**

The amount of matter contained in an object.

Units of mass:

gram	g
kilogram	kg
tonne	t
1000 g	= 1 kg
1000 kg	= 1 t

Example

This boy has a mass of 45 kilograms.

The word 'weight' is commonly but incorrectly used instead of mass. The weight of an object changes depending on gravity. Mass remains constant.

Example

While the weight of an object is less on the top of a high mountain than in an underground cave, its mass does not change.

The mass of an object together with its container is called the gross mass.

The actual mass of the object is called net mass. The mass of the container is called tare.

Example

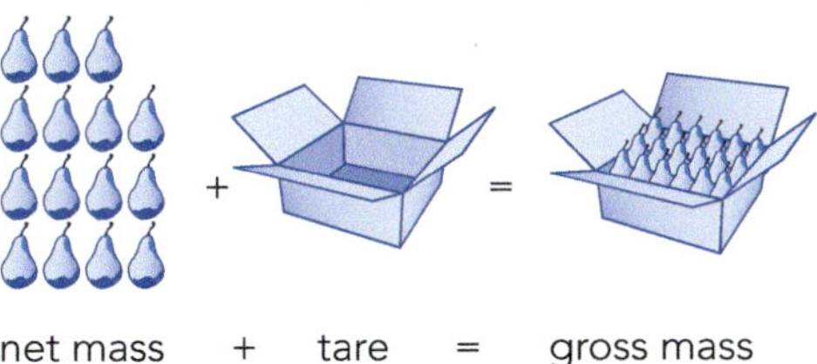

net mass + tare = gross mass

matching angles

See also **congruent**

Angles in the same position in different shapes. In congruent shapes, matching angles are the same size.

Example

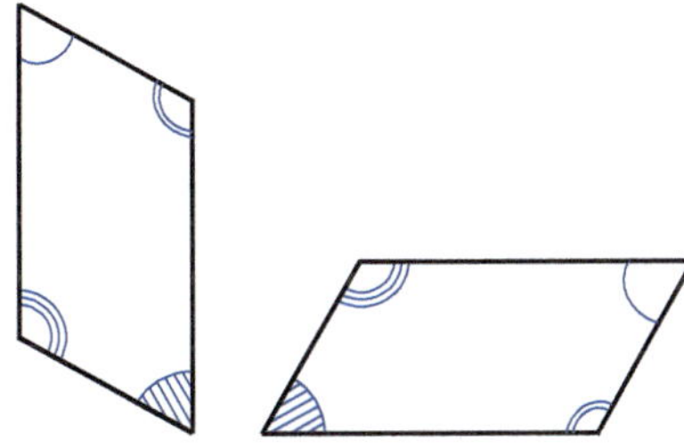

These parallelograms are congruent. Matching angles are marked by the same symbol.

matching sides

See also **congruent**

Sides of congruent shapes that are in the same position relative to the angles and therefore of the same length.

Example

In these triangles, *AB* and *XY*, *BC* and *YZ*, and *CA* and *ZX* are pairs of matching sides.

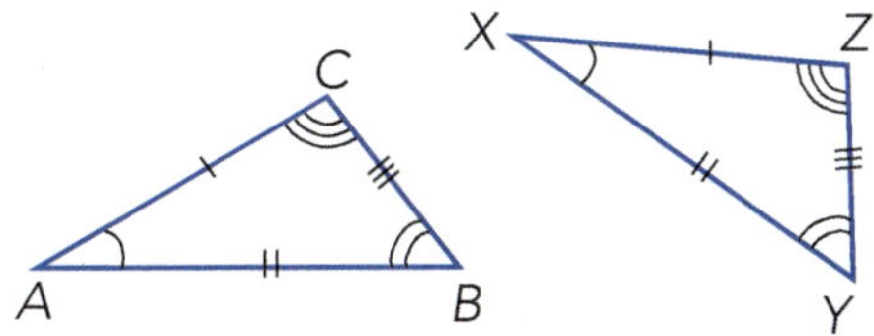

mathematical conventions

See also **order of operations, symbols**

Rules that all mathematicians in the world agree to work by so that maths symbols and processes mean the same to everyone.

Example

The order of operations used to simplify 8 ÷ 2 × (5 – 9) is the same worldwide so everyone will get the same answer.

$$\begin{aligned} 8 \div 2 \times (5 - 9) &= 8 \div 2 \times -4 \\ &= 4 \times -4 \\ &= -16 \end{aligned}$$

mathematical shorthand

See also **formula**

Instead of long sentences, mathematics uses numbers, symbols, formulas and diagrams.

Example

The sentence, 'The area of a triangle is found when its base is multiplied by its perpendicular height and then divided by two', is written in mathematical shorthand as:

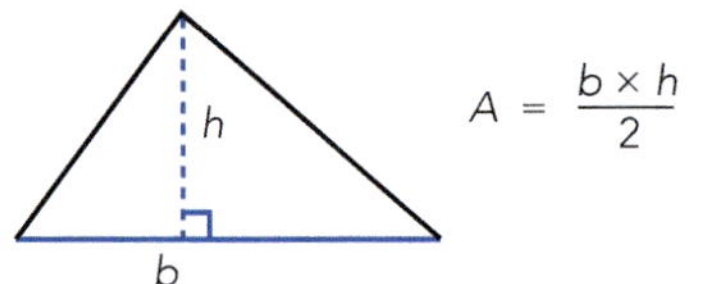

$$A = \frac{b \times h}{2}$$

maximum

See also **minimum**

The greatest or biggest value.

Examples

i The maximum temperature this month was 42°C.

ii The maximum speed is 100 kilometres per hour.

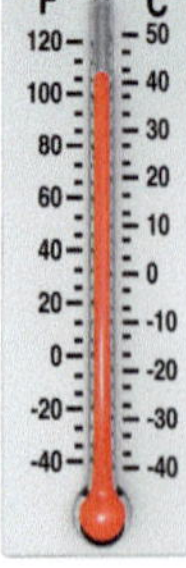

maze

See also **jigsaw**

A puzzle where a path has to be found through a network of lines.

Example

There is a path from A to B that can be followed through the maze without crossing any lines.

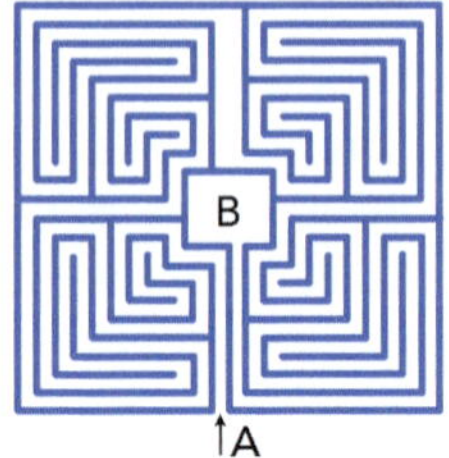

mean

See also **average, location, measures of central tendency**

The mean is the average of a set of data values. It is found by adding up all data values and dividing the sum by the number of scores.

$$\text{Mean} = \frac{\text{sum of data values}}{\text{number of data values}}$$

measure

See also **unit of measurement**

1 Find out the size of something.

Examples

Length, height, weight and time can be measured.

2 Compare quantities. A number assigned to a quantity which indicates its size compared to a chosen unit, such as a metre, a litre or a kilogram.

Example

The length of the book is 30 cm.

measures of location

See **mean, median, mode**

median

See also **average, data value, location, mean, mode, score**

In statistics, the median is the middle measurement or data value, when data values are arranged in order of size.

Example

Values: 2, 2, 4, 5, 6, 8, 10

↑

median = 5

Where there is no middle value, an average of the two central values is taken.

Example

Values: 2, 3, 4, 8, 9, 10

↑ ↑

$\text{median} = \frac{4+8}{2} = 6$

mega (Symbol: M)

See also **Decimal system prefixes** on page 000, **megalitre**

Prefix meaning one million.

megalitre (Symbol: ML)

See also **capacity**

A unit of capacity.

1 megalitre = 1 000 000 litres
1 ML = 1 000 000 L

Example

Volume (capacity) of this swimming pool is:

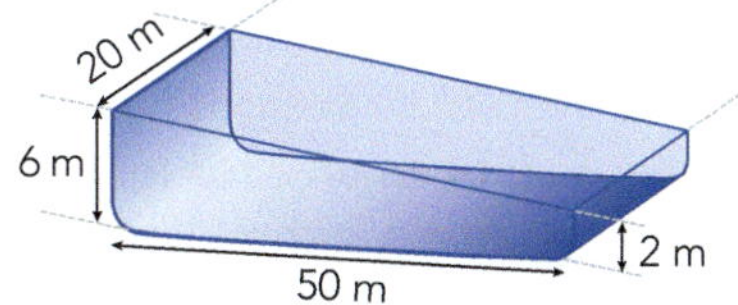

$$\begin{aligned}\text{Volume} &= [50 \times 20 \times (\tfrac{6+2}{2})]\ \text{m}^3 \\ &= 4000\ \text{m}^3 \\ &= 4\,000\,000\ \text{L} \\ &= 4\ \text{ML}\end{aligned}$$

This swimming pool contains four megalitres (4 ML) of water.

mensuration

See also **measurement**

The branch of mathematics concerned with the measurement of lengths, areas and volumes.

metre (Symbol: m)

See also **distance, unit**

The base unit of length (distance).

1 m = 100 cm
1 m = 1000 mm

Example

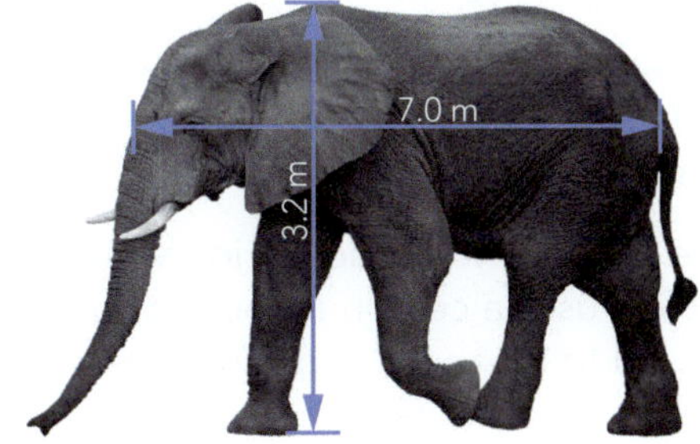

This elephant is 7 metres long and 3.2 metres high.

metric system

See also **decimal system, SI, unit of measurement**

A decimal system of weights and measures. The base unit for length is the metre, for mass is the kilogram, and for time is the second.

midpoint

See also **bisect, bisector**

A point in the middle of an interval, or exactly in between two other points.

Example

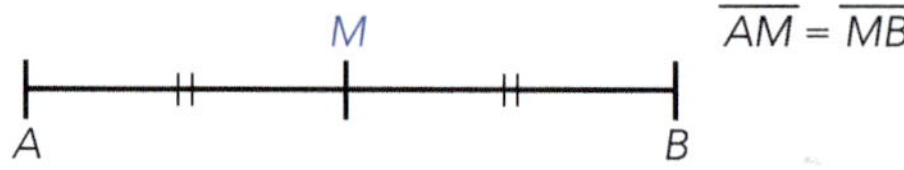

The point M is the midpoint of the interval AB.

The midpoint $m(x, y)$ between the points (x_1, y_1) and (x_2, y_2) is given by the formula

$$m(x, y) = \left(\frac{x_1 + x_2}{2}, \frac{y_1 + y_2}{2}\right)$$

mile

See also **foot, inch**

A unit of length in the imperial system.

1 mile ≈ 1.6 km

mileage

See also **gallon, mile**

The distance travelled during which the car uses a certain amount of petrol. It used to mean miles per gallon of petrol. It now means the number of kilometres per litre of petrol, or the consumption of petrol (in litres) per 100 kilometres.

milli (Symbol: m)

See also **Decimal system prefixes** on page 192, **milligram, millilitre**

Prefix meaning one-thousandth.

milligram (Symbol: mg)

See also **gram**

A very small unit of mass. It is one-thousandth of a gram.

$1 \text{ mg} = \frac{1}{1000} \text{ g}$

$1 \text{ mg} = 0.001 \text{ g}$

millilitre (Symbol: mL)

See also **centimetre, volume**

A unit of capacity, equivalent to a volume of 1 cubic centimetre.

$1 \text{ mL} = 1 \text{ cm}^3$

$1000 \text{ mL} = 1 \text{ L}$

Note: One millilitre of water at 4°C has a mass of one gram.

Examples

A teaspoon holds 5 mL.

This water bottle holds 600 mL.

millimetre (Symbol: mm)

See also **centimetre, length**

A unit of length.

10 mm = 1 cm

Examples

million

See also **billion**

One thousand thousands: 1 000 000.

minimum

See also **maximum**

The smallest or least value.

Example

The minimum temperature in July was 4°C.

minuend

See also **difference, subtract, subtrahend**

A number from which another number is to be subtracted.

Example

29	–	7	=	22
↑		↑		↑
minuend		subtrahend		difference

29 is the minuend.

minus (Symbol: –)

See also **subtract**

Subtract or take away.

Example

Eight minus two is written as 8 – 2 and means two subtracted from eight.

8 – 2 = 6

minute (Symbol: min, ′)

1 A measure of time.

one minute = sixty seconds
1 min = 60 s

There are sixty minutes in one hour.

2 Angle measurement.

$1'$ (min) $= \frac{1}{60^\circ}$ (degree)
1° (degree) $= 60'$

mirror image

See also **image, reflection**

A reflection, as in a mirror.

mixed number

See also **fraction, improper fraction, whole numbers**

A number that consists of a whole number part and a fraction part.

Examples

$1\frac{1}{2}$ $3\frac{5}{2}$

Mixed numbers are another way of writing improper fractions:

$\frac{3}{2} = 1\frac{1}{2}$ $\frac{35}{30} = 1\frac{5}{30} = 1\frac{1}{6}$

möbius (moebius) strip

A surface with only one side. It is made by giving a strip of paper or any other flexible material a half twist and then fastening the ends together.

If a line is drawn down the middle of the strip, it will come back to the starting point, having covered both sides of the strip, without the pencil being lifted.

Example

A thin strip of paper ...

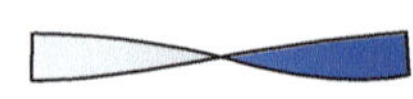
can be given a twist ...

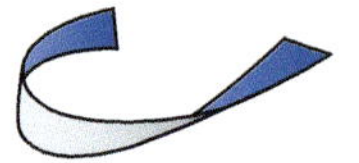
and have the ends ...

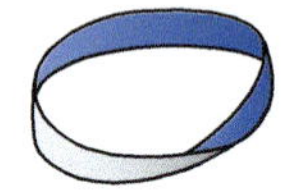
joined to make a möbius strip.

mode

See also **average, bimodal, location, mean, median**

In statistics, the data value that occurs most often in a collection. It is not a measure of location but it is often used as one.

Example
In data values
1, 1, 2, 4, 4, 6, 6, 6, 6, 7, 7, 7, 8, 10
6 is the mode.

model

See also **cube, net, scale drawing, three-dimensional**

A three-dimensional representation of an actual or designed object. It may be a physical structure, for example, a model of a cube made from cardboard or an architect's model of a house.

Examples

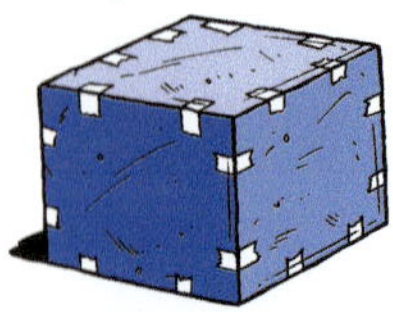
a model of a cube

a model of a house

monic

See also **leading term, non-monic, polynomial, quadratic expression**

Used to describe polynomial expressions in which the coefficient of the leading term is 1. In the general form of a quadratic expression, $ax^2 + bx + c$, $a = 1$.

Examples
$x^4 + 3x^2 - 5x$, $x^3 - 8x^2 + 4x - 5$, $x^2 + 4x - 7$, $x^2 - 9$, $x^2 + 5x$ are all monic expressions.

month

See also **calendar, day, leap year, year**

A measure of time. There are 12 months in a year. The lengths of different months vary from 28 to 31 days.

An easy way to remember the number of days in each month is to learn the following rhyme.

Thirty days has September,
April, June and November.
All the rest have thirty-one,
Except for February alone,
Which has but twenty-eight days clear,
And twenty-nine in each leap year.

more

Greater in amount.

Example
Four dollars is more than three dollars.

most

The greatest amount.

Example
Jack has twenty dollars.
Kylie has thirty-five dollars.
Ben has thirty dollars.
Kylie has the most money.

multibase arithmetic blocks (MAB)

See also **base**

A set of wooden blocks used to give a concrete representation of numbers. They can be used for any base.

Example
Base 3 blocks

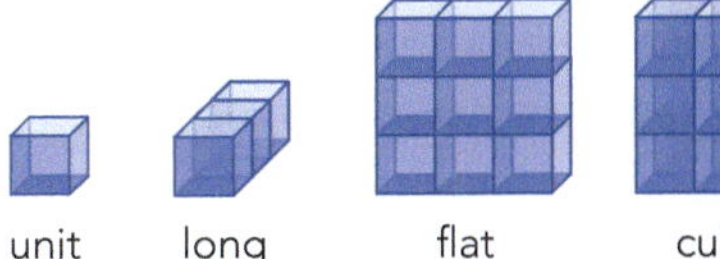

The most commonly used MAB blocks are the base ten blocks.

A set of base ten blocks consists of:

small cubes – units or ones

longs – 10 small cubes joined together

flats or squares – 100 small cubes formed into a square

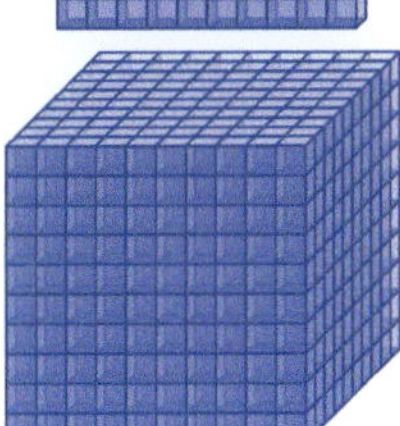

large cubes – 1000 small cubes formed into a large cube

multilateral

Having many sides.

multiple

See also **division, lowest common multiple**

A multiple of a given number is any number into which it will divide exactly. They are the numbers in the multiplication table of a given number.

Examples
Multiples of two are 2, 4, 6, 8, 10, 12 …
Multiples of three are 3, 6, 9, 12, 15, 18 …
Multiples of four are 4, 8, 12, 16, 20, 24 …

multiplicand

See also **multiplication, multiplier, product**

The number that is to be multiplied.

Example

8	×	7	=	56
↑		↑		↑
multiplicand		multiplier		product

multiplication (Symbol: ×)

See also **addition, operation**

Multiplication is repeated addition.

Example

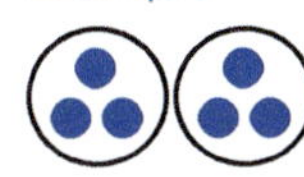

means

i 3 + 3, 2 groups of 3, 2 × 3 or 6
ii 3 multiplied by 2, 3 × 2 = 6 or
iii 3 made 2 times bigger.

The multiplication symbol × means this many lots of.

multiplication facts

See **table**

multiplication property of one

See also **equivalent fractions**

When a number is multiplied by one, the product is equal to the original number. This is the multiplication property of one.

Examples

$7 \times 1 = 7$
$1 \times 138 = 138$

Use of the property is made when a fraction is converted to an equivalent form.

Example

$\frac{2}{3} = \frac{\square}{12}$

$\frac{2}{3} \times 1 = \frac{2}{3} \times \frac{4}{4}$

$= \frac{8}{12}$

$\frac{2}{3}$ has been multiplied by one (or by $\frac{4}{4}$, which is equal to one).

multiplier

See also **multiplicand, multiplication, product**

The number by which another number is multiplied.

Example

5	×	7	=	35
↑		↑		↑
multiplicand		multiplier		product

multiply

See also **addition, multiplication**

To perform repeated addition. Carry out the process of multiplication.

Example

Multiply 5 by 7

$5 \times 7 = 35$

mutually exclusive

See also **events, outcome, probability**

Two events that cannot occur at the same time are mutually exclusive; if one event occurs, then the other cannot.

Example

A jar contains eight red lollies, five green lollies and seven yellow lollies. If a lolly is drawn at random, it must be red, green or yellow. If it is red, it cannot be green or yellow. Drawing a red lolly, a green lolly or a yellow lolly are mutually exclusive events.

natural number

See also **counting number, positive numbers**

One of the counting numbers.

Examples

1, 2, 3, 4, 5, 6, 7, 8, 9 …

nautical mile

See also **knot**

Unit of length. Used for aviation (flying) and maritime (shipping) purposes. A nautical mile is based on the circumference of the Earth. One nautical mile equals 1852 metres or 1.852 kilometres.

negative numbers

See also **integers, positive numbers, zero**

A negative number is a number less than zero. Negative numbers are written with the negative sign (–) in front of them.

Examples

i -0.1, -0.2, …-0.9, …-1, -1.1, … -2, …-2.55 …

ii

-5 -4 -3 -2 -1 0 1 2 3 4 5

net

See also **cube, model, pattern, pyramid**

A two-dimensional (2D) drawing of a three-dimensional (3D) solid, showing all of the faces of the solid. A three-dimensional model of the solid can be constructed by folding up the net.

Examples

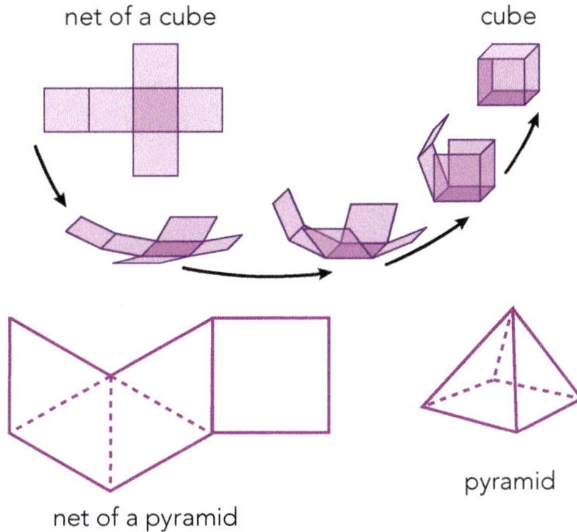

net income

See also **deductions, gross income, tax**

Total earnings in salary or wages, investments and bonuses after tax and other deductions have been made; also known as take-home pay.

Example

Robert has a gross income of $104 000. He pays $26 427 in tax. His net income is $77 573.

network

See also **intersection, node, topology**

A system of lines or arcs and intersections (nodes) drawn to represent paths and their intersections.

Examples

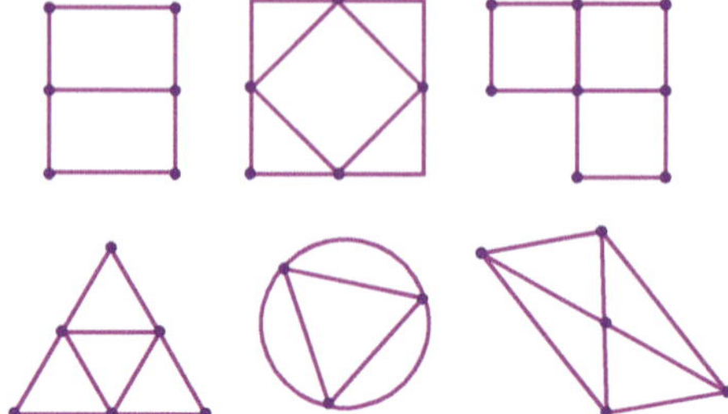

The properties of networks are studied as part of a branch of mathematics called topology.

node

See also **intersect, network**

A point where straight lines or curves intersect. It is also called a junction.

Examples

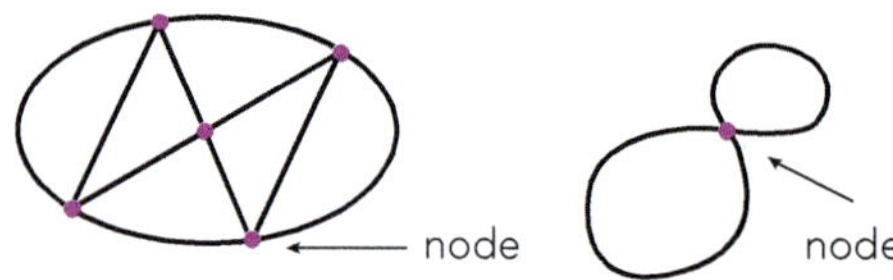

nonagon

See also **polygon**

A polygon with nine sides and nine angles. A regular nonagon has nine equal sides and nine equal angles.

Examples

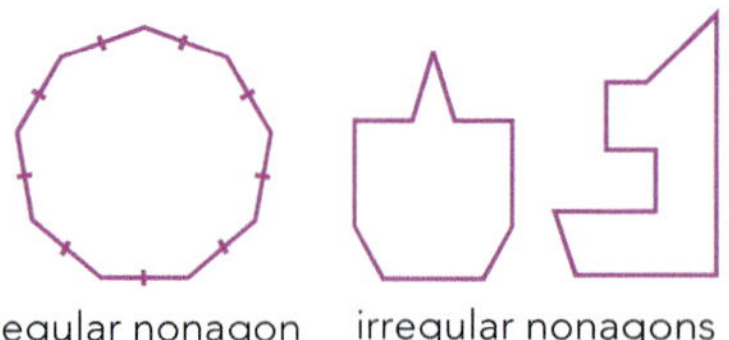

none

See also **zero**

Nothing. Not one. Not any.

Example

non-monic

See also **leading term, monic, polynomial, quadratic expression**

Used to describe polynomials in which the coefficient of the leading term is not 1. In the general form of a quadratic expression, $ax^2 + bx + c$, the polynomial is non-monic if $a \neq 1$.

non-planar figure

See also **planar figure**

A three-dimensional figure. A solid or space figure.

Examples

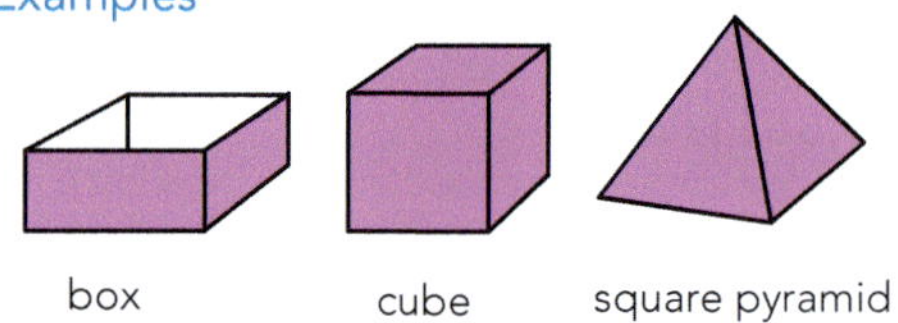

Non-planar means 'not in one plane'.

non-terminating decimal

See also **irrational number, recurring decimal, surd**

A decimal that has no final digit. It could be a recurring decimal, such as 0.3333333…, or a non-recurring decimal, such as π, or another irrational number, such as a surd.

Examples

$\frac{1}{11} = 0.181\,818\,181\,8\ldots$

$\sqrt{2} = 1.414\,213\,562\ldots$

not equal to (Symbol: ≠)

See also **inequality**

Not of equal value. Unequal. The symbol ≠ is used to indicate that two amounts are not of equal value.

Example

$4 \neq 5$

Four is not equal to five.

nothing (Symbol: 0)

See also **zero**

Not one. Having not a thing. Not anything. None. Zero.

null factor law

See also **factors, zero**

If the product of factors is zero, then at least one of the factors is zero.

Example

If $ab = 0$, then $a = 0$ or $b = 0$

number

See also **composite number, even number, irrational number, integers, natural number, odd number, prime number, rational number, square number, whole numbers**

A measure of quantity.
Numbers are grouped into many different sets:

- Natural (counting) numbers:
  1, 2, 3, 4, 5, 6, ...
- Whole numbers:
  0, 1, 2, 3, 4, 5, ...
- Integers:
  ...-4, -3, -2, -1, 0, +1, +2, +3, ...
- Rational numbers, which include fractions and ratios:
  $\frac{1}{100}$ 1 : 3
- Irrational numbers which include surds:
  $\sqrt{2}$, π, $\sqrt[3]{6}$

Other kinds of numbers include composite, prime, odd, even and square numbers.

Examples

2 is the only even number that is also a prime number.
1 is neither a prime or composite number.

number line

See also **integers, operation, order**

A line on which equally spaced points are marked. The points correspond, in order, to the numbers shown.

Example

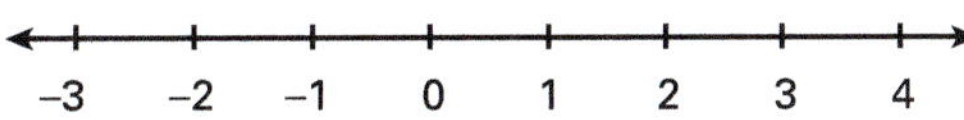

On a number line, the points are labelled from zero and move left of zero for negative numbers and right of zero for positive numbers. The numbers show the distance from zero to each point (the distance between successive points is one unit).

Operations with numbers can be shown on a number line.

number line continued ▶

Example

Add 3 and 4.

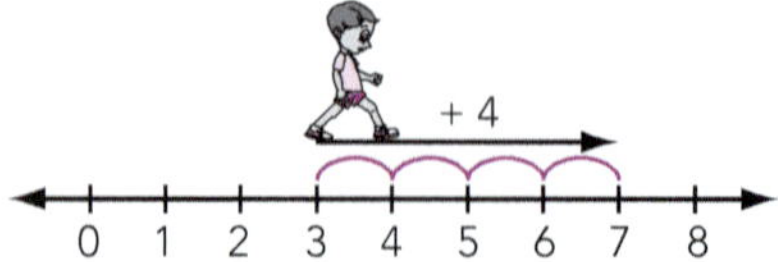

Start at the first number. Add the second number by walking that number of steps in the positive direction.

$3 + 4 = 7$

number machine

See also **calculator, flowchart, rule**

Number machines can carry out operations such as addition, subtraction, multiplication and division. Calculators and computers are types of number machines. A flowchart can be used to show the operations of a number machine.

Example

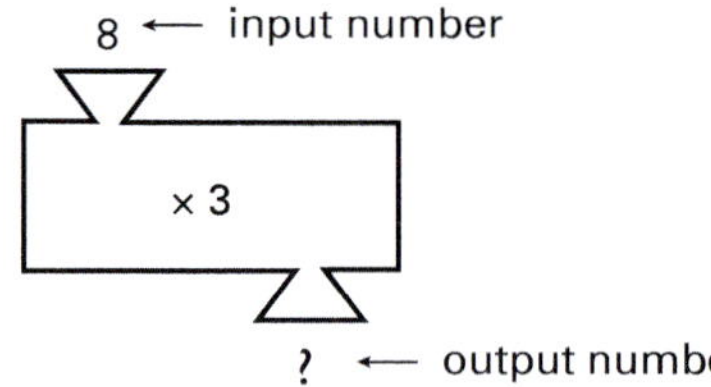

i The number 8 is put into the machine. This is the input number.

ii The number is multiplied by 3. This is the rule.

iii What comes out is the answer.

number pattern

See **pattern**

number sentence

See also **equation, solve, symbol**

A statement about numbers, usually in symbols rather than words.

A number sentence has a left hand side (LHS) and a right hand side (RHS), separated by an equals sign. A true number sentence has a LHS and a RHS that are equal in value. In a false number sentence, the LHS is not equal to the RHS. An open number sentence, or equation, contains one or more variables.

Examples

$6 + 7 = 13$ (true)

$4 \neq 9$ (true)

$5 + \square = 9$ (open)

$7 + 9 = 10$ (false)

$3 + 1 < 3 \times 1$ (false)

numeral

See also **numeration, Roman numerals** on page 187, **symbol**

A symbol used to represent a number.

Example

5 is the numeral which represents the number five.

5 apples

5 and V (Roman) are numerals for the number five.

numeration

See also **Hindu–Arabic system, symbol**

A system of symbols used to represent numbers. Our system uses the symbols 0, 1, 2, 3, 4, 5, 6, 7, 8 and 9.

numerator

See also **denominator, fraction**

The top number in a fraction. It tells how many parts of the whole there are.

Example

$\frac{3}{4}$ ← numerator / ← denominator

In $\frac{3}{4}$ the numerator is 3.

Three out of four equal parts are coloured.

numerical data

See also **categorical variable, continuous data, discrete data**

In statistics, a type of data that is either counted or measured, such as the number of people living in each house on a street (counted), or the height of each person in a house (measured).

Data that is counted is called discrete data. Data that is measured is called continuous data.

Numerical data can be used for calculations, such as finding the mean or median.

It is important to distinguish between truly numerical data, and categorical data where categories have numerical names. For example, postcodes give a data set of numbers, but it is not sensible to perform any calculations on them, such as finding a 'mean (average) postcode'.

Example

Maximum daily temperature (shown in the table below) is an example of a continuous numerical variable. Recording the daily maximum temperatures for the week would give a set of continuous data.

Day	Daily maximum temperatures
Monday	27 °C
Tuesday	29 °C
Wednesday	31 °C
Thursday	34 °C
Friday	33 °C
Saturday	23 °C
Sunday	24 °C

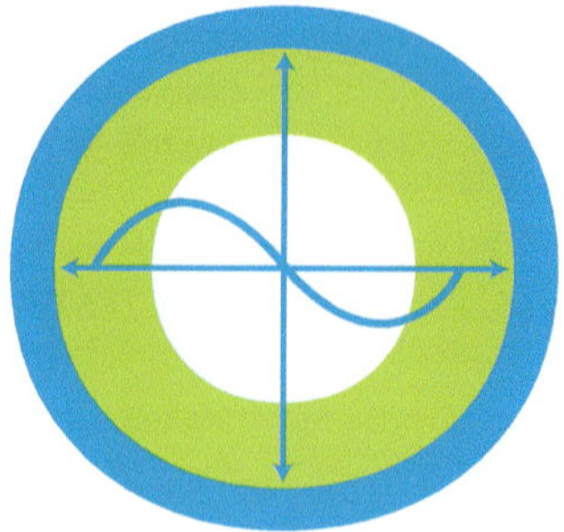

oblique

See also **horizontal, vertical**

A slanting line that is neither vertical nor horizontal.

Examples

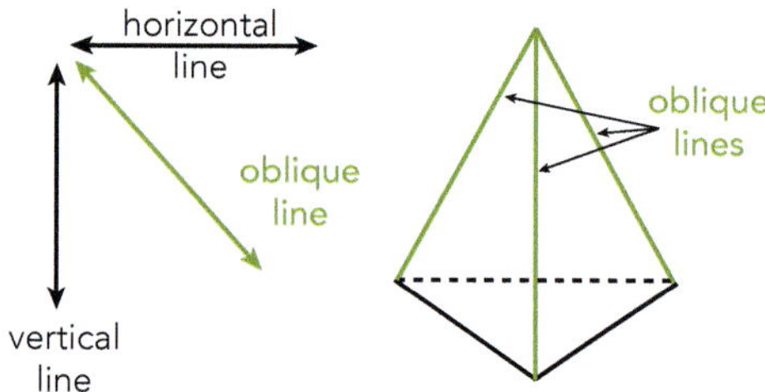

oblong

See also **rectangle**

Another word for a rectangle or for rectangular.

Example

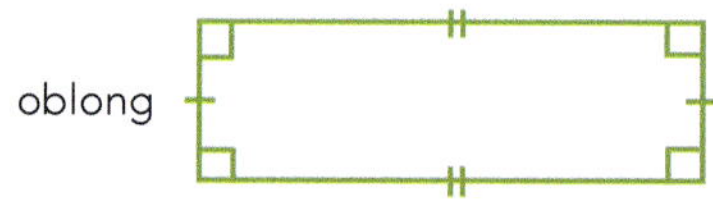

obtuse angle

See also **acute angle, angle, reflex angle, right angle, revolution, straight angle**

An angle bigger than a right angle (90°) but smaller than a straight angle (180°).

Examples

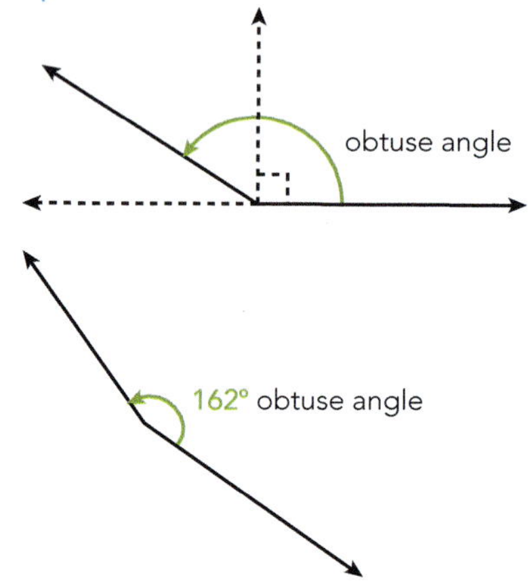

obtuse-angled triangle

See also **acute-angled triangle, right-angled triangle**

A triangle with one obtuse (larger than 90°) angle.

Examples

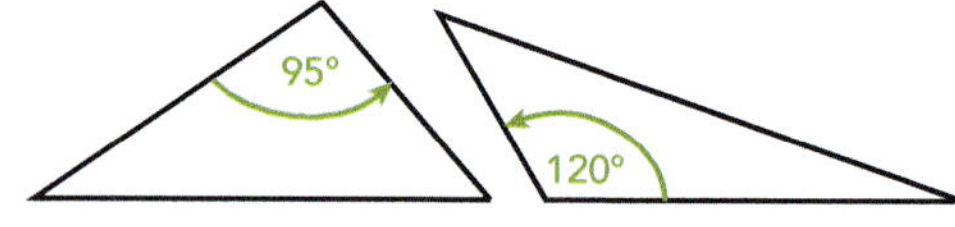

o'clock

See also **hour, time interval**

Used when telling the time but only when talking about full hours. It is not used to describe part hours, such as six fifteen, ten past four.

Examples

Six o'clock, ten o'clock ...

octagon
See also **plane shape, polygon**

A plane shape (polygon) with eight sides and eight angles. A regular octagon has eight equal sides and eight equal angles.

Examples

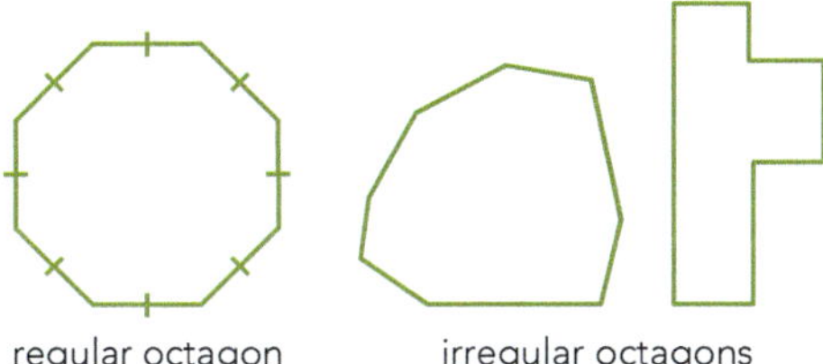

regular octagon irregular octagons

octahedron
See also **polyhedron, regular polyhedron**

A solid (polyhedron) with eight faces. A regular octahedron is formed by eight congruent equilateral triangles. It is one of the five Platonic solids.

Examples

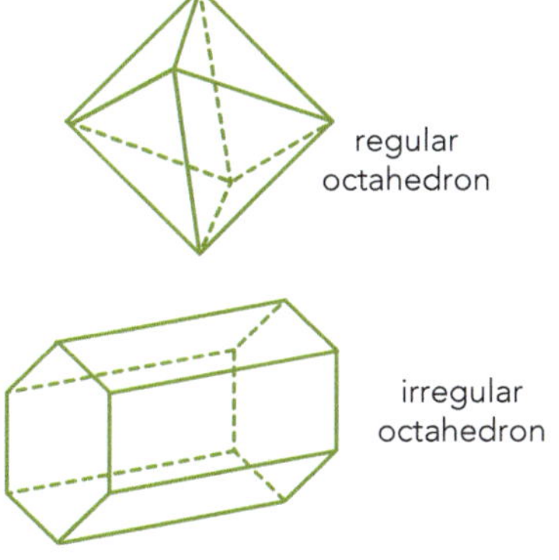

octal
See also **binary, decimal, hexadecimal**

Containing eight parts or digits. It is a base eight number system that is made up of eight digits. The digits represented by this number system are 0 to 7. This number system is used primarily by computer systems, particularly by certain programming languages.

Example

Digits represented: 0, 1, 2, 3, 4, 5, 6, 7

odd number
See also **even number**

A number which, when divided by two, leaves a remainder of 1.

All odd numbers finish with one of the digits 1, 3, 5, 7 or 9.

one-dimensional (1D)
See also **dimension, plane**

A figure which has only length is said to be one-dimensional.

Examples

A line has only length; therefore, it has only one dimension.

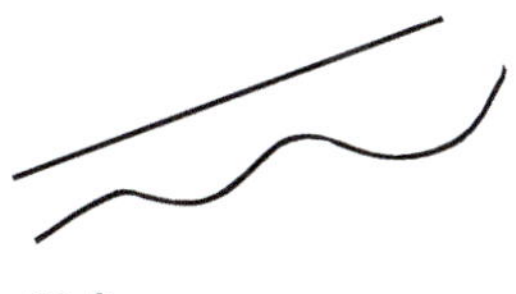

1D figures

one-to-many correspondence

See also **correspondence**

A matching between two sets for which one member of a set is paired with many members of another set.

Example

A duck can have many ducklings

one-to-one correspondence

See also **correspondence, many-to-one correspondence, many-to-many correspondence, one-to-many correspondence, sets**

A matching between two sets for which each member of one set is paired with only one member of the other set. Arrows are used to show the corresponding objects.

Examples

A key and a lock

A dog and a registration tag
A person and a fingerprint

open curve

See also **closed curve, curve**

A curve which has a beginning and an end which do not meet.

Examples

operation

See also **addition, arithmetic, basic facts, division, multiplication, order of operations, subtraction**

A mathematical procedure. Here are four arithmetic operations.

		Examples
Addition	+	2 + 4
Subtraction	–	7 – 3
Multiplication	×	10 × 5
Division	÷	8 ÷ 4

operators

See also **operation**

The signs used in arithmetic operations.

+ – × ÷

Examples

10 + 2 7 × 3

8 – 4 18 ÷ 6

opposite numbers

See also **additive inverse**

Two numbers that add to zero.

Examples

-5 + 5 = 0

The opposite to -5 is 5;
the opposite to 320 is -320.

order

See also **ascending order, descending order, number line, pattern, sequence**

1 Arrange in a pattern or a sequence, or place objects according to their size, value, speed, etc.

2 A pattern or a sequence.

3 Numbers on a number line.

Example

The rabbits have been ordered from smallest to largest.

ordered pair

See also **axis, brackets, coordinates**

Two numbers (called the *x*-coordinate and the *y*-coordinate) that indicate the position of a point on a plane.

Ordered pairs are written in brackets. The *x*-coordinate is always written first. It indicates the distance along the horizontal axis. The *y*-coordinate indicates the distance up or down the vertical axis.

Example

Show (5, 3) and (3, 5) on a Cartesian plane. The ordered pair (3, 5) is not the same as the ordered pair (5, 3).

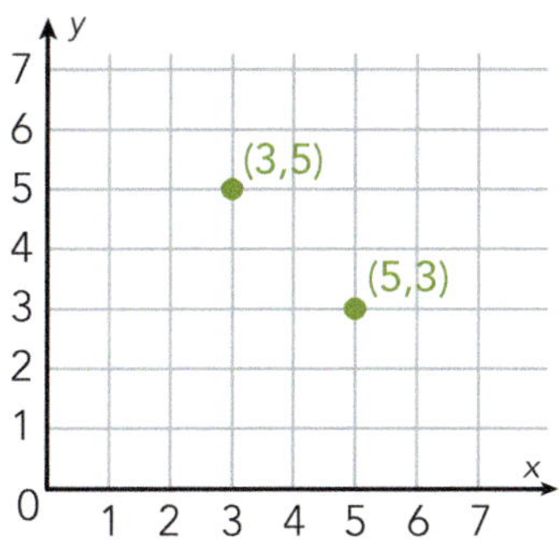

order of operations

See also **brackets, operation, parentheses**

When a calculation contains more than one operation, mathematicians use the following set of rules, known as the 'order of operations'.

Step 1 Any calculations in brackets are done first.

Step 2 Then, perform any calculations with powers (indices).

Step 3 Next, do multiplication and division, in order from left to right, as they appear.

Step 4 Finally, do the addition and subtraction, in order from left to right as they appear.

Example

$24 - 7 + 3 \times (6 + 4) \div 5 + 2^2$
$= 24 - 7 + 3 \times 10 \div 5 + 2^2$ (brackets)
$= 24 - 7 + 3 \times 10 \div 5 + 4$ (powers)
$= 24 - 7 + 6 + 4$ (multiplication and division)
$= 27$ (addition and subtraction)

When more than one set of brackets is used, working is done from the inside bracket to the outside bracket.

Example

$5\{3 - [(4 \times 9) - (20 - 4)] + 19\}$
$= 5\{3 - [36 - 16] + 19\}$
$= 5\{3 - 20 + 19\}$
$= 5 \times 2$
$= 10$

order of reflectional symmetry

See also **axis, image, line of symmetry, mirror image, reflection, symmetry**

The number of axes (lines) of symmetry that can be drawn through a shape.

Example

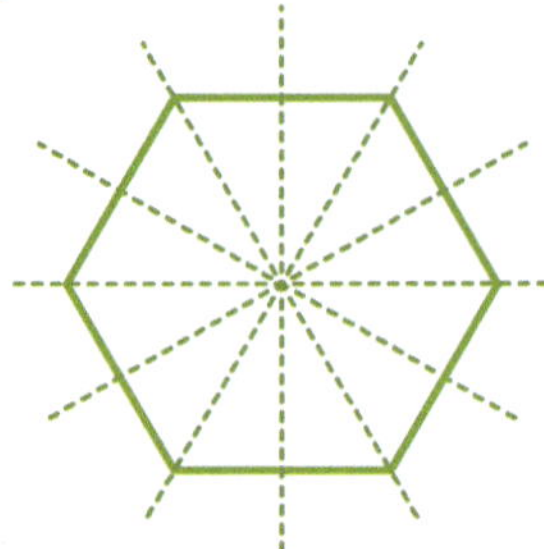

If this shape is reflected along any of the six lines of symmetry shown, an image identical to the original is formed, so the order of reflectional symmetry is 6.

order of rotational symmetry

See also **centre, centre of rotation, image, rotational symmetry, symmetry**

The number of times in a complete 360° rotation that an identical image of the original would be produced.

Example

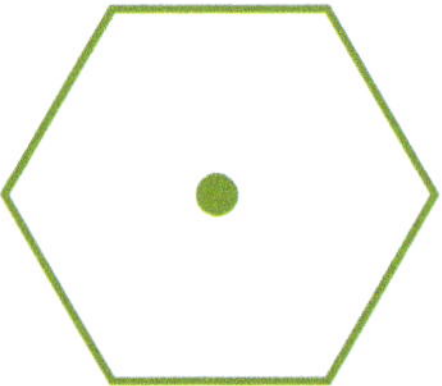

This shape can be rotated 60°, 120°, 180°, 240°, 300° and 360° around the centre of rotation to produce an image that is identical to the original, so the order of rotational symmetry is 6.

ordinal data

See also **non-numerical data**

Non-numerical data that has some sort of order associated with it.

Example

Data collected from a survey question that asks for a response that implies some order.

Regular homework improves student learning

- o strongly disagree
- o disagree
- o unsure
- o agree
- o strongly agree

ordinal number

See also **cardinal number**

A number indicating position.

Examples

ordinate

See also **abscissa, axis, coordinates, *x*-coordinate, *y*-coordinate**

The vertical coordinate of a point. The y-coordinate of a point (x, y) in a Cartesian system. The y-axis is sometimes called the ordinate axis.

Example

For the point (2,3), 3 is the ordinate.

origin

See also **axis, coordinates, intersect, ordered pair**

1 A point in time or space at which something begins.

2 The intersection of the *x*-axis and the *y*-axis in the Cartesian plane. The coordinates of the origin are (0, 0).

Example

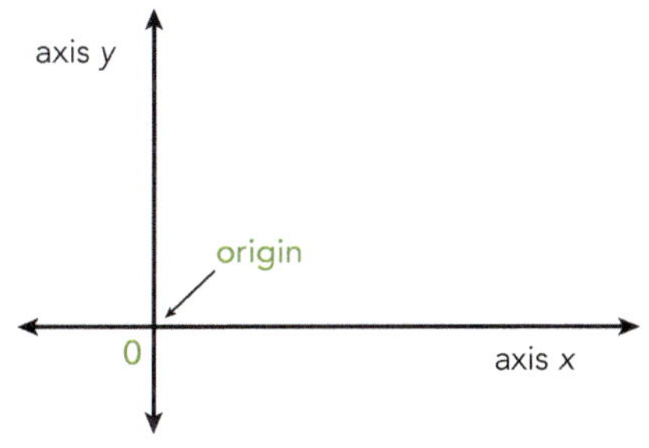

outcome

See also **data, statistics, trial**

The result of an experiment or trial involving the unknown.

Example

When tossing a coin, there are two possible outcomes, either heads or tails.

outlier

See also **box plot, interquartile range, continuous data**

A value in a data set that seems unusually high or low compared to the others. Outliers are often most clearly seen when the data is displayed in a frequency table or a graph.

When constructing a box plot, a data value is considered to be an outlier if it lies more than 1.5 times the interquartile range beyond the upper or lower quartile. This means that a data value is an outlier if it is less than $Q_1 - 1.5(Q_3 - Q_1)$ or greater than $Q_3 + 1.5(Q_3 - Q_1)$.

There may be an explanation for outliers in a data set. In a set of continuous data, outliers may be due to an error in measurement.

Example

This box plot shows the distances travelled by car each week by 30 employees of the same company. There are three outliers: 245, 438, 1880.

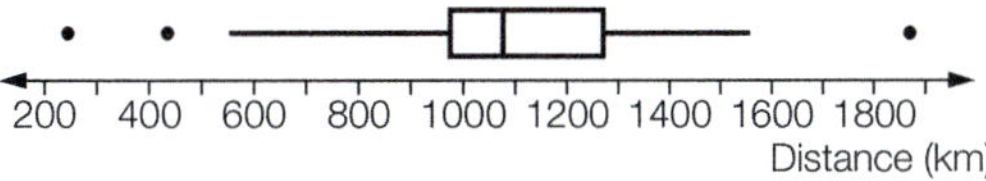

output

See also **number machine**

The answer given for a calculation done by a number machine such as a calculator or computer.

Example

When 3.145 was multiplied by 593.2 on a calculator, the output was 1865.614.

oval

See also **axis, ellipse, symmetry**

1 An egg-shaped figure which is symmetrical about one axis. One end is more pointed than the other.

Example

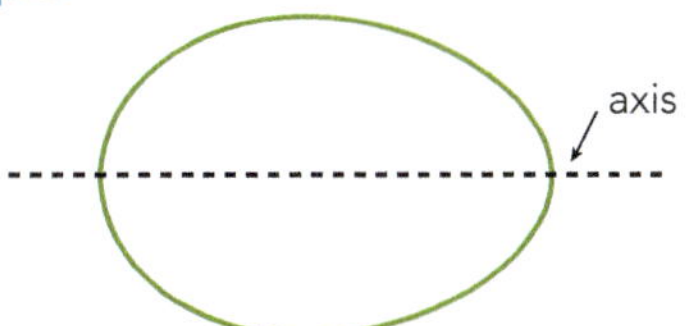

2 Another word for an ellipse, which is symmetrical about two axes.

Example

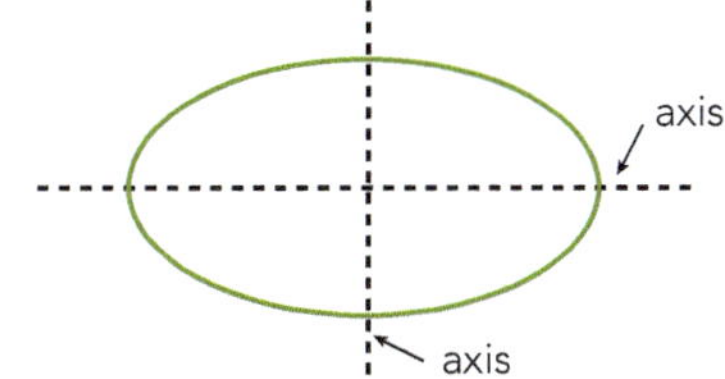

p.a.

Abbreviation of the Latin phrase per annum, meaning 'for each year'.

Example
The bank charges 7% interest p.a.

pace

See also **distance, estimate, informal unit**

The distance between your feet when you take a step. It is measured from heel to heel. It is used as an informal unit for estimating distances.

Example

pair

Two things that belong together.

Example

a pair of socks

palindrome

A date, number or word that reads the same forward as backward.

Examples
1991 19.9.1991 madam

parabola

See also **axis of symmetry, conic section, quadratic equation**

The shape of the graph of a quadratic equation. It is a symmetric curve, with an axis of symmetry that divides it into two identical halves. The point where the graph changes direction (at the very top or bottom of the curve) is called the turning point or vertex.

Example

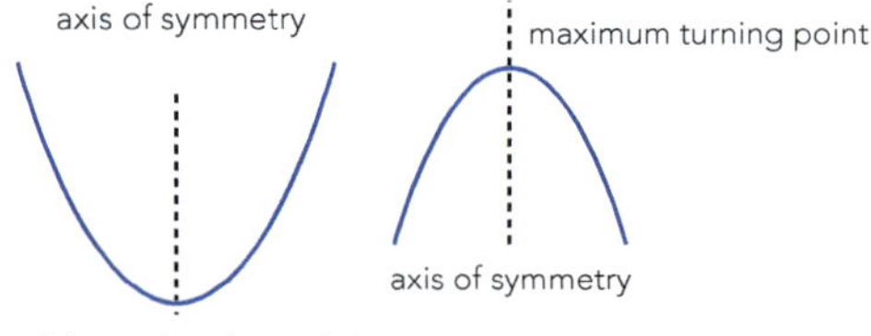

A parabola is also a conic section made by the intersection of a right circular cone and a plane.

Example

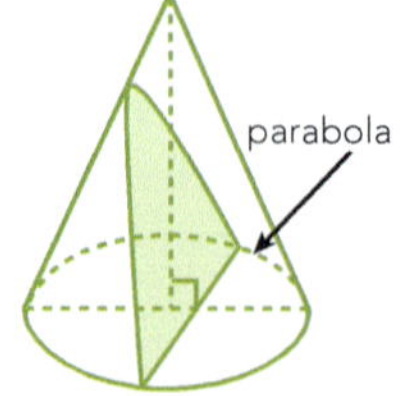

parallel box plot

See also **box plot**

A visual display used to compare two sets of data. Two box plots are drawn on the same scale.

Example

This parallel box plot compares the heights of students in classes 8A and 8B.

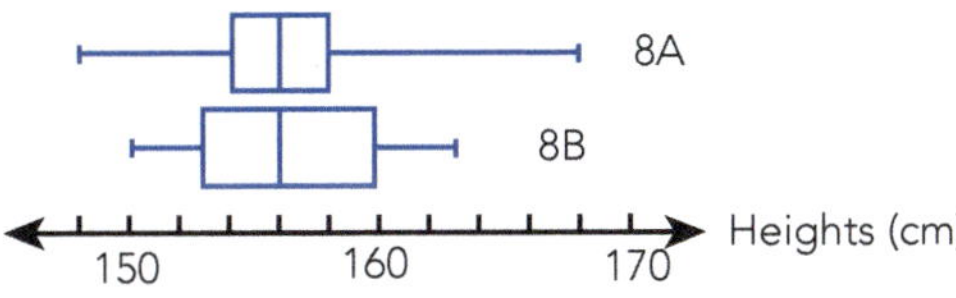

parallelepiped

See also **parallelogram, prism**

A prism for which the faces are parallelograms.

Example

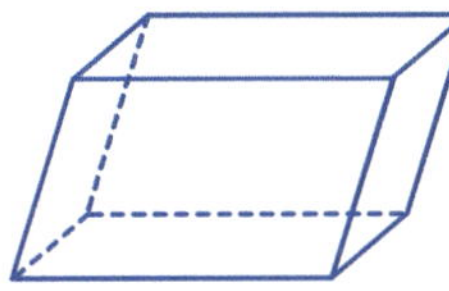

parallel lines (Symbols: ⫽ ⇉)

See also **alternate angles, cointerior angles, corresponding angles, transversal**

Two or more lines that go in exactly the same direction. Parallel lines always remain the same distance apart. They never meet.

Examples

When parallel lines are crossed by a transversal, pairs of angles are formed. These pairs can be classified as three different types of angles. Each type has a special name and a special property.

- corresponding angles (make F-shape). They are equal.

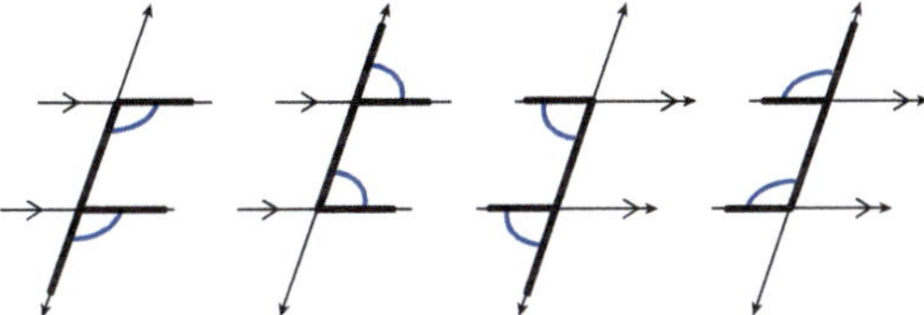

- alternate angles (make Z-shape). They are equal.

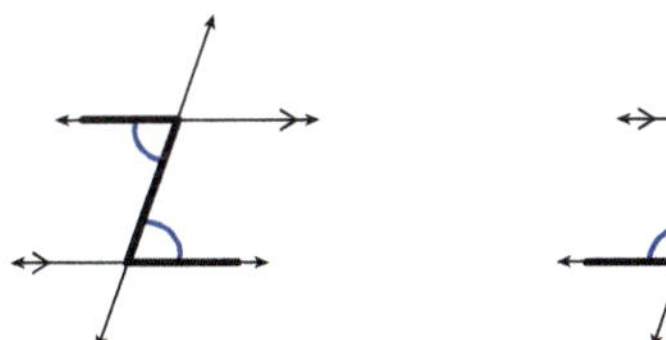

- cointerior (allied) angles (make C-shape). They add to 180°.

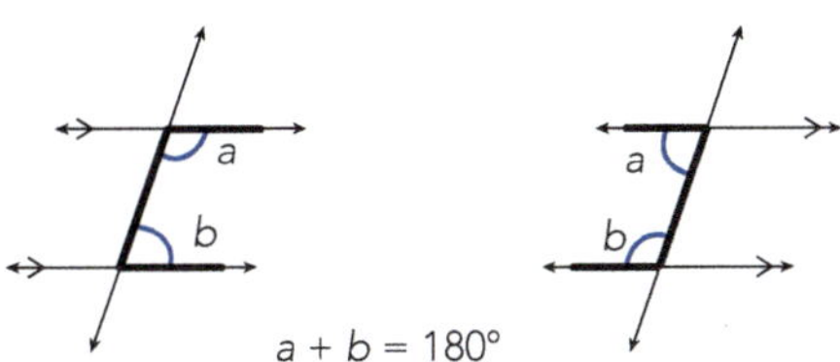

parallelogram

See also **parallel lines, quadrilateral, rectangle**

A four-sided figure (quadrilateral) in which both pairs of opposite sides are parallel and equal, and the opposite angles are equal.

Examples

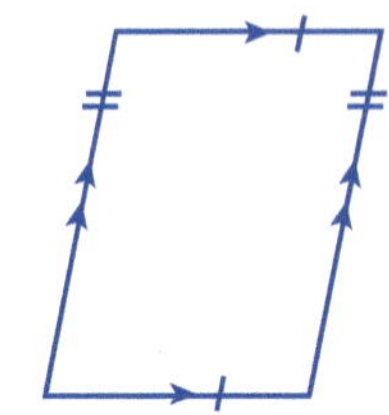

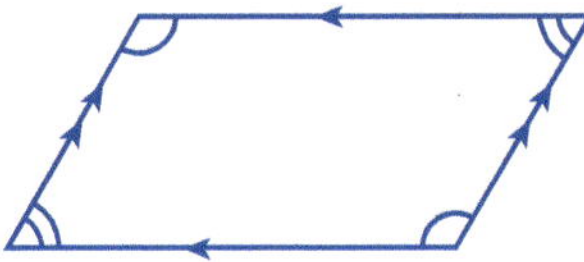

The arrow marks show which pairs of lines are parallel.

A right-angled parallelogram is a rectangle.

Example

parentheses

See also **brackets, order of operations**

Word for ordinary brackets used for grouping numbers together.

Example

( )
parentheses, or ordinary brackets

(2 + 3) – (5 + 2)
= 5 – 7
= -2

partition

See **division**

Pascal's triangle

Used in probability and algebra.

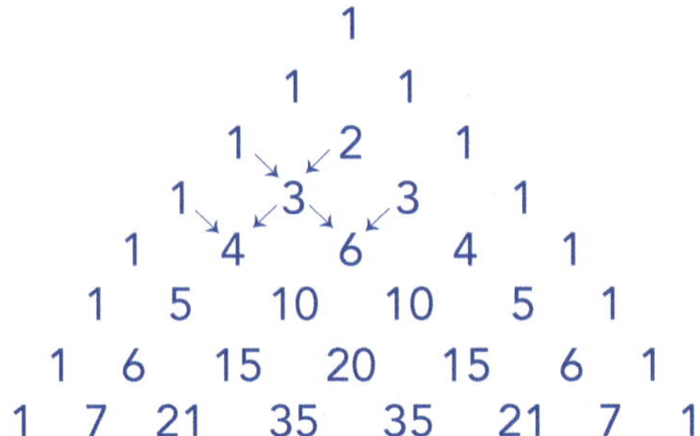

After the second line the new numbers are made by adding the two numbers to the left and right in the row above.

path

See also **graph, line, relationship, route**

A connected set of points.
The route or line along which a person or object moves.

Example

pattern

See also **rule, sequence**

A repeated design or arrangement using shapes, lines, colours, numbers, etc.

Examples

i Shape pattern

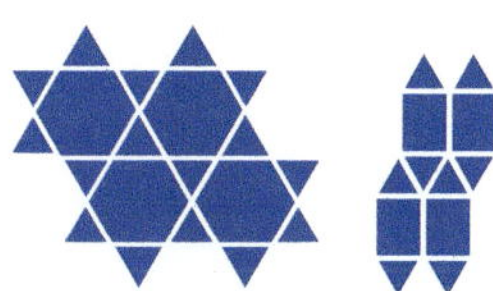

ii Colour pattern

iii A 'number pattern' is a sequence of numbers formed by following a 'rule':
1, 4, 7, 10 … (rule: add three)
16, 8, 4, 2, 1, $\frac{1}{2}$, $\frac{1}{4}$, $\frac{1}{8}$ … (rule: divide by two)

pendulum

See also **second**

A small heavy object attached to a string suspended from a fixed point.

Example

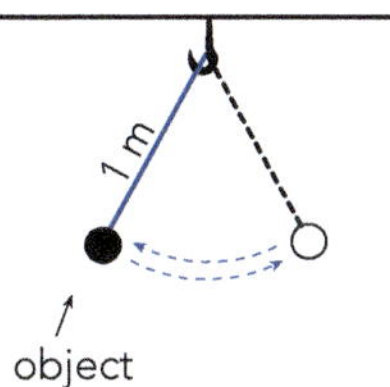

If the string is 1 metre in length, then it takes about 1 second to make a single complete swing, over and back.

pentagon

See also **polygon**

A shape (polygon) with five straight sides and five angles. A regular pentagon has five equal sides and five equal angles.

Examples

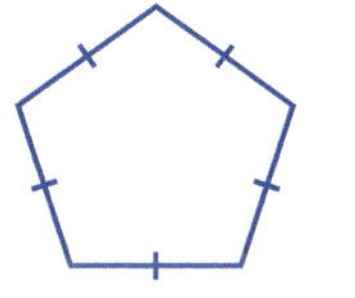

regular pentagon

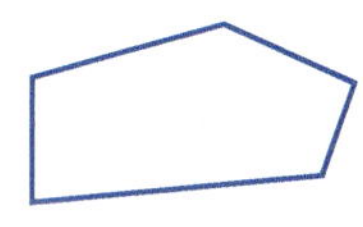

irregular pentagon

per annum

See **p.a.**

percentage (per cent) (Symbol: %)

See also **decimal fraction, fraction**

'For every hundred'. A number out of one hundred.

Example

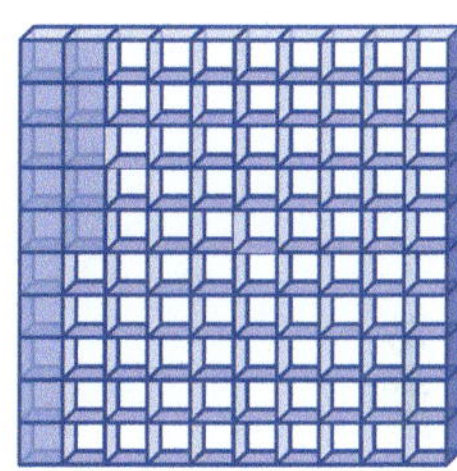

This is a 'hundred square'. Fifteen out of the hundred little squares have been coloured in. They represent:

$$\frac{15}{100} = 15\,\% = 0.15$$

↑ fraction ↑ percentage ↑ decimal fraction

To represent a fraction as a percentage, it must first be converted to a fraction out of 100.

$$\frac{14}{25} = \frac{56}{100} = 56\%$$

perfect square

See also **quadratic expression, square number, trinomial**

1. A whole number that is obtained by multiplying a number by itself.
2. A quadratic trinomial expression in the form of $a^2 \pm 2ab + b^2$ that can be factorised to give $(a \pm b)^2$.

Examples

i 36 is a perfect square because it is the square of 6.

$$\begin{aligned} 6^2 &= 6 \times 6 \\ &= 36 \end{aligned}$$

ii $x^2 - 14x + 49$ is a perfect square because it is the square of $(x - 7)$.

$$\begin{aligned} (x - 7)^2 &= (x - 7)(x - 7) \\ &= x^2 - 14x + 49 \end{aligned}$$

perimeter

See also **boundary, circumference**

The distance around a closed shape, or the length of its boundary.

Example

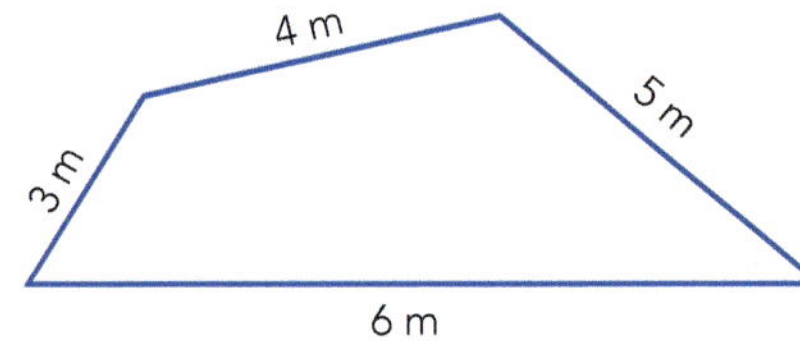

To find the perimeter of a shape, add the lengths of all its sides.

The perimeter is:
3 m + 4 m + 5 m + 6 m = 18 m

period

See also **axis, cosine, sine, tangent, trigonometry**

The horizontal distance covered by one entire cycle of the graph of a trigonometric function. When the horizontal axis is time, the period is the time taken to complete a full cycle of the graph.

Example

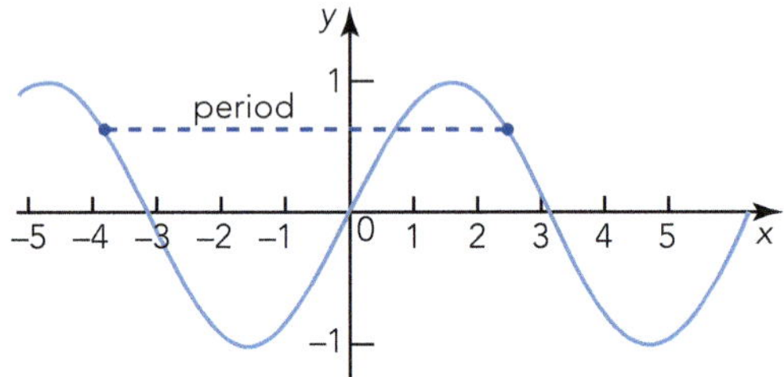

permutation

See also **combination**

An ordered arrangement or sequence of a group of objects.

Example

Three shapes 

can be arranged in six different ways, or have six permutations.

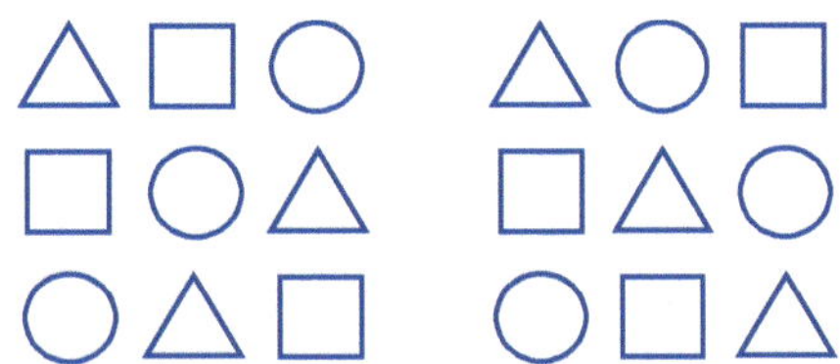

The order in which the shapes are arranged in a permutation is important. When the order is not important, the arrangement is called a combination.

perpendicular

See also **altitude, apex, bisector, cone, line segment, pyramid, triangle, vertex**

Forming a right angle.

1 Perpendicular height.
The line segment drawn from the vertex (top) of a figure to the opposite side at a 90° angle.

Examples

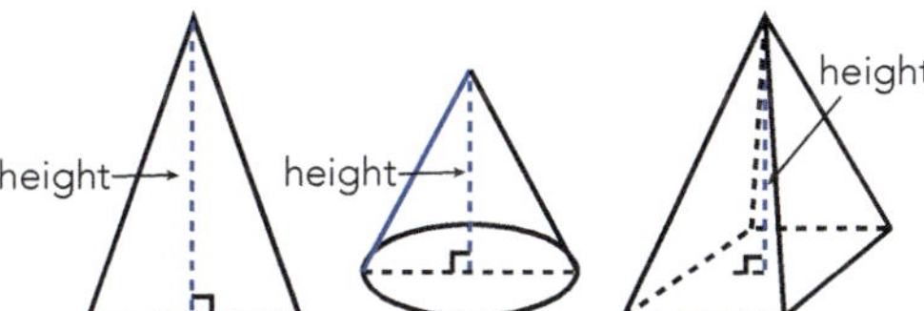

The height of a triangle, cone or pyramid

2 Perpendicular lines.
Lines which intersect to make right angles.

Examples

perspective

See also **converging lines**

When drawing on paper, we can show depth by drawing several parallel lines running into one or several points on the horizon. These points are called vanishing points. The drawing looks as if it is three-dimensional. We say it has perspective. Photos also have perspective as they appear three dimensional.

Example

pi (Symbol: Π)

See also **circle, circumference, diameter, non-terminating decimal, radius**

The ratio of the circumference of a circle to its diameter is a special irrational number known as π (the Greek letter pi).

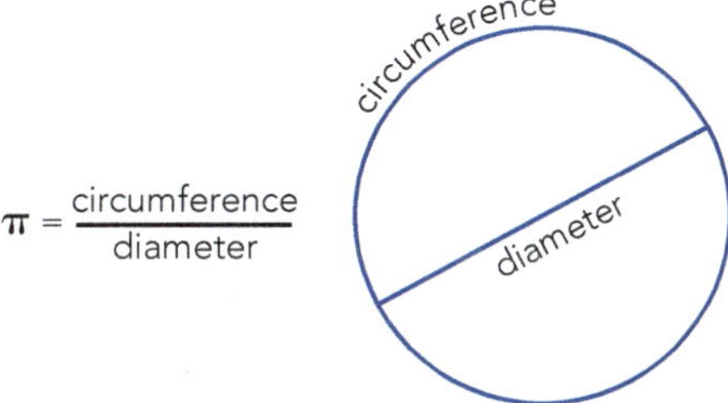

$$\pi = \frac{\text{circumference}}{\text{diameter}}$$

The approximate value of π is 3.14.

The exact value cannot be calculated as π is an irrational number.

pictograph

See **picture graph**

picture graph

See also **graph**

A graph drawn with pictures that represent real objects. Each picture may represent one or several things.

Example

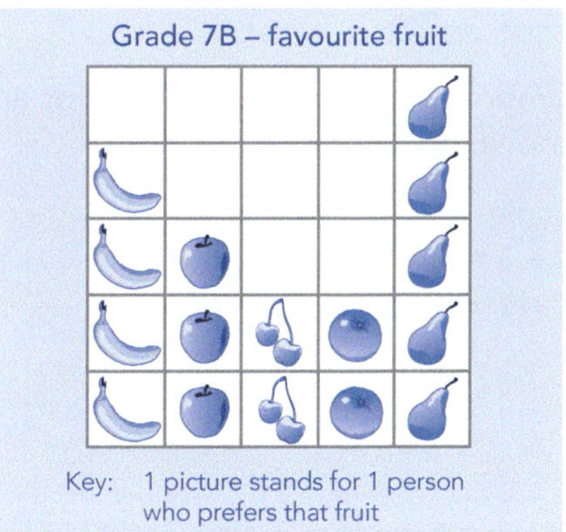

A picture graph must have a heading and a key.

piece work

See also **salary, wages**

Work for a payment per item produced.

Example

Gina is paid $20.00 for every shirt she makes. In a week, she made fifteen shirts. Her weekly wage was $300.00.

pie graph (pie chart)

See also **graph**

A circle graph. Also called a sector graph. A pie graph shows how a whole dataset is divided into various parts.

Example

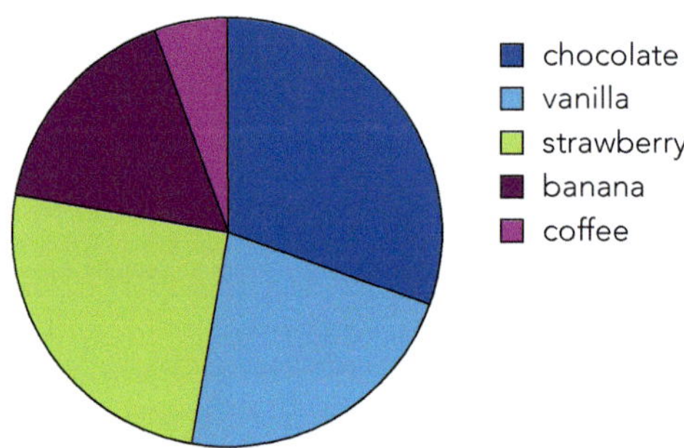

Flavours of ice-cream bought at the beach café on Saturday

place holder

See also **equation, variable**

A symbol which holds the place for an unknown number.

Examples

In $w + 3 = 7$, w is the place holder.
In □ – 6 = 10, □ is the place holder.

place value

See also **decimal place-value system, digit, value**

The value of each digit in a number depends on its place or position in that number.

Examples

hundreds	tens	ones
4	8	6
	1	8
8	2	3

i In the number 486 the value of digit 8 is 80 (eight tens).

ii In the number 18 the value of digit 8 is 8 (eight units).

iii In the number 823 the value of digit 8 is 800 (eight hundreds).

plane

See also **dimension, infinite, plane shape, two-dimensional**

A flat surface, like the floor of a house or a wall.

A plane extends infinitely in all directions.

Two-dimensional shapes are called plane shapes because they can be drawn in one plane. They have only length and width (no depth).

Example

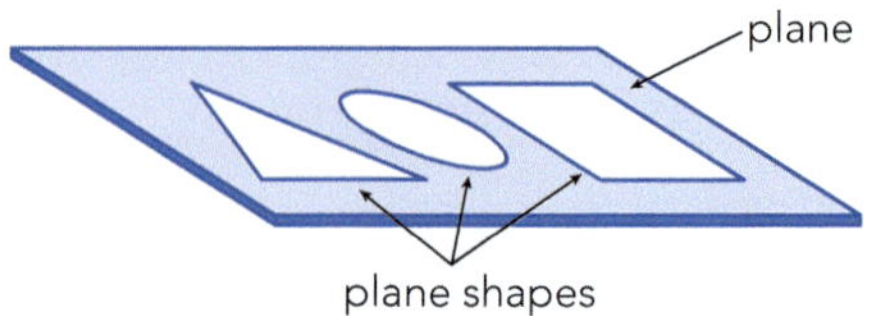

plane shape

See also **non-planar figure**

A plane shape is a closed shape that can be drawn on a flat surface. It is two-dimensional.

Examples

plan view

See also **cross-section of a solid, diagram, front view, side view, top view**

A diagram of an object as seen from the top, front or side.

Example

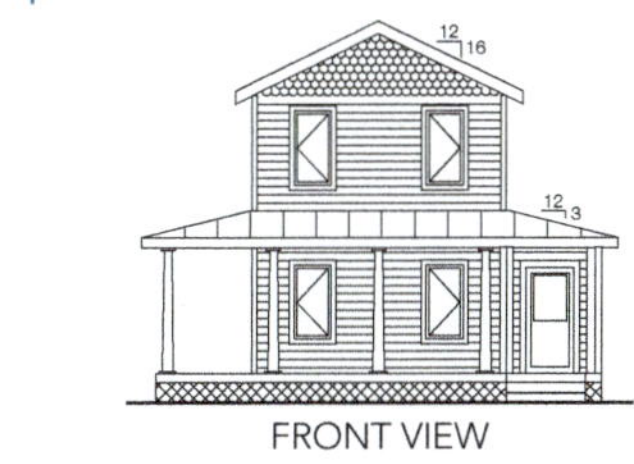

FRONT VIEW

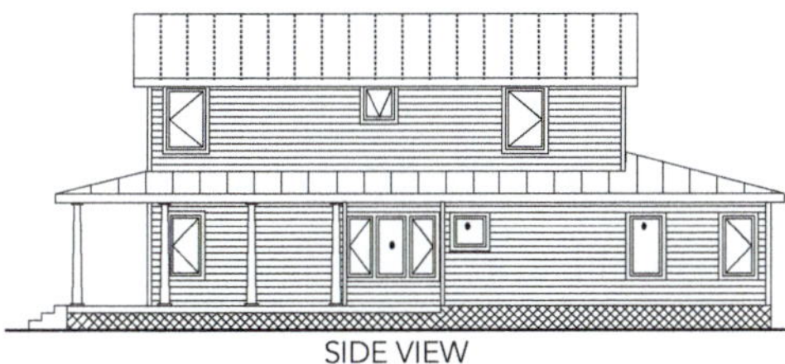
SIDE VIEW

Platonic solids

See **regular polyhedron**

plus (Symbol: +)

See also **addition**

The name of the symbol that means addition.

Example

$4 + 6 = 10$

We say 'four plus six equals ten'.

p.m. (post meridiem)

See also **a.m.**

The time from immediately after midday until immediately before midnight.

The abbreviation p.m. is used only with 12-hour time.

Example

The time is half past seven in the evening so it is 7.30 p.m.

point

See also **decimal point**

1 A position in space. A dot on a surface represents a point. It has no dimension (no length, width or depth).

. *P*

2 A decimal point separates the whole number part from the part less than one.

Example

$$27.659 = 27 + \frac{6}{10} + \frac{5}{100} + \frac{9}{1000}$$

point graph

See also **line graph, variable**

A statistical graph using points that are not joined. Individual points show information relating to two variables.

point graph continued ▶

Example

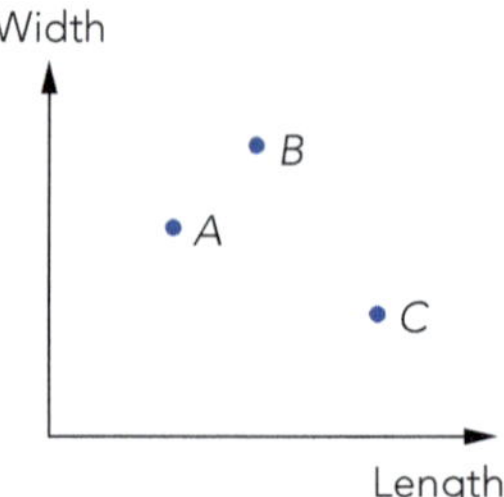

polygon

See also **closed shape, hexagon, irregular polygon, line segment, octagon, pentagon, quadrilateral, regular polygon, triangle**

A plane shape which has three or more straight sides; for example, a triangle, quadrilateral, pentagon or hexagon.

Examples

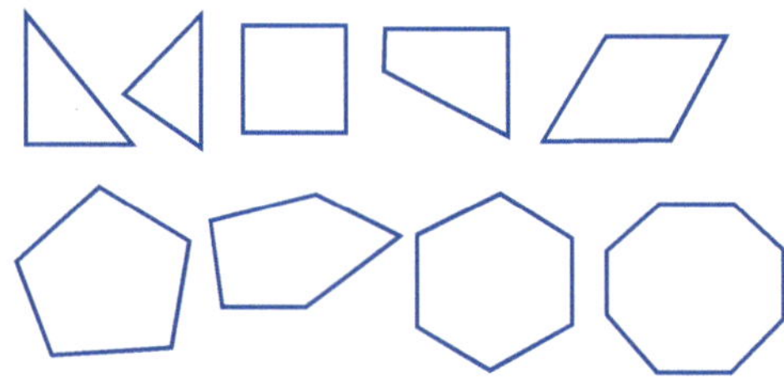

polyhedron (Plural: polyhedrons or polyhedra)

See also **cube, dodecahedron, icosahedron, prism, pyramid, regular polyhedron**

A three-dimensional shape with polygons as the faces.

Examples

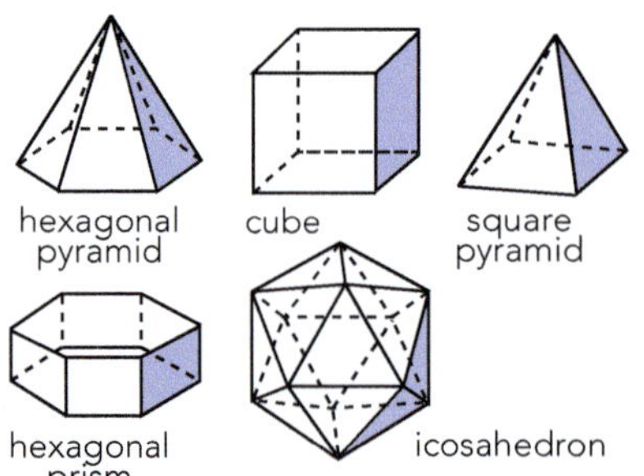

polynomial

See also **algebraic expression, leading coefficient, leading term, power**

An algebraic expression that contains only one type of variable, and consists of a sum of terms. In each term the variable is raised to a different, non-negative, integer power.

Examples

$7x^2 - 5x + 6$, $x^3 + x - 1$, $2x^5 + 3x^4 - x$ are all polynomials.

A polynomial can be written in the general form

$$P(x) = a_n x^n + a_{n-1} x^{n-1} + \ldots + a_2 x^2 + a_1 x^1 + a_0,$$

where a_n, a_{n-1} … are the coefficients of each term.

a_n is called the leading coefficient, and $a_n x^n$ is called the leading term. The last term, a_0, is a constant (because $x^0 = 1$).

Although the general form above shows the powers of x decreasing with each term, a polynomial may not contain every consecutive power from n.

Example

$7x^4$	$-\ 5x^3$	$+$	x	$-\ 3$
$a_n x^n$	$a_{n-1}x^{n-1}$	$a_{n-2}x^{n-2}$	$a_{n-3}x^{n-3}$	$a_{n-4} = a_0 x^0$
$a_n = a_4$ $= 7$	$a_{n-1} = a_3$ $= -5$	$a_{n-2} = a_2$ $= 0$	$a_{n-3} = a_1$ $= 1$	$a_{n-4} = a_0$ $= -3$

Note that here, $x^{n-4} = x^0 = 1$

The highest power in the expression is called the degree of the polynomial. The above example shows a polynomial of degree 4.

polyomino

See also **plane shape**

A plane shape made of squares of the same size, each square being connected to at least one of the others by a common edge.

Examples

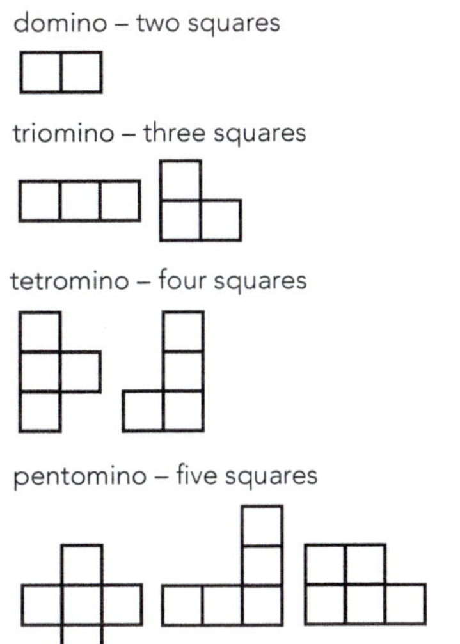

population

See also **census, sample**

In statistics, the entire category or group of people, animals or things from which data is collected.

Example

In August 2011, a census was held in Australia. At that time the population was found to be 21 507 717.

position

See also **Cartesian plane, coordinates, grid, ordered pair**

Describes the place where something is located.

Example

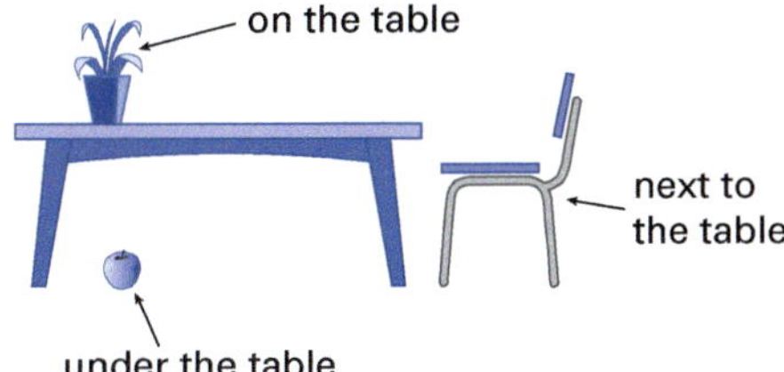

1 On, under, above, behind, in front of, between, next to, outside and inside all help to describe an object's position.

2 A Cartesian plane or grid reference system can be used to specifically describe the position of a point or object.

positive numbers

See also **integers, negative numbers, zero**

Numbers greater than zero. We sometimes write the positive sign (+) in front of them; however, we assume that a number is positive unless there is a negative sign in front of it.

Examples

i

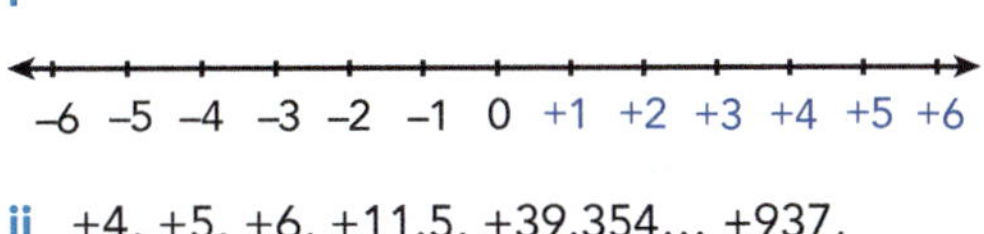

ii +4, +5, +6, +11.5, +39.354… +937, +938 …

power of a number

See also **base, cubic number, index, index notation, square number, zero power**

In 2^4 the power is 4. It is also called the index or exponent. 2 is called the base.
It means $2 \times 2 \times 2 \times 2 = 16$
Say: two to the power of four.
When the power is zero, the value is one, whatever the value of the base.
$10^0 = 1$ $1000^0 = 1$

prediction

See also **estimate, probability**

In mathematics we can predict or estimate possible answers to problems, or outcomes of probability events based on past events or outcomes.

prefix

See also **Prefixes tables** on pages 192, 193

A group of letters with a particular meaning placed in front of another word that shows the relationship between the two words.

Example

The prefix 'milli' means 'one thousandth' so a millimeter is one thousandth of a metre.

prime factor of a number

See also **factor tree, factors, prime number**

A prime number that will divide exactly into a given number. All numbers can be written as a product of prime numbers. The prime factors of a number can be found by constructing a factor tree.

Example

2, 3 and 5 are the prime factors of thirty. (10 is a factor of thirty, but not a prime factor.)

30

3 × 10

3 × 2 × 5

Prime factors of 30
$30 = 3 \times 2 \times 5$

prime number

See also **composite number, counting number, factors**

A counting number that can only be divided by one and itself. It has no other factors.

Examples

2, 3, 5, 7, 11, 13, 17 ...

The factors of two are 2 and 1.

The factors of five are 5 and 1.

Note: 1 is neither prime nor composite.

principal

See also **interest, interest rate**

The amount borrowed or invested is called the principal.

Example

Joe borrowed $10 000 from a bank. The principal is $10 000.

prism

See also **cuboid, cylinder, face, parallel lines, polygon, polyhedron, three-dimensional, uniform cross-section**

A polyhedron with two polygon faces that are parallel and the same in size and shape. These faces can be any polygon. They give the solid a uniform cross-section.

Examples

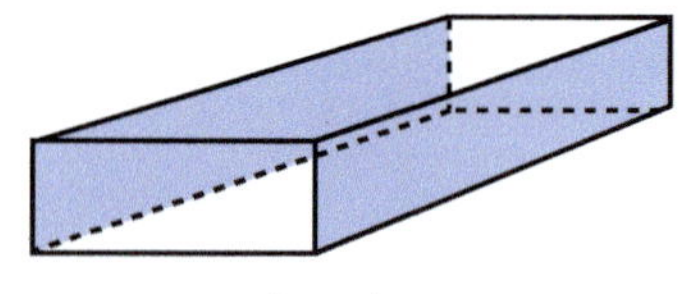

rectangular prism

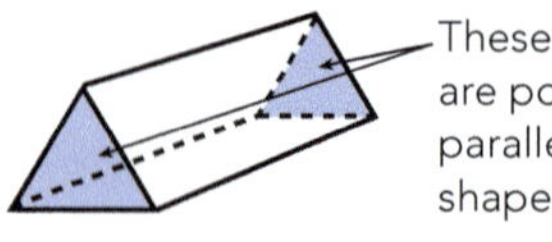

These two faces are polygons, are parallel and are the same shape and size.

triangular prism

All cuboids are prisms. A cylinder is not a prism although it also has a uniform cross-section. A cylinder has two parallel faces that are circles, not polygons.

probability

See also **chance event, equally likely**

The likelihood of an event occurring. The probability of an event occurring is given a value between 0 (impossible) and 1 (certain). Probability can be written as a fraction, decimal or percentage.

Example

If a coin is tossed, the probability of getting tails is $\frac{1}{2}$.

problem solving

See also **solution**

Using your knowledge of mathematical concepts and a range of strategies to find a solution in a new or unfamiliar situation.

product

See also **associative law of multiplication, commutative law of multiplication, multiplicand, multiplication, multiplier**

The answer to a multiplication calculation.

Example

3	×	2	=	6
↑		↑		↑
multiplicand		multiplier		product

Six is the product of three and two.

profit

See also **cost price, loss, selling price**

If the selling price is higher than the cost price the seller makes a profit.

Example

A car dealer buys a car for \$10 000 and sells the same car for \$12 000. The dealer makes a profit of \$2000.

pronumeral

See also **algebraic expression, symbol, variable**

A symbol used in algebra to represent a variable (an unknown value). The pronumeral stands for a particular value or particular values in an equation.

Examples

$2a = 6$	$7 - x = 5$	$12 \times \square = 24$
$a = 3$	$x = 2$	$\square = 2$

a, *x* and □ are pronumerals.

proof

See also **prove, theorem**

A logical, step-by-step connection of true statements used to verify that another statement is always true.

Example

There are over 90 different proofs of Pythagoras' theorem: 'The square on the hypotenuse of a right-angled triangle is equal to the sum of the squares on the other two sides.'

$c^2 = a^2 + b^2$

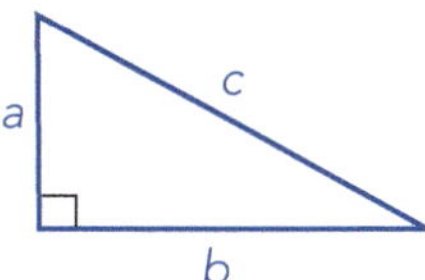

proper fraction

See also **denominator, fraction, improper fraction, numerator, simple fraction**

A fraction where the numerator is less than the denominator. Proper fractions represent positive numbers less than 1.

Examples

$\frac{4}{5}$ 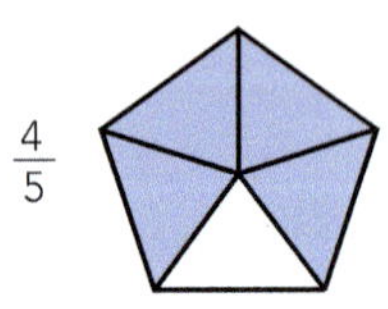

$\frac{36}{100}$ 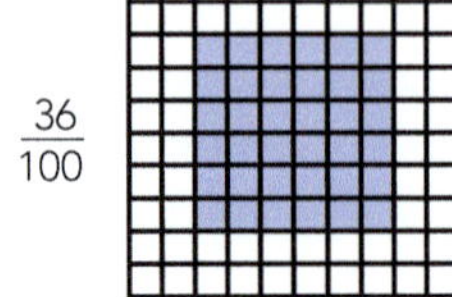

property

See also **attribute, classification, classify**

A characteristic of an object.

proportion

See also **inverse, ratio, variable**

A statement of equality between two variables.

1 Direct proportion.
When a relation between two variables remains constant, they are said to be in direct proportion. As one increases, the other also increases by the same factor.

Example

Mary reads three pages of a book every 10 minutes.

The ratio $\frac{\text{pages}}{\text{time}}$ is constant.

$$\frac{3 \text{ pages}}{10 \text{ min}} = \frac{6 \text{ pages}}{20 \text{ min}} = \frac{9 \text{ pages}}{30 \text{ min}} = \frac{12 \text{ pages}}{40 \text{ min}} \ldots$$

2 Inverse (or indirect) proportion.
When the product of two variables is a constant value, the variables are said to be in inverse proportion.

Example

It takes 4 hours for one person to mow the lawn.
It takes 2 hours for two people to mow the lawn.

Number of people	1	2	3	4	8
Time in hours	4	2	$1\frac{1}{3}$	1	$\frac{1}{2}$

protractor

See also **angle**

An instrument used to measure and draw angles.

Example

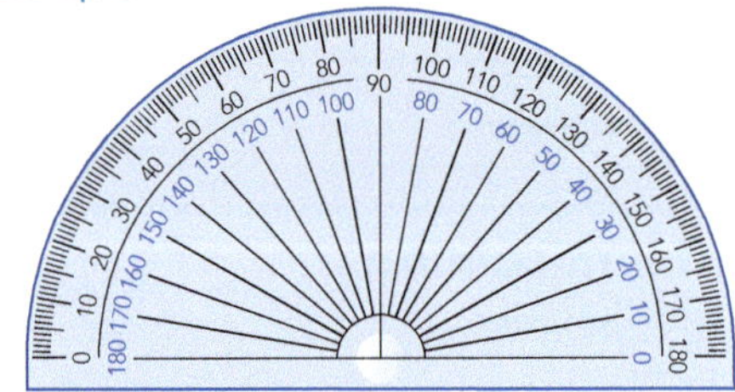

prove

See also **proof**

To set out a logical series of steps and true statements in order to demonstrate that another statement is always true.

pyramid

See also **apex, base, face, net, polygon, solid, tetrahedron, vertex**

A solid (3D object) which has a polygon for a base and triangles for all the other faces. These faces all meet at a single vertex above the base, called the apex.

Examples

This pyramid has a square base and the other faces are congruent triangles.

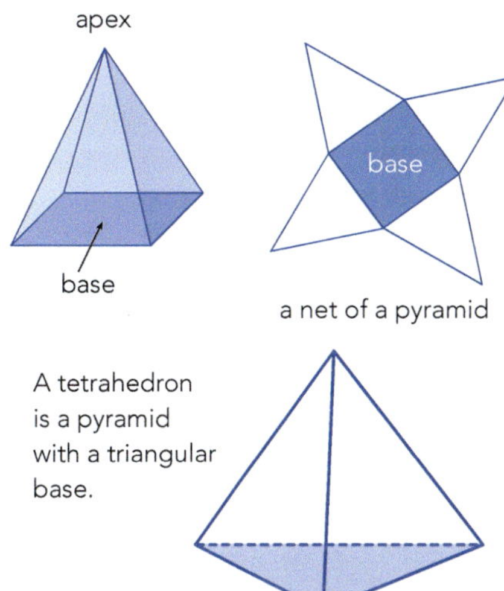

The base of a pyramid can be any polygon.

Pythagoras' theorem

See also **converse, right-angled triangle, hypotenuse**

In any right-angled triangle, the square of the hypotenuse (side c) is equal to the sum of the squares of the other two sides (sides a and b).

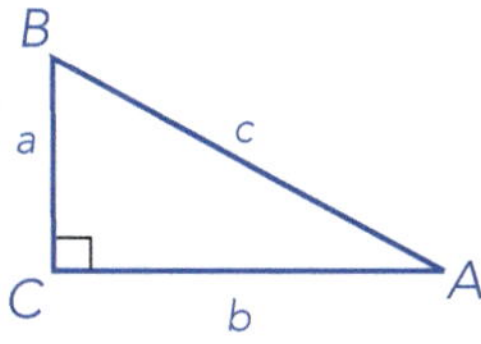

$$c^2 = a^2 + b^2$$
$$a^2 = c^2 - b^2$$
$$b^2 = c^2 - a^2$$
$$a = \sqrt{c^2 - b^2}$$
$$b = \sqrt{c^2 - a^2}$$
$$c = \sqrt{a^2 + b^2}$$

Example

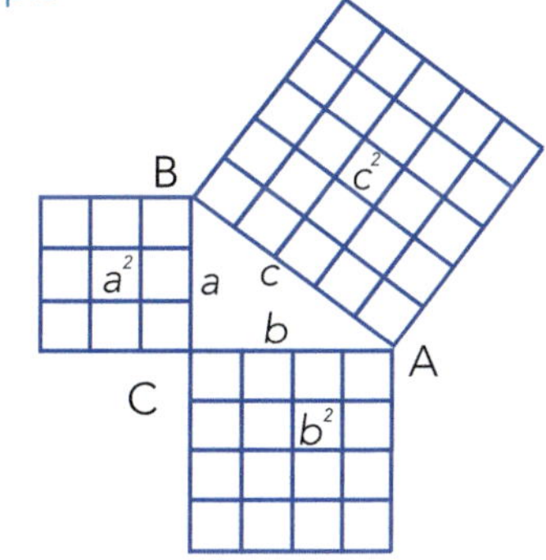

$$\begin{aligned} & a^2 + b^2 \\ &= 3^2 + 4^2 \\ &= 9 + 16 \\ &= 25 \\ c^2 &= 5^2 \\ &= 25 \\ 3^2 + 4^2 &= 5^2 \end{aligned}$$

The converse of the theorem is that if $c^2 = a^2 + b^2$, then the triangle must be right angled.

quadrant

See also **arc, coordinates, ordered pair, radius**

1 A quarter of the circumference of a circle.

Example

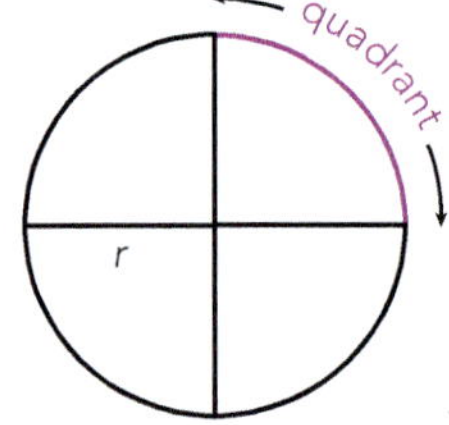

2 A plane figure made by two radii of a circle at a 90° angle and the arc cut off by them.

Example

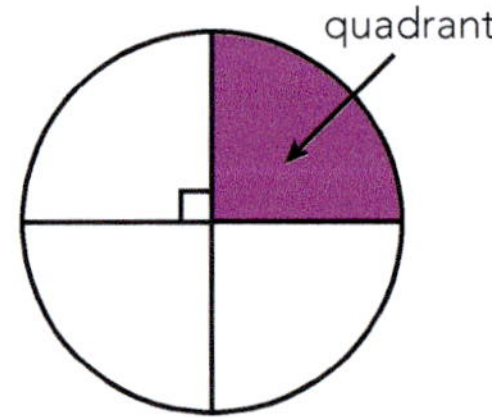

3 The intersection of the *x*- and *y*-axes divides the Cartesian plane into four quadrants. Quadrants are numbered in an anticlockwise direction.

Example

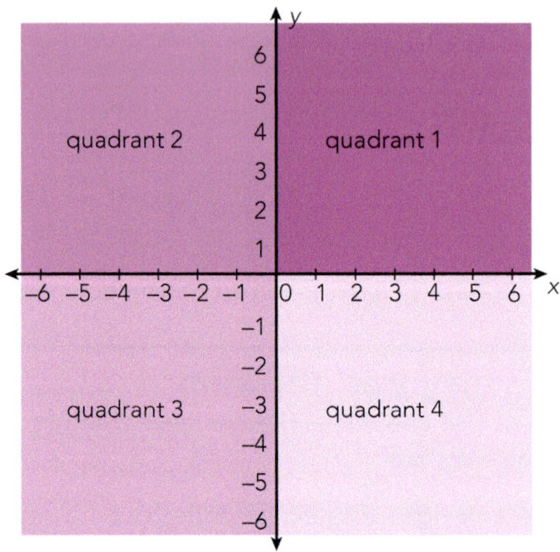

quadrilateral

See also **kite, parallelogram, plane shape, rectangle, rhombus, square, trapezium**

A plane (2D) shape with four sides and four angles.

Example

Some special quadrilaterals are:

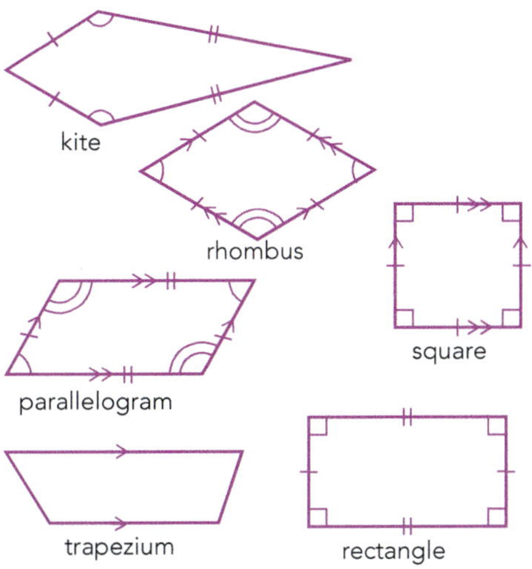

quadratic equation

See also **factorising, null factor law, polynomial, quadratic formula**

An equation containing only one variable in which the highest power of the variable is 2 and all powers are positive integers.

Examples

$x^2 + 6x = -9$ $2x - x^2 = 3,$
$4x^2 - 48 = 0$ $x^2 + 15x + 56 = 0$

To solve a quadratic equation, we write it in the general form
$ax^2 + bx + c = 0$ $(a \neq 0)$.

We can then solve by factorising and using the null factor law, or by using the quadratic formula.

quadratic expression

See also **algebraic expression, power, variable**

An expression containing one variable in which the highest power of the variable in any of the terms is 2 and all powers are positive integers.

Examples

$x^2 + 5x + 6$
$8 - x^2 - 6x$
$4x^2 - 48$

quadratic formula

See also **polynomial, quadratic equation, quadratic expression**

A formula for solving all quadratic equations in the form of
$ax^2 + bx + c = 0$

$$x = \frac{-b \pm \sqrt{b^2 - 4ac}}{2a}$$

quadruple

See also **double, treble**

Increase the amount by a factor of 4. Multiply the amount by 4. Double it then double it again.

Example

To quadruple \$20 means 4 × \$20 = \$80.

qualitative data

See **categorical data**

quantitative data

See **numerical data**

quantity

The amount or number of something.

Example

The quantity of mineral water in the bottle is 2 litres.

quarter

One of four equal parts.

Examples

$\frac{1}{4}$ is shaded

One quarter of the boys are sitting.

quartile

See also **median**

In an ordered data set, the quartiles are the values that divide the data into four equal parts. There are three quartiles.

- The lower quartile, Q_L, is the 25th percentile. One quarter of the data values are less than or equal to this figure.
- The second quartile is the median, or the 50th percentile. Half of the data is less than or equal to this figure.
- The upper quartile, Q_U, is the 75th percentile. One quarter of the data values are greater than or equal to this figure.

To find the quartiles:

Step 1 Arrange the data values from smallest to greatest.

Step 2 Find the median.

Step 3 The median splits the data into two halves. Find the median of the lower half of the data. This value is the lower quartile, Q_L.

Step 4 Find the median of the upper half. This value is the upper quartile, Q_U.

Example

8 10 11 13 14 16 17 17 19 21 22 25

↑ $Q_L = 12$ ↑ median = 16.5 ↑ $Q_U = 20$

The data set above contains 12 data values. The median lies between the 6th and 7th values. Q_L lies between the 3rd and 4th values, and Q_U between the 9th and 10th values.

quotient

See also **dividend, division, divisor**

The answer to a division calculation.

Example

$10 \div 2 = 5$

10 ↑ dividend, 2 ↑ divisor, 5 ↑ quotient

Five is the quotient.

quotition

See **division**

radian

See also **arc, radius**

The radian is the angle at the centre of a circle (approximately 57.3°), when the length of the arc is equal to the radius.

Example

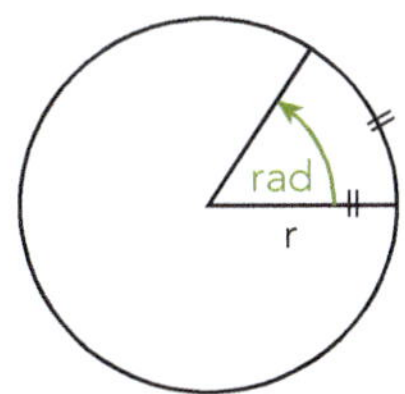

radius (Plural: radii)

See also **circle, circumference, diameter, line segment, sphere**

1 The distance from the centre of a circle to its circumference (or from the centre to the surface of a sphere).

Example

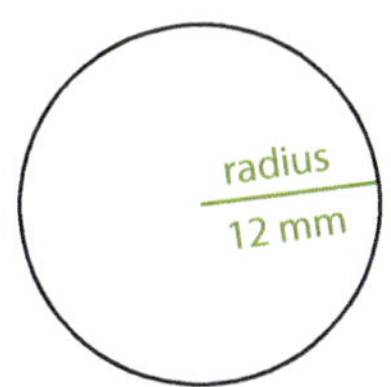

2 The line segment joining the centre and a point on the circle (like the spoke of a wheel) or a line segment joining the centre of a sphere to a point on its surface.

Example

radiant point

See also **ray, radius**

A point from which rays or radii start.

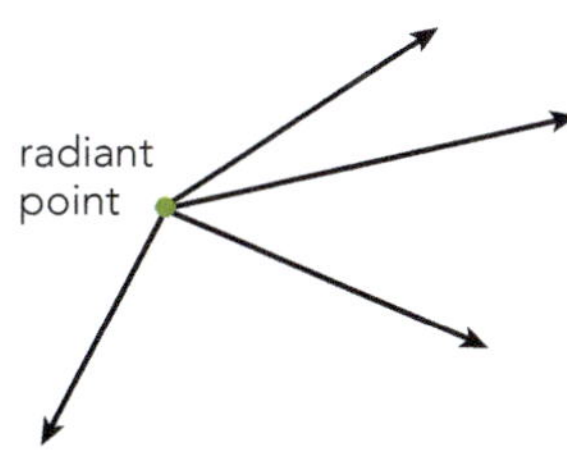

random sample

See also **statistics, sample**

A term in statistics meaning a sample (a part or portion) chosen to represent the whole population. There is no pattern, intent, or bias in the way in which the sample is selected. Every member in the population has an equal chance of being selected.

Example
A bag with twenty black and twenty white balls. A random sample would be selected by removing balls from a bag without looking. A random sample of five balls may consist of three white and two black balls.

range

See also **data, interquartile range, statistics**

The range is the difference between the largest and the smallest number in a data set.

Example
17, 16, 14, 11, 22, 19, 18, 13, 25
The smallest number is 11.
The largest number is 25.
The range is 25 – 11 = 14.

rate

See also **comparison**

The comparison between two different quantities, which usually have different units.

The word 'per' is used when describing a rate. 'Per' means 'for every'.

1 Speed
Speed is a rate that compares distance and time. It describes how fast something is travelling.

Example
A car travelling at a rate of 60 kilometres per hour (60 km/h) covers a distance of 60 km in one hour.

2 Exchange rate
An exchange rate describes how much of one type of currency (money) you would receive in exchange for one unit of another type.

Example
AUD (Australian dollars) and GBP (British pounds)
AUD$1 = £0.48
One Australian dollar can be exchanged for 0.48 British pounds, or 48 pence.

3 Unit pricing
Supermarkets are required to display the prices of items as a price per unit, where the unit might be kilograms, litres or 100 g or 100 mL. This allows for the easy comparison of prices of differently sized items.

Example
A 250 g jar of jam costs $4.98. This is $1.99 per 100 g.
A 400 g jar of jam costs $5.74. This is $1.44 per 100 g.

4 Percentage rate of increase or decrease
The change in a quantity over time can be described as percentage change per day, week, month or year.

Example
The number of students enrolled at a school increases from 600 to 645 over a year. This is an increase of 7.5% per year ($\frac{45}{600} \times \frac{100\%}{1}$).

ratio (Symbol: :)

See also **comparison**

A comparison of two quantities.

Example

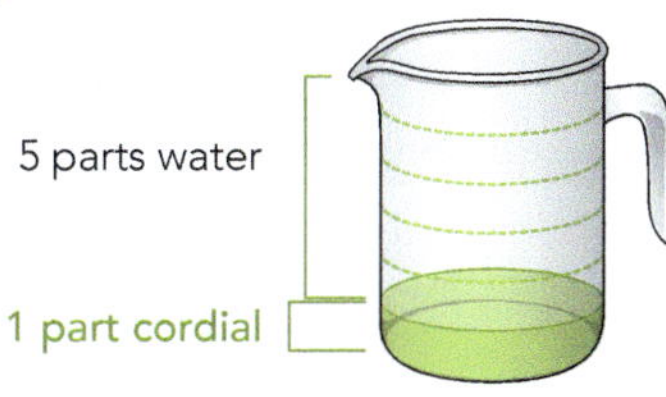

To make a jug of cordial, mix the cordial and water in the ratio of 1 : 5. This means that you mix one part of cordial to five parts of water.

The order of the numbers is important: 1 : 5 ≠ 5 : 1.

There are no units in a ratio. The two quantities are assumed to be measured in the same unit.

rational approximation

See also **approximation, irrational number, rational number**

An approximate value for an irrational number.

Examples

i $\pi \approx 3.14$ (correct to two decimal places)
$\pi \approx 3.1412$ (correct to four decimal places)

ii $\sqrt{3} \approx 1.732$ (correct to three decimal places)

rational number

See also **fraction, ratio, recurring decimal, terminating decimal**

A number that can be expressed as a fraction or ratio of integers.

Examples

$\frac{3}{4}$ $\quad 0.5 = \frac{1}{2}$ $\quad 8 = \frac{8}{1}$

All rational numbers can be represented by either:

- decimal numbers that terminate

Examples

$\frac{3}{4} = 0.75$ $\quad \frac{1}{8} = 0.125$

- non-terminating, recurring decimals.

Examples

$\frac{2}{3} = 0.\dot{6}$ $\quad -\frac{4}{11} = -0.\dot{3}\dot{6}$

ray

See also **angle, line, line segment, radiant point**

A line that has a starting point but no end. It extends in one direction only.

Examples

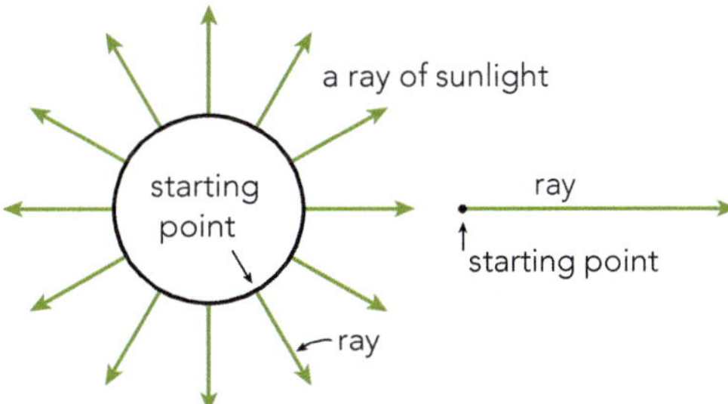

real number

See also **irrational number, rational number**

The set of real numbers is made up of all rational and irrational numbers.

reciprocal

See also **invert**

The reciprocal of a fraction is the fraction obtained by inverting or 'flipping' the numerator and denominator.

Example

i Since we can write 4 as $\frac{4}{1}$ the reciprocal of 4 is $\frac{1}{4}$.

ii The reciprocal of $\frac{2}{3}$ is $\frac{3}{2}$ or $1\frac{1}{2}$.

iii The reciprocal of $2\frac{1}{4}$ is $\frac{4}{9}$.

rectangle

See also **parallel lines, quadrilateral, right angle, square**

A quadrilateral with two pairs of equal and parallel sides, and four right angles.

Example

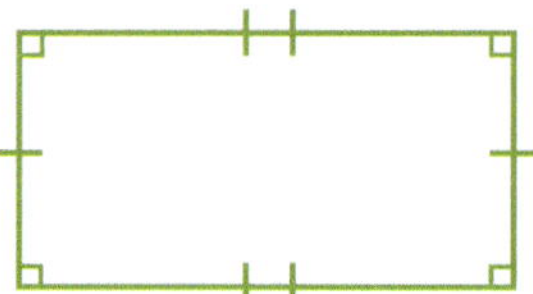

A rectangle is sometimes called an oblong. A square is a rectangle with all sides equal in length.

rectangular hyperbola

See also **asymptote**

The shape of the graph produced by an inverse relationship, where one variable increases as the other decreases. The simplest rectangular hyperbola is the graph of the equation $y = \frac{1}{x}$.

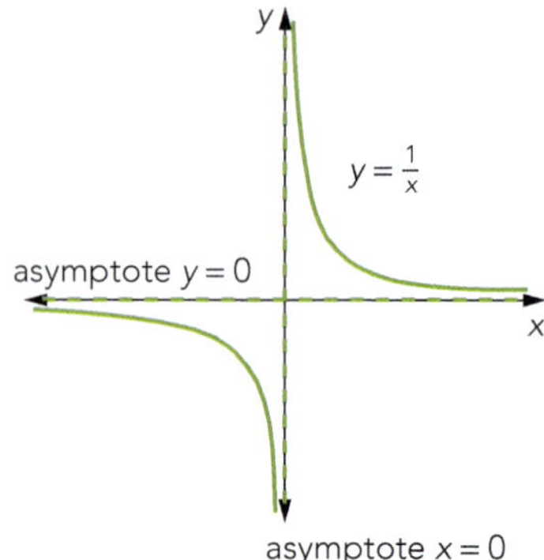

Note that the graph $\frac{1}{x}$ approaches, but does not touch, the x-axis (where $y = 0$) and the y-axis (where $x = 0$). The graphs of the equations $x = 0$ and $y = 0$ are known as asymptotes.

Example

For a fixed pressure, the temperature of a gas in a container is inversely proportional to the volume of the container.

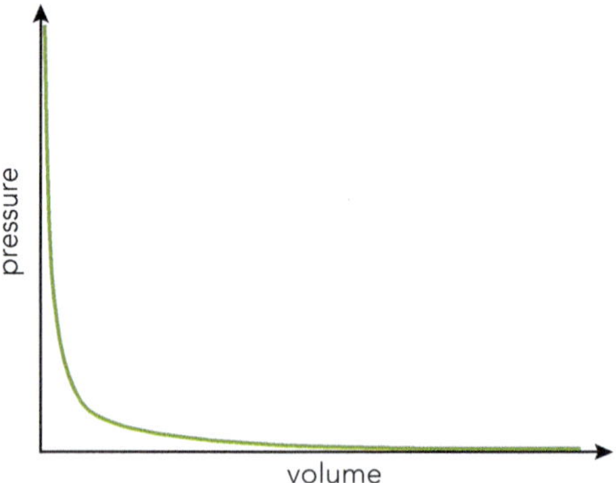

rectangular prism

See also **cuboid, prism, rectangle**

A prism whose base is a rectangle. Another name for a cuboid.

Examples

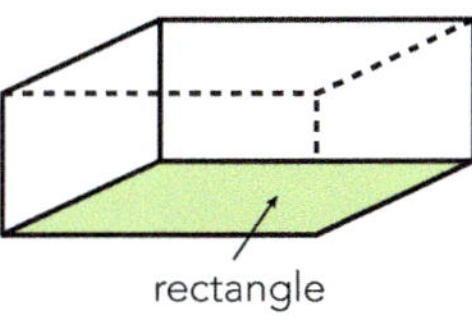

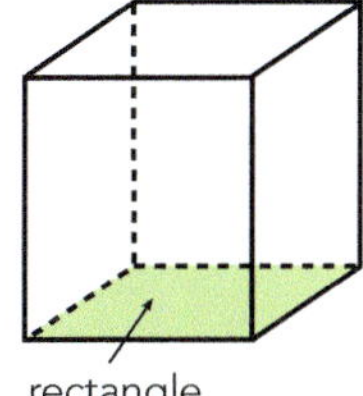

recurring decimal

See also **decimal fraction, digit, rational number, terminating decimal**

A non-terminating decimal that has a repeating pattern of digits. It can be written as a fraction in the form of $\frac{a}{b}$ where *a* and *b* are integers.

Examples

i $\frac{1}{3} = 0.33333\ldots = 0.\dot{3}$

It is written $0.\dot{3}$. The dot shows that the digit is repeated.

ii $0.\dot{1}\dot{7}$

These dots show that the digits 1 and 7 are repeated.

0.1717171717 …

iii $\frac{1}{7} = 0.142857142857\ldots$

It is written either as $0.\dot{1}4285\dot{7}$ or $0.\overline{142857}$ to show the repeated digits.

reduce

See also **cancelling, enlargement, fraction, transformation**

1 Simplify. Express a fraction in its simplest form.

Example

$\frac{5}{30}$ can be reduced to $\frac{1}{6}$

2 Make smaller. An enlargement by a scale factor between 0 and 1 produces a reduced image.

reflection

See also **flip, mirror image**

The image of a reflected object.

Example

reflectional symmetry

See also **asymmetry, axis, line of symmetry, rotational symmetry**

A shape has reflectional symmetry when one half of the shape can fit exactly over the other half when folded along an axis of symmetry. Shapes are symmetrical if they have one or more axes (lines) of symmetry.

Examples

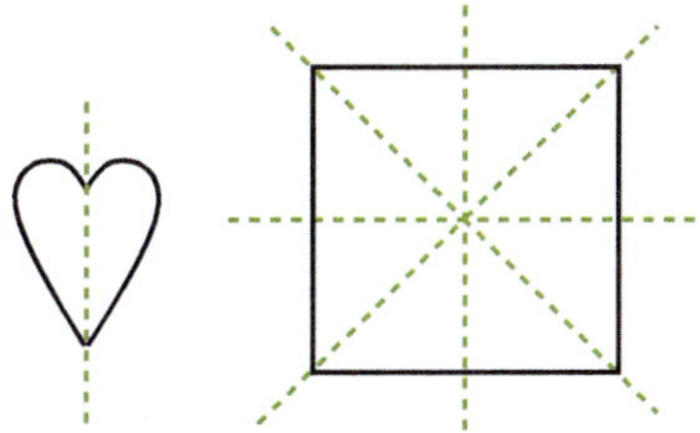

reflex angle

See also **angle, revolution, straight angle**

An angle greater than a straight angle (180°) but less than a revolution (360°).

Examples

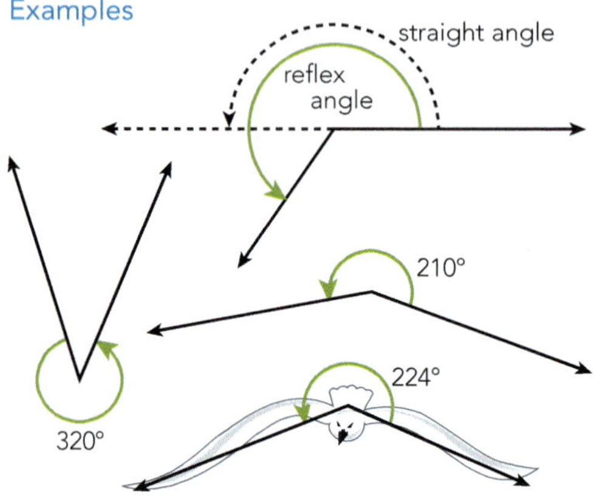

region

See also **boundary, plane, solid, surface**

1 Plane region. All the points inside a simple closed shape together with all of the points on the boundary of the shape.

Examples

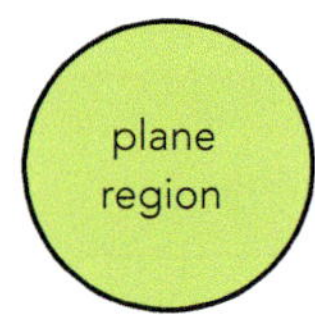

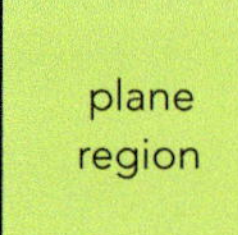

2 Solid region. All the points inside a closed object together with all the points on the surface of that object.

Example

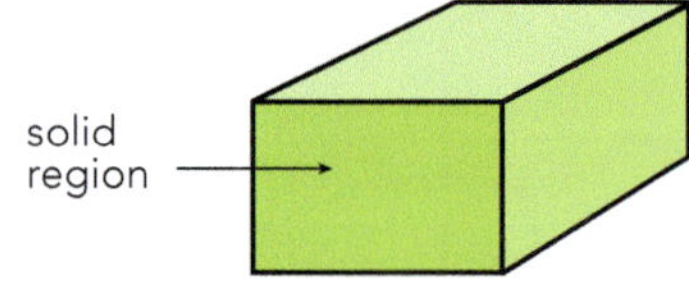

regroup

See also **carrying, group, multibase arithmetic blocks (MAB)**

Exchange.

Examples

i Twelve unit blocks can be regrouped (exchanged) for one long (10) and two units.

ii Before subtracting fifteen from eighty-two, the eight tens and two units have been regrouped into seven tens and twelve units.

$$\begin{array}{r} {}^{7}\not{8}{}^{1}\not{2}{}^{12} \\ -\ 15 \\ \hline 67 \end{array}$$

regular polygon

See also **equilateral triangle, hexagon, irregular polygon, pentagon, square**

A polygon is regular if its sides are equal in length and its angles are equal in size.

Some common regular polygons are:

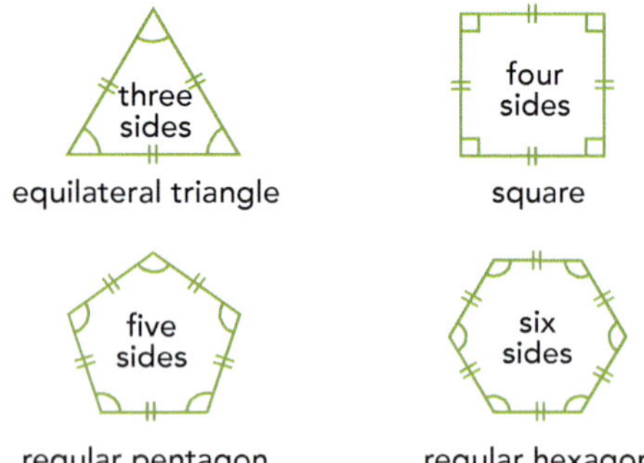

regular polyhedron

See also **congruent, dodecahedron, face, hexahedron, icosahedron, octahedron, polyhedron, tetrahedron**

A polyhedron whose faces are congruent regular polygons. Internal angles are also the same in size. Regular polyhedrons are also called Platonic solids.

There are only five Platonic solids.

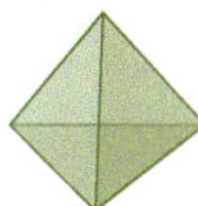

tetrahedron

4 equilateral triangle faces

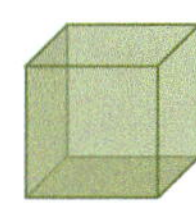

hexahedron (cube)

6 square faces

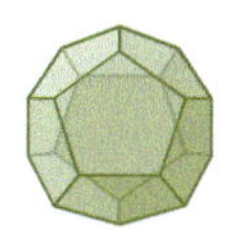

dodecahedron

12 regular pentagon faces

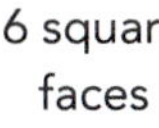

octahedron

8 equilateral triangle faces

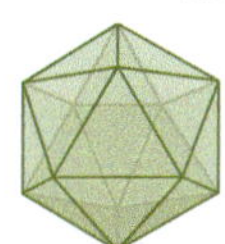

icosahedron

20 equilateral triangle faces

regular shape

See **regular polygon**

related denominators

See also **denominator, fraction**

A pair of denominators where one is a multiple of the other. Fractions with related denominators are easy to add or subtract, as only one fraction needs to be rewritten as an equivalent fraction.

Example

$\frac{2}{5}$ and $\frac{3}{10}$ have related denominators because 10 is a multiple of 5.

$$\frac{2}{5} + \frac{3}{10} = \frac{4}{10} + \frac{3}{10} = \frac{7}{10}$$

Rewrite $\frac{2}{5}$ as $\frac{4}{10}$.

relation

See also **arrow diagram, correspondence**

Connection, correspondence or contrast between a pair of objects, measures, numbers, etc. Also called a relationship.

Examples

i Family relationship:
Judi is the sister of Lea.

ii Size relation:
Jan is taller than Helen.

iii Mathematical relation.

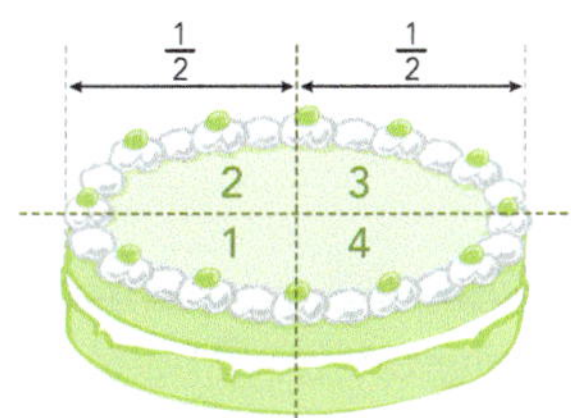

Two quarters are half of four quarters
2 is half of 4

iv Relation between pairs of numbers.
Often presented in a table of values.

x	1	2	3	4	5
y	6	7	8	9	10

$y = x + 5$

The numbers are related by the rule.

relative frequency

See also **frequency, proportion, trials**

A proportion found by dividing the frequency of a particular result by the total number of trials.

Example

In a probability experiment when a fair coin was tossed 100 times, heads were recorded 49 times. The relative frequency was 0.49 or 49%.

remainder

See also **division**

The amount left over after division.

Example

$$\begin{array}{r} 25 \\ 5\overline{)128} \\ -\underline{10} \\ 28 \\ -\underline{25} \\ \underline{3} \end{array} \leftarrow \text{remainder}$$

There are different ways of expressing the remainder in the answer. They depend on the question.

remainder theorem

See also **factor theorem, polynomial, remainder**

The remainder theorem is used to factorise polynomials. The theorem states that for a polynomial P(x):

If $P(x) \div (x - a)$, $P(a)$ gives the remainder.

If $P(x) \div (ax - b)$, $P(\frac{b}{a})$ gives the remainder.

If $P(a) = 0$ or $P(\frac{b}{a}) = 0$, then $(x - a)$ or $(ax - b)$ is a factor of the polynomial.

Example

The remainder for $x^3 - 6x^2 + 4x + 9 \div (x - 2)$ can be found by finding P(2).

$$\begin{aligned} P(2) &= (2)^3 - 6(2)^2 + 4(2) + 9 \\ &= 8 - 24 + 8 + 9 \\ &= 1 \end{aligned}$$

So the remainder for $x^3 - 6x^2 + 4x + 9 \div (x - 2)$ is 1.

repeating decimal

See **recurring decimal**

retainer

See also **commission, salary, wages**

A fixed amount paid to an employee on a regular basis as a basic payment to which commission is added.

Example

Suri has a job selling household cleaning products to retail stores. She is paid a $300 weekly retainer and 10% of the value of goods she sells.
In a week that she sells $12 000 worth of products she earns $300 + $1200 = $1500.
In a week that she sells $500 worth of product, she earns $300 + $50 = $350.

reverse

See also **backtracking**

The other way round, or opposite way round. Working or moving backwards instead of forwards.

Example

The reverse of 385 is 583.

revolution

See also **angle, right angle**

One complete turn. There are 360° in one revolution.

There are four right angles in one revolution.

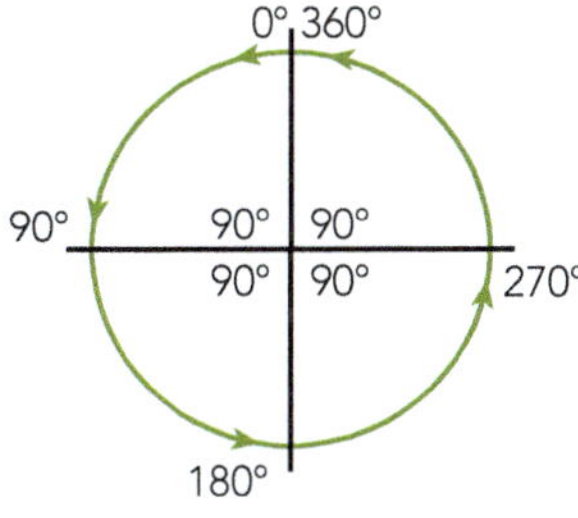

right-angled triangle

See also **hypotenuse, Pythagoras' theorem, right angle, trigonometric ratios**

A triangle with a right angle, indicated by the ⊾.

Examples

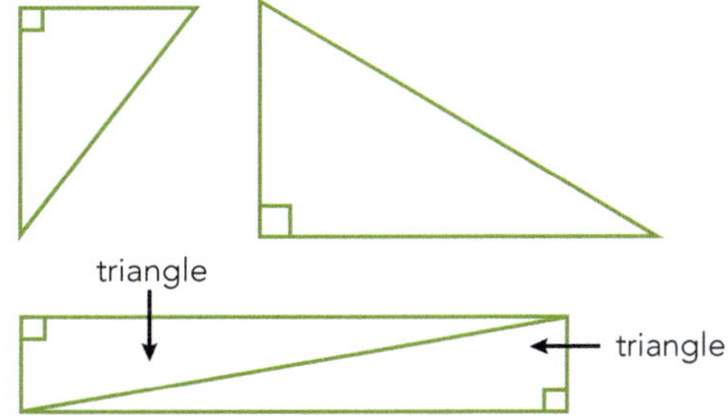

rhombus

See also **diamond, parallelogram**

A parallelogram with four equal sides. Opposite angles are equal. A square is a special type of rhombus.

Examples

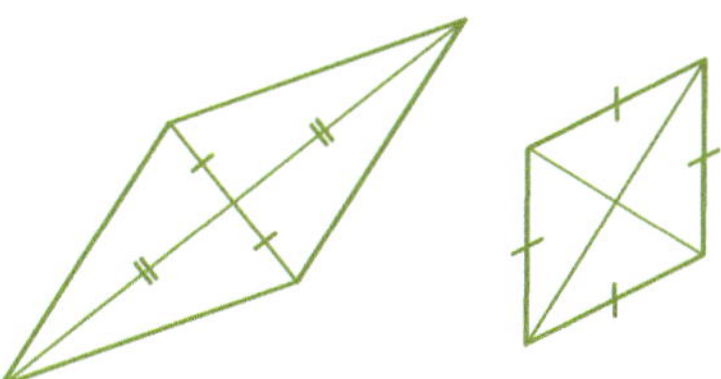

right 3D object

See also **cone, cylinder, prism**

A solid with the ends or base perpendicular to height.

Examples

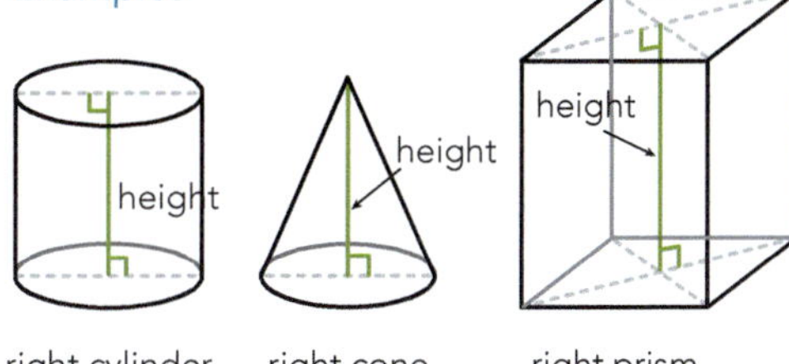

right cylinder right cone right prism

right angle (Symbol: ⊾)

See also **angle**

An angle measuring exactly 90°.

Examples

rigid

See also **flexible**

Not flexible. A structure is rigid when its angles cannot be changed.

A triangle forms a rigid structure.

Examples

rigid shape non-rigid shape (flexible)

rise

See also **gradient, run**

The vertical distance between two points found by subtracting the y-coordinate of the first point from the y-coordinate of the second point, written as $y_2 - y_1$.

Example

Given (2, 5) and (6, 3)

$$\text{rise} = 3 - 5$$
$$= -2$$

A negative rise means a fall as indicated by the arrow shown on the graph below.

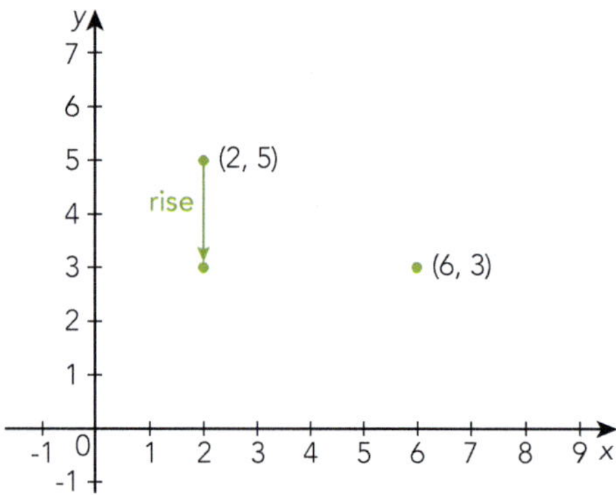

Roman numerals

See also **numeration, Roman numerals** on page 000

An ancient system of numeration, where the numbers are represented by letters of the Roman alphabet.

The numerals are made up of a combination of these symbols.

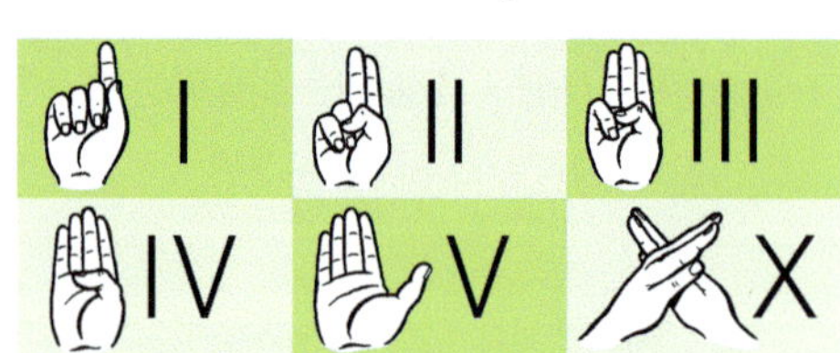

I	(1)	C	(100) centum
V	(5)	D	(500)
X	(10)	M	(1000) mille
L	(50)		

Examples

IX = 9	XVII = 17
MM = 2000	XXXIV = 34
LXI = 61	XLIX = 49
MCMXLIX = 1949	CD = 400

rotate

See also **turn**

Turn or spin around an axis or centre.

Example

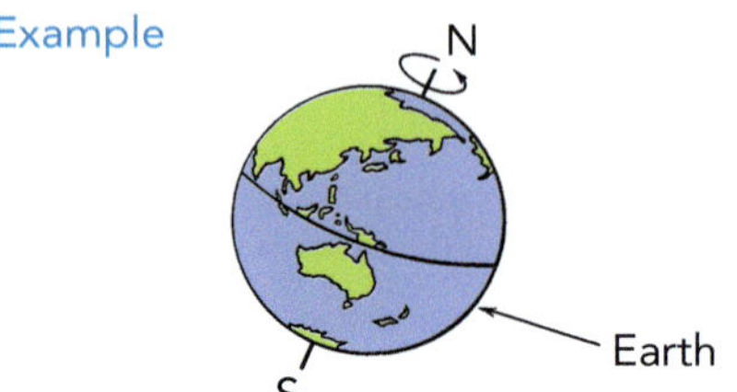

The Earth rotates on its axis.

rotation

See also **centre of rotation, rotate, rotational symmetry, transformation, turn**

The process by which an object changes position by turning about a fixed point, called the centre of rotation, through a given angle.

Examples

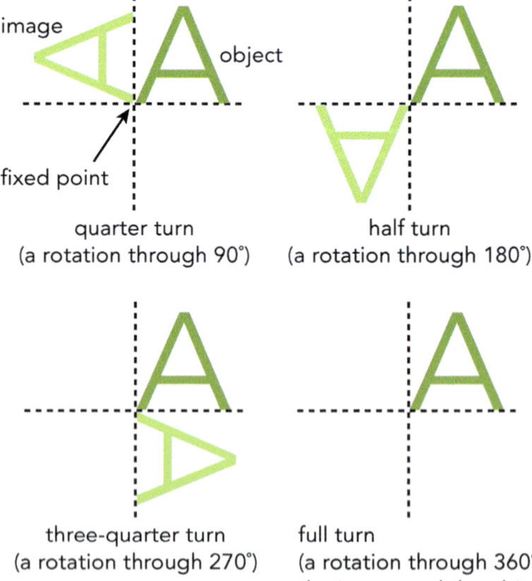

rotational symmetry

See also **order of rotational symmetry, symmetry, transformation**

The property of a shape if, when turned through an angle less than 360°, the image formed is identical to the original shape.

Example

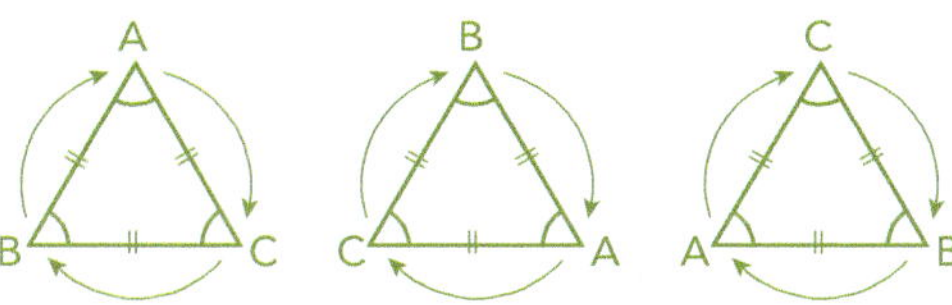

An equilateral triangle has rotational symmetry.

The number of times the same shape is achieved in one rotation is called the order of rotational symmetry. The order of symmetry of an equilateral triangle is 3.

rounding

See also **accurate, estimate, significant figure**

Writing an answer to a given degree of accuracy.

Example

2764 rounded to the nearest ten becomes 2760
rounded to the nearest hundred becomes 2800
rounded to the nearest thousand becomes 3000

- Numbers ending in 1, 2, 3 and 4 round down to the lower number.

Examples

i 54 ↑ rounded to the nearest ten becomes 50.

ii 348 ↑ rounded to the nearest hundred becomes 300.

- Numbers ending in 5, 6, 7, 8 and 9 round up to the higher number.

Examples

i 55 ↑ rounded to the nearest 10 becomes 60.

ii 356 ↑ rounded to the nearest 100 becomes 400.

The arrows point to the digits that determine whether to round up or down.

route

See also **traversable**

A path. A way taken from start to finish, which is traversable.

Example

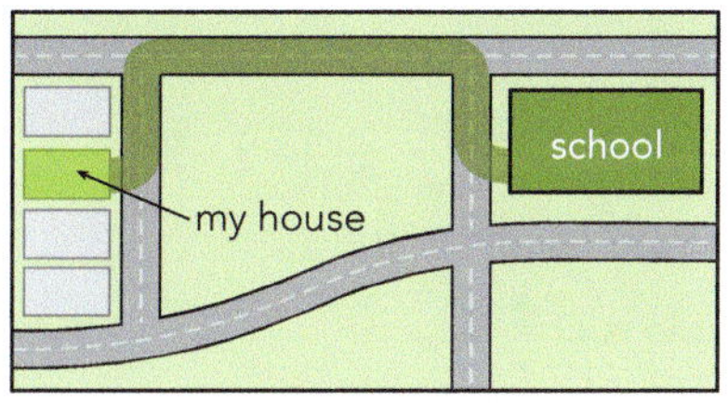

My route to school

row

See also **column, horizontal line**

1 A horizontal arrangement.

Example

Three rows of pears

2 Things arranged so that they make a line going from left to right.

Examples

i A row of numbers: 4, 5, 6, 7, 8, 9, …

ii A row of seats in a theatre

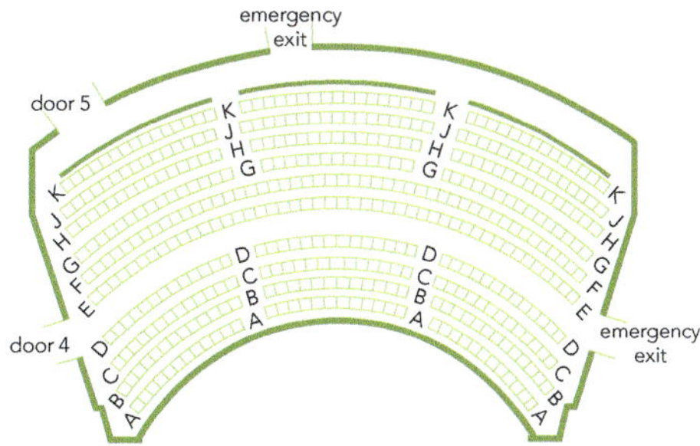

rule

See also **number machine, progression, sequence**

1 An instruction to do something in a particular way.

Example

Find the rule for this sequence.

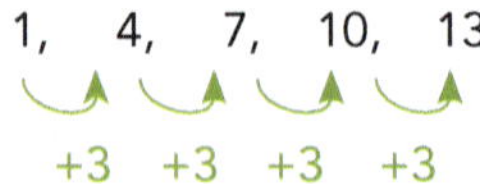

The rule is 'add 3'.

2 Numbers in a relation are following a rule.

Example

t	1	2	3	4	5	6
D	15	30	45	60	75	90

The rule is $D = 15t$.

3 To draw a line using a ruler.

Example

ruler

See also **graduated, scale**

An instrument for drawing straight lines, usually made of plastic or wood. It has a scale for measuring length.

run

See also **gradient**

The horizontal distance between two points found by subtracting the x-coordinate of the first point from the x-coordinate of the second one written as $x_2 - x_1$.

Example

Given (2, 5) and (6, 3)

$$\text{run} = 6 - 2$$
$$= 4$$

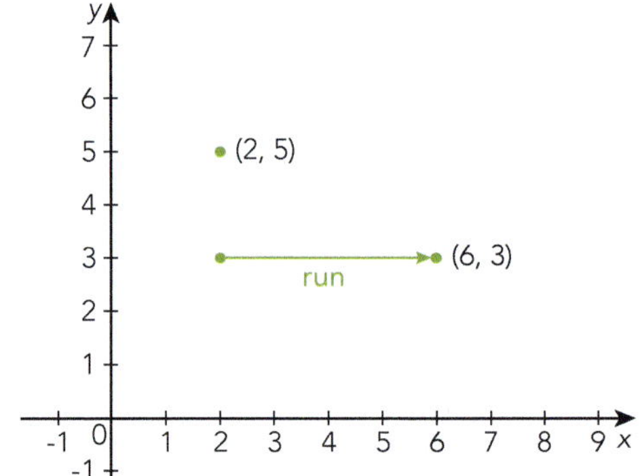

s

Symbol for second.

salary

See also **income, wages**

A fixed annual income that is divided up and paid at regular intervals. No penalty rates or overtime are paid to workers who earn a salary.

Example

Financial Accountant

Experienced Financial Accountant needed for Head Office Finance section. Key functions of this role are balance sheet reconciliations, general ledger reconciliations, asset management and end of month processes.

You will need to be an enthusiastic finance professional with experience in managing a small processing team and CA or CPA qualified.

Salary $56,000+. Apply using link below.
Reference Number: 163369

sale price

See also **discount, selling price**

The price of an article after a discount has been applied to the selling price.

Example

The sale price of a pair of shoes that normally sells for $85 is $68 after a 20% discount has been applied.

same

See also **congruent**

Identical, alike, unchanged, not different.

Example

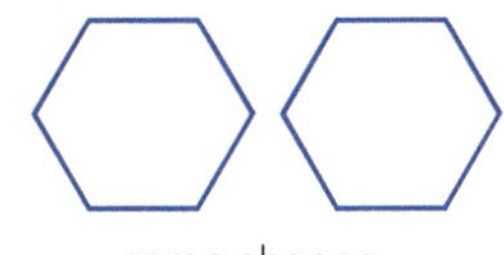

same shapes

sample

See also **population, random sample**

A selection of a few items or individuals taken from a population.

Example

In a biscuit factory, a sample of each batch of biscuits is taken and checked for quality.

sample space

See also **tree diagram, two-way table**

A list of all of the possible outcomes of a probability experiment. The sample space is written inside a pair of curly brackets known as braces.

Examples

i The sample space for rolling an ordinary die is {1, 2, 3, 4, 5, 6}.

ii The sample space for tossing two coins is {HH, HT, TH, TT}.

When two or more events are being considered (such as tossing two coins, rolling a die and tossing a coin, or randomly selecting three items from a drawer), a two-way table or tree diagram is useful for ensuring that all of the possible outcomes are listed.

satisfy

In mathematics it means 'make the equation true'.

Example

The whole numbers 1, 2, 3 and 4 satisfy the inequality $x < 5$ because $1 < 5$, $2 < 5$, $3 < 5$ and $4 < 5$ are all true number sentences.

The number 6 would not satisfy the inequality because $6 < 5$ is not true.

scale

See also **balance, enlargement, graph, number line, reduce, ruler, scale drawing, scale factor, thermometer**

1 A series of evenly spaced marks on a measuring instrument. A thermometer, a ruler and a set of bathroom scales each have a scale marked on them to measure temperature, length and weight, respectively.

Examples

2 A number line used on a graph.

Example

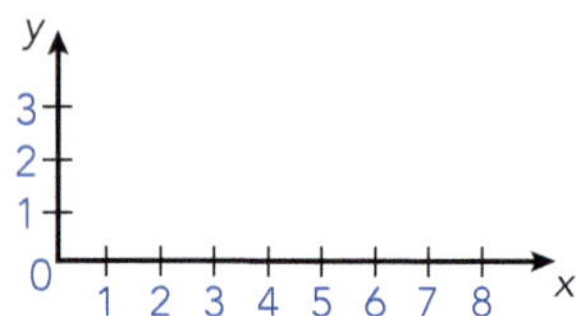

3 The scale on a map or a plan indicates the real-life distance shown by a certain distance (e.g.1 cm) on the map. The ratio indicates the factor by which the real-life distances have been reduced to produce the map.

Example

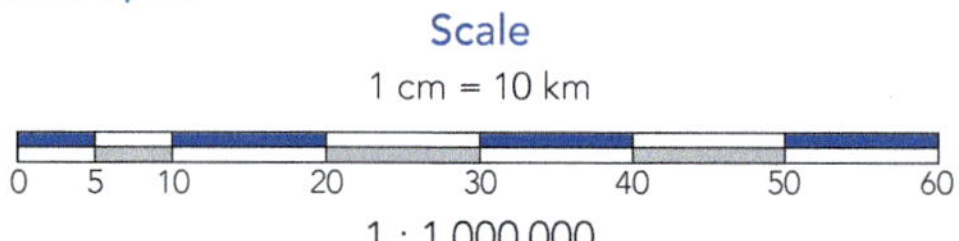

scale drawing

See also **enlargement, proportion, ratio, reduce, scale factor**

A drawing or plan on which the real object is enlarged or reduced while keeping the same proportions. This means that every measurement on the drawing has been enlarged or reduced by the same factor.

Example

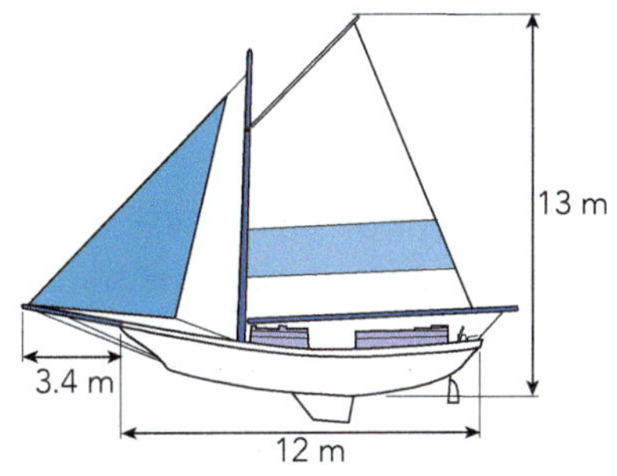

scale factor

See also **scale, scale drawing**

The number by which the dimensions of a figure are multiplied to obtain a larger or smaller similar figure.

Example

A model aeroplane is built using a scale factor of $\frac{1}{100}$ on the dimensions of an actual aeroplane.

scalene triangle

See also **triangle**

A triangle with each side different in length.

Example

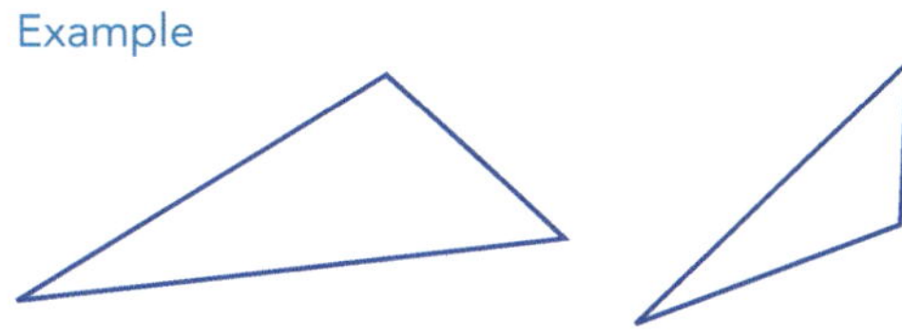

scales

See also **mass, weight**

Instruments used for finding or comparing weights or masses.

Examples

scatter plot

See also **bivariate data, data, line of best fit**

A graph of bivariate data where each data pair is represented by a point on the graph.

Example

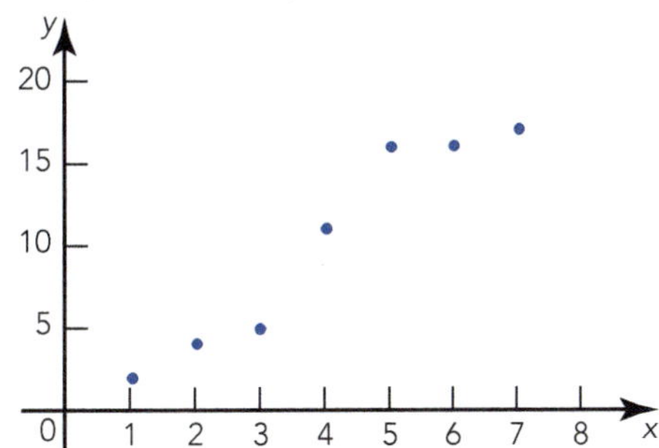

scientific notation

See also **expanded notation, index notation**

A shorthand way of writing very large or very small numbers using powers of ten. Also called standard form.
To write a number in scientific notation, write it as the product of a number between 1 and 10 and a power of 10.

Examples

i 6 300 000 = 6.3 × 1 000 000
= 6.3×10^6
6 places

ii 0.000 567 = 5.67 × 0.0001
= 5.67×10^{-4}
4 places

score

See also **average, data, mean, median, mode**

1 An old English word for the number 20.

Example
Four score years = 4 × 20 = 80 years

2 A word for an individual data value in a data set.

Example
Tim's batting scores for the last six cricket matches were 29, 34, 63, 48, 5 and 72.

second

See also **degree, ordinal number, pendulum**

1 second (2nd): the ordinal number which comes after first (1st) and before third (3rd).

Example

1st 2nd 3rd

2 second (symbol: s): A measurement of time. There are sixty seconds in one minute.

Example

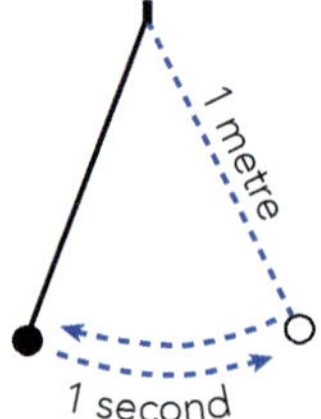

One second is the time taken by a pendulum about one metre long to make one complete swing, over and back.

3 An angle measurement (symbol: "). A second is $\frac{1}{60}$ of a minute, which is $\frac{1}{60}$ of a degree.

secondary data set

See also **primary data set**

Data that has not been collected directly by the user, but has been accessed from a book, the internet, the media, or some other source.

Example

Evan used the internet to collect data about how many people in Victoria had installed a water tank.

section

See also **cross-section ellipse, frustum, solid, surface, uniform cross-section**

1 A flat surface obtained by cutting through a solid in any direction.

Example

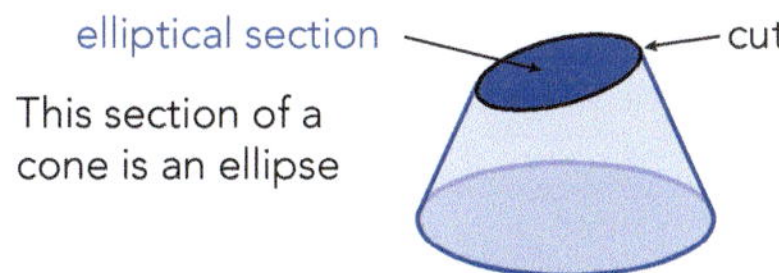

2 The 2D shape formed when the cut is parallel to the base of the solid.

Example

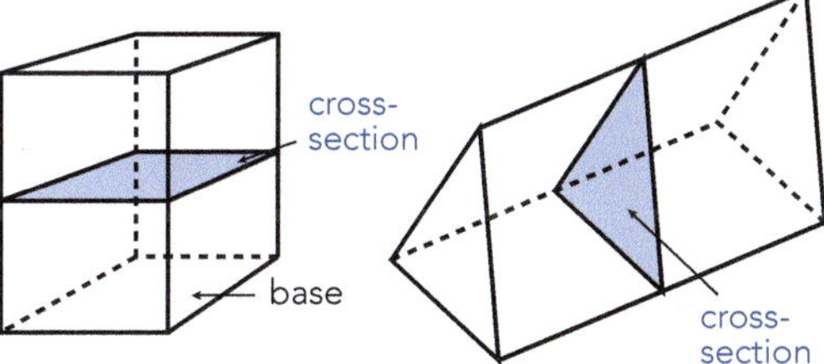

sector

See also **arc, circle, radii**

The area contained between two radii of a circle and the arc that joins the end points.

Example

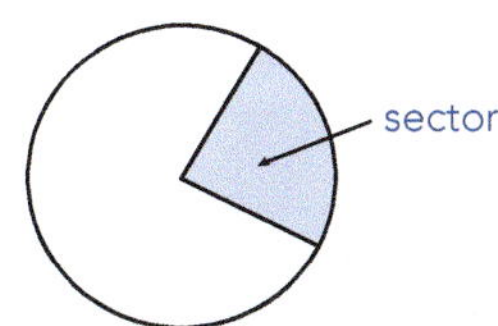

sector graph

See **pie graph**

segment

See also **arc, chord**

A part, a section of something.

Examples

i A line segment

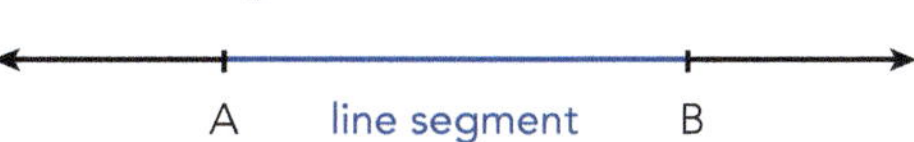

ii A segment of a circle is the part of the circle between an arc and its chord.

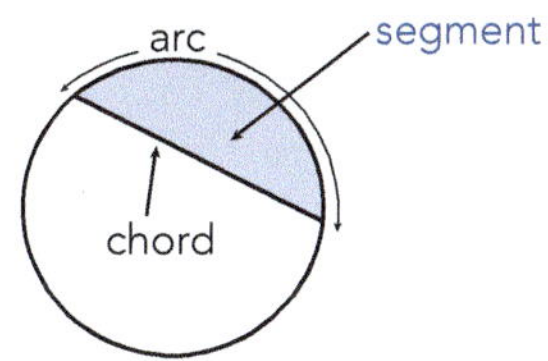

selling price

See also **cost price, loss, profit, sale price**

Price at which something is sold.

Example

The selling price of a car in a car yard is $12 000.

semicircle

See also **circle, diameter**

Half a circle.
When a circle is cut along a diameter, two semicircles are formed. They are identical to each other.

Example

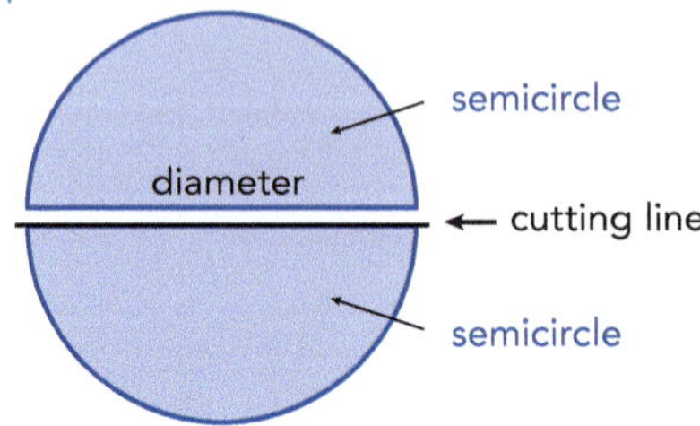

sequence

See also **order, pattern, progression, rule**

A string of numbers in a pattern that increases or decreases in a constant way.

1 If the rule is 'add a number', it is called an arithmetic sequence.

Examples
Rule: add 3 1, 4, 7, 10, 13, 16, …
Rule: subtract 2 21, 19, 17, 15, 13, 11, …

2 If the rule is 'multiply by a number', it is called a geometric sequence.

Examples
Rule: multiply by 4 1, 4, 16, 64, 256, …
Rule: divide by 2 12, 6, 3, 1.5, 0.75, …

A sequence is sometimes known as a progression.

set (Symbol: { })

See also **braces, element of a set, subset, whole numbers**

A group of objects or numbers. Each object in a set is called a member or an element of the set. The elements of a set are written inside braces { }.

Example
Set of whole numbers = {0, 1, 2, 3, 4 …}

set square

See also **parallel lines, right angle**

An drawing instrument in the shape of a right-angled triangle used for geometrical drawings of parallel lines and angles.

Examples

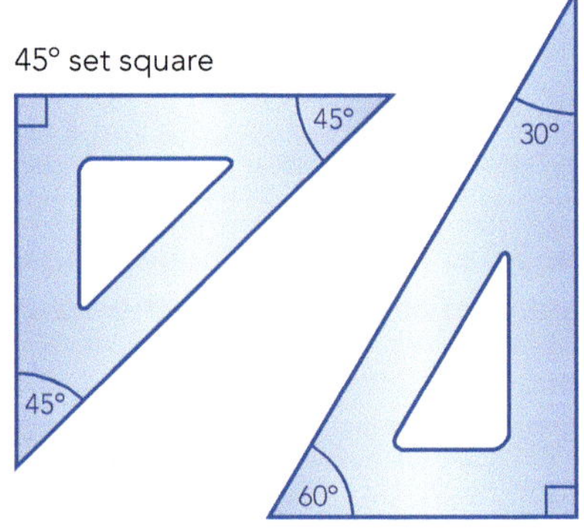

shadow stick measuring

See also **ratio, similar**

A useful, old method for calculating heights that cannot be directly measured. It is based on the properties of similar triangles.

Example

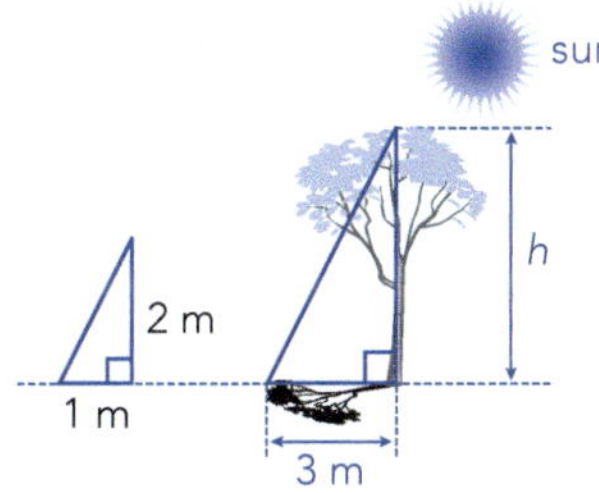

We measure the shadow of a stick of a known length and the shadow cast by the tall object. The length of the stick and the object, and the length of their shadows, are in the same ratio.

$$\frac{\text{height of tree}}{\text{height of tree's shadow}} = \frac{\text{height of stick}}{\text{height of stick's shadow}}$$

$$\frac{h}{3} = \frac{2}{1}$$

$$h = 3 \times \frac{2}{1}$$

$$= 6$$

The tree is 6 m high.

shape (geometry)

See also **cube, dimension, polygon, prism, pyramid, quadrilateral, three-dimensional, triangle, two-dimensional**

The form of an object.

Examples

2D shapes: triangles, quadrilaterals

3D shapes: cubes, prisms, pyramids

shape (statistics)

See also **dot plot, histogram, skew, stem plot, symmetry (statistics)**

The shape of a statistical graph (such as a histogram, stem plot or dot plot) tells us about the way that the data is distributed across the range.

If it is evenly spread to the left and right of the median (the middle value), the data is said to be symmetrical. If a lot of the data is clustered at the lower end of the range, it is positively skewed. If it is clustered at the higher end of the range it is negatively skewed.

Examples

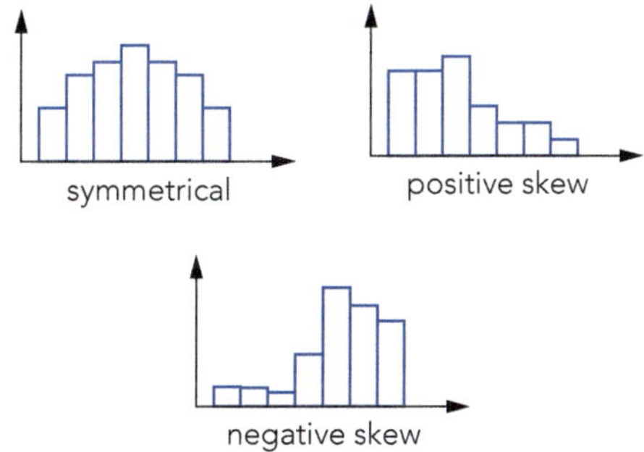

shape name

See also **angle name, quadrilateral, triangle**

Letters placed alphabetically around a shape at each vertex give the shape a specific name.

Example

The letters *A*, *B*, *C* and *D* are used to name quadrilateral *ABCD*.

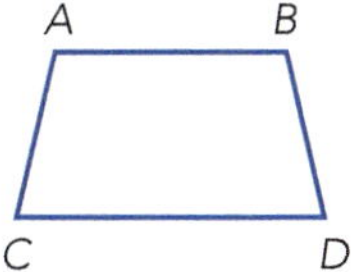

sharing

See **division**

SI

See also **metric system**

The international metric system.

The symbol SI comes from the initials of the French term *Système Internationale d'Unités* (international unit system).

This system is based on the following units: metre, gram, second, ampere, kelvin, candela and mole.

Examples

SI units are used for quantities of goods, such as 500 g of butter, and for constructions, such as a 50 m swimming pool.

side

See also **line segment, pentagon, perimeter**

A line segment which is a part of a perimeter or of a figure.

Examples

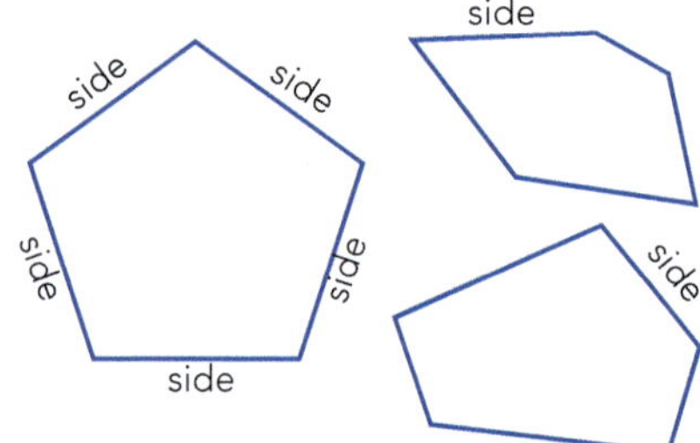

A pentagon has five sides.

side-by-side column graph

See also **column graph**

A type of column graph used to display two or more sets of data that have been collected about a particular characteristic from more than one individual or place.

Example

This side-by-side column graph compares how the staff from three different companies come to work.

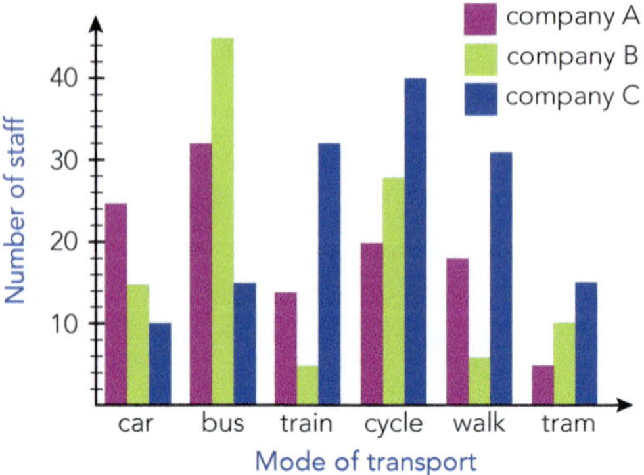

side view

See also **cross-section of a solid, front view, plan view, top view**

A diagram of a 3D object, as seen from the side.

Example

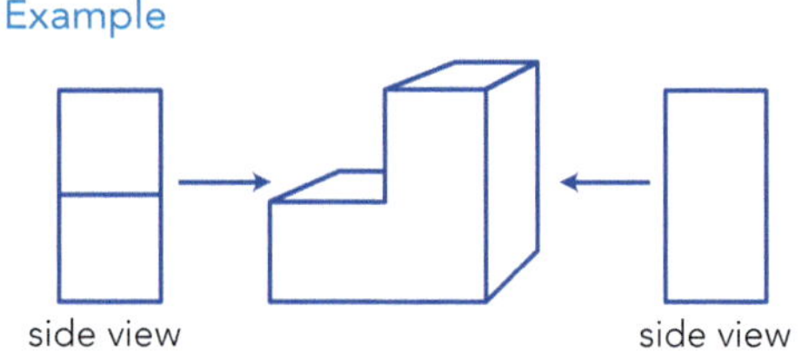

sign

See also **List of symbols** on page 186, **operation, symbol**

A symbol used to show an operation or a statement.

Examples

Addition sign	+
Subtraction sign	−
Multiplication sign	×
Division signs	÷ ⟌ ⟌
Equal sign	=

significant figure

See also **approximately, rounding**

A digit in a number that is considered important when rounding off or making an approximation.

Examples

i 3745 rounded to two significant figures is 3700.

ii 0.165 of a metre rounded to one significant figure is 0.2 of a metre.

similar

See also **congruent, enlargement, matching angles, matching sides, ratio, reduce**

Identical in shape but not necessarily in size.

Examples

Similar figures have:

- each pair of matching angles (that is, angles in the same position) equal
- each pair of matching sides in the same ratio.

Example

These arrows are similar because one can be enlarged or reduced to form the other.

similarity

See also **matching angles, matching sides, similar, similar triangles**

A property of a pair or group of figures or objects. Two figures or objects are similar if they are exactly the same shape, but are the same or different in size. If two figures are similar and different in size, enlarging or reducing one will make it congruent to the other.

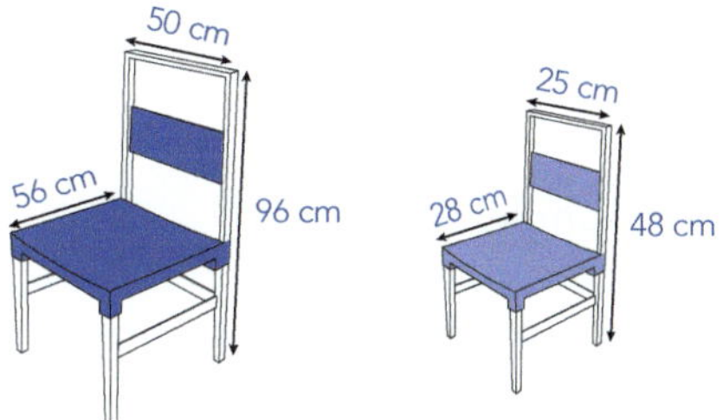

similar triangles

See also **matching angles, matching sides, similarity**

A pair or group of triangles in which triangles of different sizes can be enlarged or reduced to make them congruent. The matching sides are in the same ratio and matching angles are equal. To classify triangles as similar, one of the following four tests can be used.

1 Angle, angle, angle (AAA)
Three pairs of angles are of the same magnitude. (Only two pairs of angles are needed because the angle sum of a triangle is 180°.)

Example

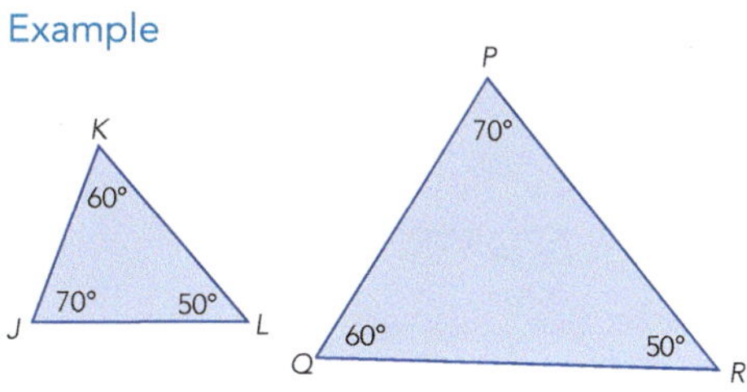

$\Delta JKL \sim \Delta PQR$ (AAA)

similar triangles continued ▶

2 Side, side, side (SSS)
Three pairs of matching sides are in the same ratio.

Example

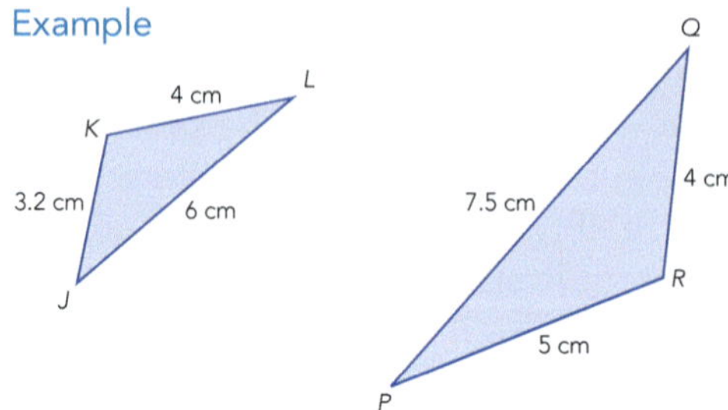

ΔJKL ~ ΔPQR (SSS)

3 Side, angle, side (SAS)
Two pairs of matching sides have lengths in the same ratio and the included angles are equal.

Example

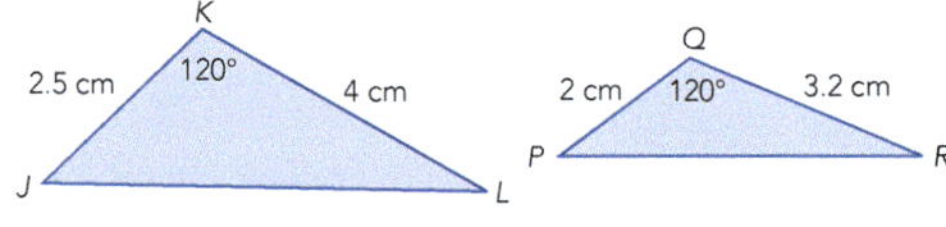

ΔJKL ~ ΔPQR (SAS)

4 Right angle, hypotenuse, side (RHS)
The hypotenuse and one side of a right-angled triangle are in the same ratio as the hypotenuse and one side of another right-angled triangle.

Example

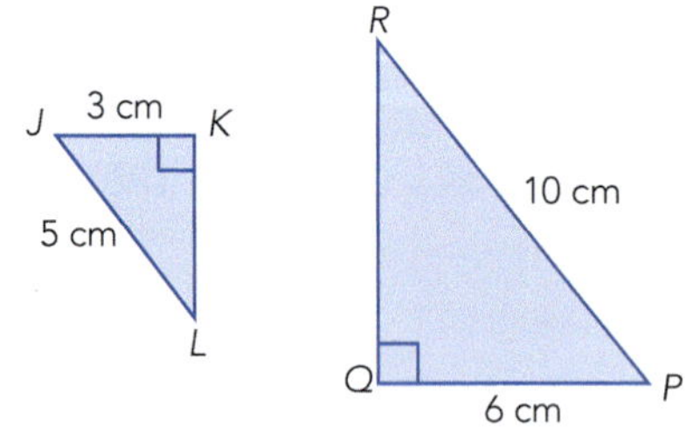

ΔJKL ~ ΔPQR (RHS)

simple fraction

See also **complex fraction, denominator, fraction, improper fraction, numerator, proper fraction**

A fraction where both numerator and denominator are integers. It can be a proper or improper fraction.

Examples

$\frac{3}{4}$, $\frac{1}{2}$, $\frac{7}{10}$, $\frac{9}{5}$

simple interest

See also **interest, interest rate, principal**

Interest payable on the principal alone and charged each time period for the period of the loan. Simple interest is calculated using the formula:

$$I = PRT$$

where P is the principal, R is the rate over a time period and T is the time period (usually a year).

Example

John borrows $10 000 from his bank to buy a car at a simple interest rate of 6 per cent over a period of 5 years.

$$\begin{aligned} I &= PRT \\ &= 10\,000 \times 0.06 \times 5 \\ &= 3000 \end{aligned}$$

John has to pay a total amount of $3000 simple interest on the loan.

simplest form

See also **denominator, factor, numerator, ratio, simplify**

A fraction or ratio in which all common factors have been divided into both the numerator and denominator.

Example

$\frac{1}{2}$ is the simplest form of $\frac{3}{6}$ after both the numerator and denominator have been divided by three.

simplify

See also **denominator, fraction, numerator**

A method of changing a fraction to its simplest form, by dividing both the numerator and denominator by common factors.

Examples

i Divide both numerator and denominator by three (common factor).

$$\frac{\cancel{15}^{5}}{\cancel{21}_{7}} = \frac{5}{7}$$

ii Simplify the fractions to be multiplied by dividing by common factors first. Here, we divide 15 and 40 by 5, and 33 and 22 by 11.

$$\frac{\cancel{15}^{3}}{\cancel{22}_{2}} \times \frac{\cancel{33}^{3}}{\cancel{40}_{8}} = \frac{3 \times 3}{2 \times 8}$$

$$= \frac{9}{16}$$

iii Simplify this algebraic fraction.

$$\frac{a^2b}{ab}$$

$$= \frac{a \times \cancel{a}^1 \times \cancel{b}^1}{\cancel{a}_1 \times \cancel{b}_1}$$

$$= a$$

simultaneous equations

See also **equation, solution**

Equations that have the same unknown quantities and are solved together.

Example

$a + b = 10$
$a - b = -4$

Adding the two equations gives

$2a = 6$
$a = 3$

Substitute $a = 3$ into the first equation:

$3 + b = 10$	Check:
$b = 10 - 3$	$a - b = -4$
$b = 7$	$3 - 7 = -4$ ✓

The solution is $a = 3$ and $b = 7$.

sine

See also **cosine, equivalent angle, hypotenuse, tangent, theta, trigonometric ratios, unit circle**

One of the three basic trigonometric ratios. In a right-angled triangle the sine of an angle θ (theta) is the ratio of the side opposite the angle θ and the hypotenuse.

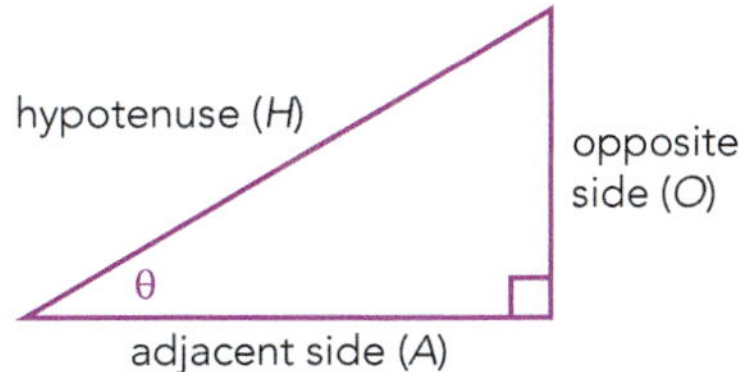

Sine is usually abbreviated to sin and the ratio written as $\sin\theta = \frac{\text{opposite}}{\text{hypotenuse}}$, $\frac{\text{opp}}{\text{hyp}}$, or simply $\frac{O}{H}$.

In unit circle trigonometry, $\sin\theta$ is the y-coordinate of a point P on the unit circle, where the position of P is determined by the angle θ.

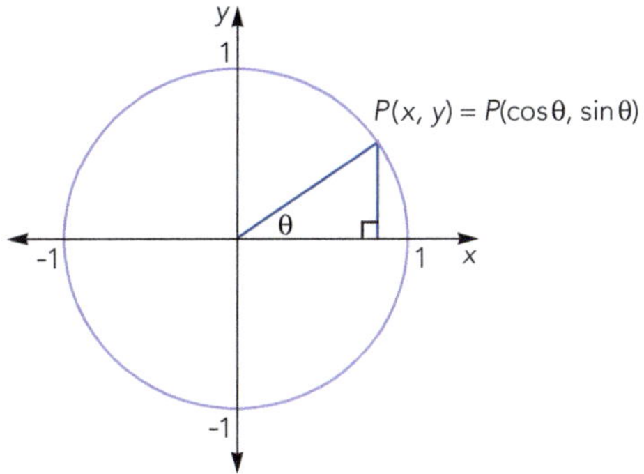

size

The amount, magnitude or dimension.

Examples

i The size of this angle is 37°.

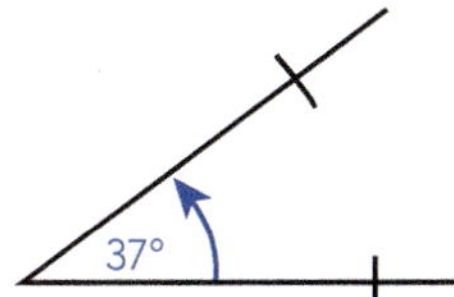

ii Helen wears size ten clothes and size seven shoes.

skew

See **shape (statistics)**

skew lines

See also **intersect, parallel lines**

Lines that do not lie in the same plane; they cannot intersect and are not parallel.

Examples

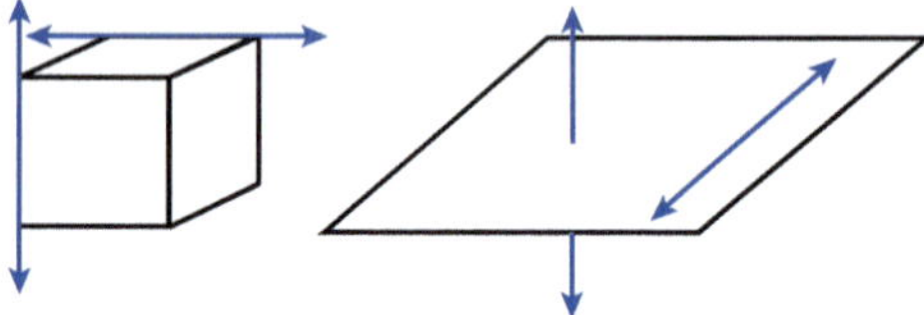

slide

See also **flip, rotation, translation, turn**

A slide is a translation, a transformation that changes the position of a figure without changing its orientation (no turning or flipping).

slope

See also **gradient, rise, run**

A measure of the steepness of the line. The slope is also called the gradient. Slope is calculated by $\frac{\text{rise}}{\text{run}}$ (the change in the vertical position divided by the change in the horizontal position).

Example

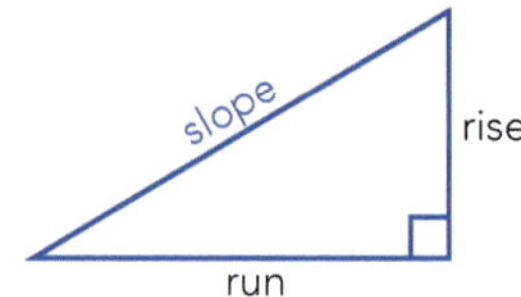

solid

See also **height, length, three-dimensional, width**

A figure with three dimensions: length, width and height (depth).

Examples

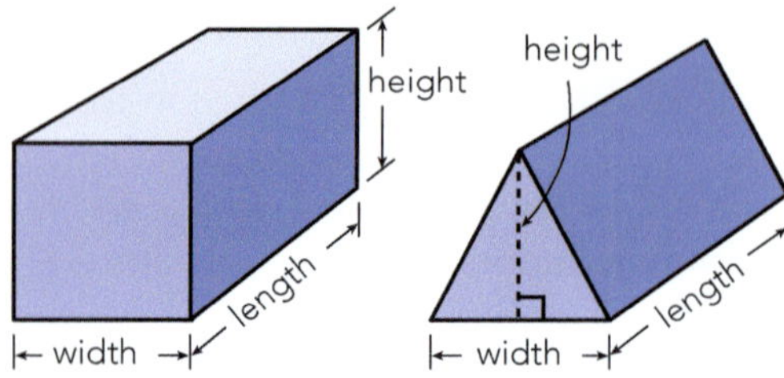

solution

See also **calculation, equation, solve**

The correct answer to a calculation, equation, problem or question.

Example

The equation $x + 4 = 9$

has a solution $x = 5$.

solve

See also **calculate, equation, number sentence, solution**

Find the answer. An equation is solved by finding the value of the variable(s) that makes the equation a true number sentence.

some

1 Not all of the whole.

Examples

a whole cake

some of the cake

2 More than one.

Example

some apples

sorting

See also **attribute, classification, classify, group, property**

Putting objects into groups according to attributes.

Example

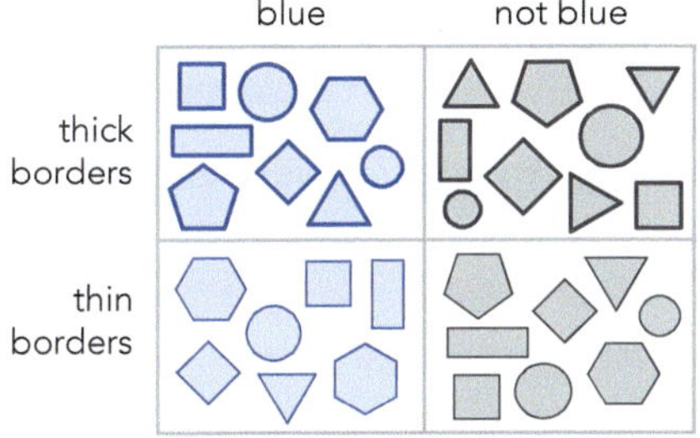

Attributes are colour and thickness.

space

See also **dimension, region, solid, three-dimensional**

A three-dimensional region.

span

See also **handspan**

Stretch from side to side, across.

spatial

See also **space**

Relating to, or happening in, space.

speed

See also **distance, knot, rate, unit of measurement**

The rate at which something travels. The distance travelled in a unit of time.

Example

A car travelled 60 kilometres in 1 hour. Its speed was 60 km/h.

sphere

See also **three-dimensional**

A three-dimensional shape like a round ball. A sphere has one curved surface and no corners or edges. Every point on the sphere's surface is the same distance from the sphere's centre.

Examples

a basketball

the Earth

spinner

See also **chance, die**

A disc marked with numbers. Used in chance games.

Examples

spiral

See also **curve, distance**

A curve like a coil on a flat surface. A spiral is a continuous curve moving around and outwards from a fixed point. Its distance from the fixed point is always increasing.

Example

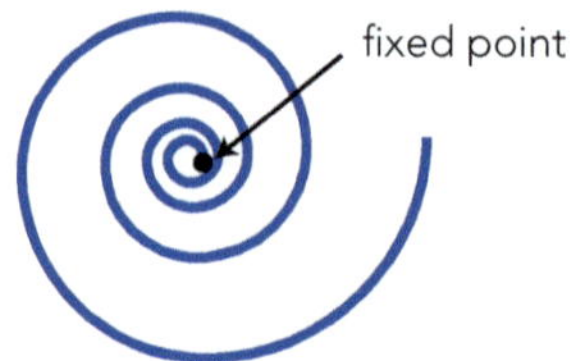

spring balance

See also **mass, weight**

An instrument that measures weight.
A spring inside it is extended by the force of gravity acting on the mass of the object.

square

See also **quadrilateral, right angle, regular polygon**

A regular quadrilateral. A square has four equal sides and four right angles. A square is a special type of rectangle.

Example

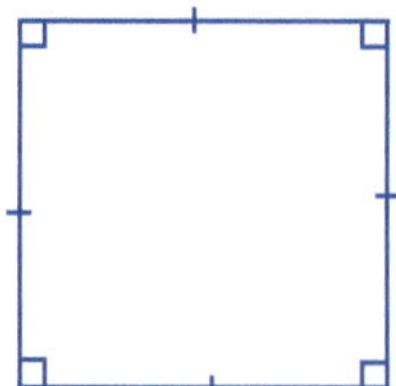

square centimetre (Symbol: cm²)

See also **area, unit of measurement**

A square centimetre is a unit for measuring area.

Examples

i The area is one square centimetre.

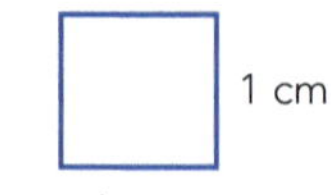

ii The area of this shape is three square centimetres.

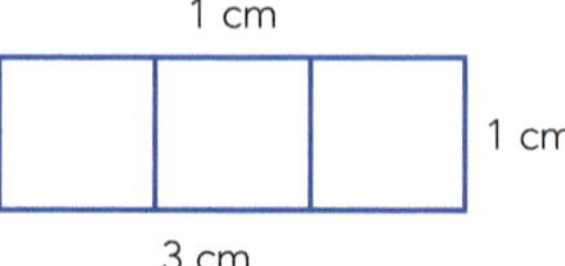

$$3 \text{ cm} \times 1 \text{ cm} = 3 \text{ cm}^2$$

square kilometre (Symbol: km²)

See also **area, unit of measurement**

A unit for measuring very large areas.

$$1 \text{ km}^2 = 1\,000\,000 \text{ m}^2$$

Examples

i

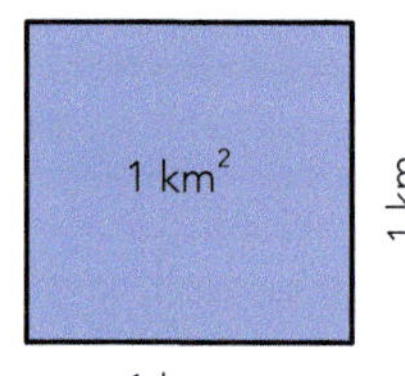

ii The area of the Northern Territory is 1 346 200 km².

Smaller areas, like the sizes of towns or suburbs, are measured in hectares.

$$1 \text{ km}^2 = 100 \text{ ha}$$

square metre (Symbol: m^2)

See also **area, square centimetre, unit of measurement**

A unit for measuring area.

$1\ m^2 = 10\,000\ cm^2$

Examples

i This man is holding a piece of cardboard which has an area of one square metre.

ii This rug has an area of $4.5\ m^2$.

square number

See also **index, index notation, triangle number**

A number that can be represented by dots in the shape of a square.

Examples

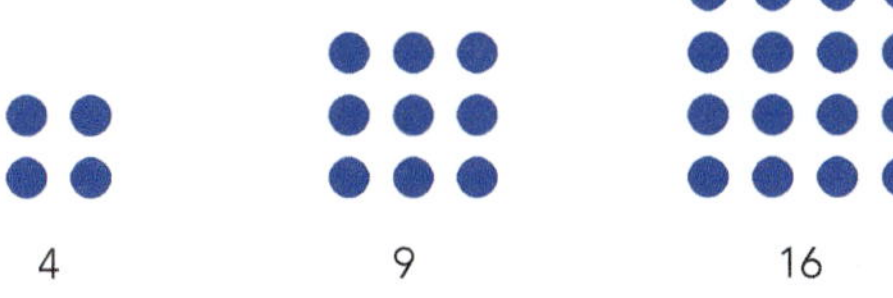

4 9 16

Square numbers are the result of multiplying a number by itself.

$4 = 2 \times 2$ or 2^2 'two squared'

$9 = 3 \times 3$ or 3^2 'three squared'

$16 = 4 \times 4$ or 4^2 'four squared'

square of a number

See also **index, index laws, square root, square number**

The answer you get when you multiply a number by itself.

square root

See also **inverse operations, square number, square of a number**

A number which, when multiplied by itself, produces the given number. The inverse operation of squaring a number.

Examples

$\sqrt{2} \times \sqrt{2} = 2$

$\sqrt{9} \times \sqrt{9} = 9$

Because negative numbers multiplied by themselves give positive answers, the square root of a number may be positive or negative.

Example

$$\begin{aligned}(+2)^2 &= 2 \times 2 \\ &= +4 \\ (-2)^2 &= -2 \times -2 \\ &= +4 \\ \therefore \sqrt{4} &= \pm 2\end{aligned}$$

standard deviation

(σ for a population, *s* for a sample)

A measure of the spread of a data set around the mean. The smaller the standard deviation, the more closely 'packed' the data is around the mean. The lower case Greek letter σ (sigma) is used to represent the standard deviation of a population, while *s* is used for the standard deviation of a sample.

standard deviation continued ▶

Standard deviation of a population is found by calculating the deviation from the mean of each data value (the difference between the mean and the data value), then squaring each deviation, adding these squared deviations together and then dividing this total by the number of data values. This is called the variance. Finally, the square root is taken (to reverse the earlier 'squaring' process).

The process is written as a formula in the following way:

$$\sigma = \sqrt{\frac{\Sigma(X-\bar{X})^2}{n}}$$

where
X is the data value,
$\bar{X}$ is the mean, Σ (upper case Greek letter sigma) means 'the sum of the following', and n is the number of values in the data set.

The process for finding the standard deviation for a sample is almost the same except that the sum of the squared deviations is divided by $n - 1$.

$$s = \sqrt{\frac{\Sigma(X-\bar{X})^2}{n-1}}$$

standard unit

See also **SI, unit, unit of measurement**

A measurement that has been internationally accepted by agreement to represent 'one' unit.

Examples

a metre, a gram, a second, a mole

statistics

See also **categorical data, data, numerical data**

The study concerned with the collection, classification, display and analysis of data. Data may be numerical (numbers) or it may be categorical. Data can be represented in a table or on a graph.

Example

Favourite foods

Meat	Vegetables	Fruit	Sweets
Paul S. John Tibor Jackie Toula Sarah David Jeremy	Carlo Hirani	Anne James Paul B. Claire Ranjit	Dean Belinda Quong Brad Ali Anna Jhiro Peter Samantha Halima

The information in the table is the data.
There are 25 children in the class.
8 children prefer meat
$\therefore \frac{8}{25} \times \frac{100}{1} = 32\%$ of the class prefer meat

2 children prefer vegetables
$\therefore \frac{2}{25} \times \frac{100}{1} = 8\%$ of the class prefer vegetables

5 children prefer fruit
$\therefore \frac{5}{25} \times \frac{100}{1} = 20\%$ of the class prefer fruit

10 children prefer sweets
$\therefore \frac{10}{25} \times \frac{100}{1} = 40\%$ of the class prefer sweets

The percentages are statistics about the food preferences of the class.

straight angle

See also **angle**

An angle of 180°.

Example

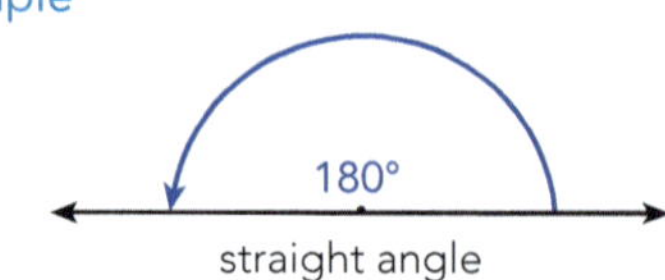

straight line
See **line**

stem-and-leaf plot (stem plot)
See also **data, histogram, statistics**

A way of displaying numerical data. Each data value is split into a 'leaf' (the last digit in the data value, usually the units value) and a 'stem' (the rest of the digits in the data value, i.e. tens, hundreds, etc.).

Example

The stem-and-leaf plot below shows the number of items in the trolleys of 20 people passing through a supermarket checkout.

Data

23, 14, 9, 32, 20, 18, 36, 25, 32, 16, 7, 36, 27, 44, 23, 36, 5, 40, 13, 34

Stem	Leaf
0	9 7 5
1	4 8 6 3
2	3 0 5 7 3
3	2 6 2 6 6 4
4	4 0

Here, the stem represents the tens values and the leaves are the units, so the data value of 32 is represented as 3|2. The top row of data values in the plot is 9, 7, 5 and the next row is 14, 18, 16, 13.

When the leaf values in each row are written from smallest to largest, the plot is an 'ordered' stem-and-leaf plot. It can then be used to find the median and quartile values.

Stem	Leaf
0	5 7 9
1	3 4 6 8
2	0 3 3 5 7
3	2 2 4 6 6 6
4	0 4

Stem-and-leaf plots are similar to histograms in that they display grouped data; but unlike in grouped histograms, no individual data values are lost. A sideways view of a stem-and-leaf plot gives the shape of a histogram and therefore gives an idea of the distribution or shape of the data.

Stem-and-leaf plots are easy to construct; however, they are not really suited to large amounts of data. Where there is a large amount of data, the stem values can be split so that they show either the lower five leaf-values (0, 1, 2, 3, 4) or the upper five leaf-values (5, 6, 7, 8, 9).
The stem-and-leaf plot above, shown in this way, would look like:

Stem	Leaf
0_L	
0_U	5 7 9
1_L	3 4
1_U	6 8
2_L	0 3 3
2_U	5 7
3_L	2 2 4
3_U	6 6 6
4_L	0 4

subitising
See also **number, counting on**

Instantly recognising the number of objects in a small group, without actually counting them.

Example

subset

See also **combination, set**

A set within a set.

Examples

i If each element of a set S (below) is also an element of a set T, then S is called a subset of T.

Set T = {natural numbers to twenty-five}
Set S = {square numbers to twenty-five}

Set T: 15, 11, 2, 3, 20, 14, 7, 6, 19, 23, 12, 21, 24, 18, 10, 5, 8, 13, 17, 22

Set S: 9, 4, 16, 1, 25

ii Set A = {all children in your class}
Set B = {all girls in your class}

Set B is a subset of set A, because all the elements in set B are also in set A.

substitution

See also **algebraic expression, formula, number sentence, variable**

1 Something standing in place of another.

2 The replacement of a variable in an algebraic expression or formula by a number.

Examples

i If $a = 5$ and $b = 2$, what is value of $2a + 2b$?

$$\begin{aligned} 2a + 2b &= 2 \times 5 + 2 \times 2 \\ &= 10 + 4 \\ &= 14 \end{aligned}$$

ii If $s = \frac{d}{t}$, find s when $d = 84$ and $t = 7$

$$\begin{aligned} s &= \frac{d}{t} \\ &= \frac{84}{7} \\ &= 12 \end{aligned}$$

subtract

See also **difference, subtraction**

Take away. Find the difference.

subtraction

See also **complementary addition, difference, number line**

1 Taking one amount away from another to find what amount is left.

Example

Jessica had five pencils and gave three to Mario. How many pencils did Jessica keep?

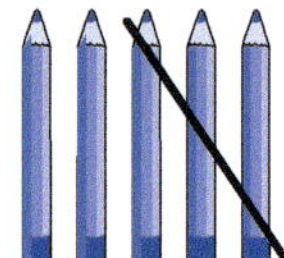

$5 - 3 = \square$

$5 - 3 = 2$

Jessica kept two pencils.

2 Difference (comparison).

Example

Remy has seven pencils and Robin has three pencils. How many more pencils has Remy than Robin?

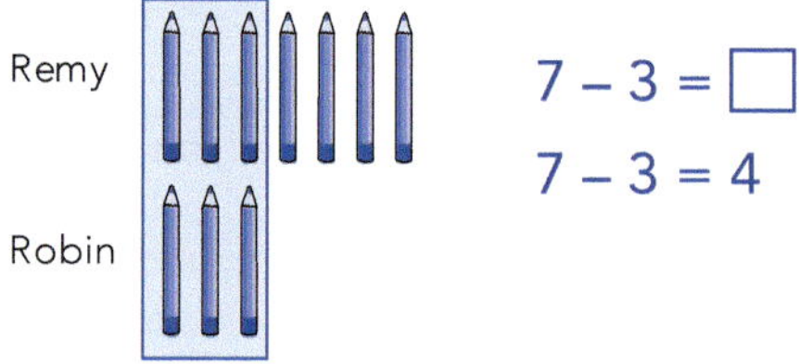

$7 - 3 = \square$

$7 - 3 = 4$

Remy has four more pencils than Robin.

3 Complementary addition (missing addend, counting on).

Example

Rowan has three pencils, but needs seven. How many more must he get?

$3 + \square = 7$

$3 + 4 = 7$

Rowan must get four more pencils.

Subtraction may be represented on a number line.

Example

Show on the number line:

$11 - 9$

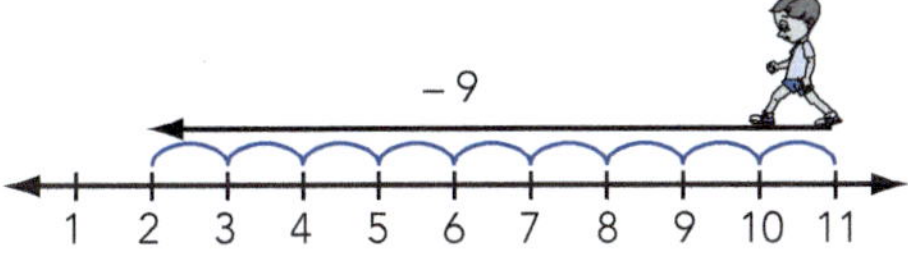

subtrahend

See also **difference, minuend, subtract**

A number which is to be subtracted from another number.

Example

12	−	4	=	8
↑		↑		↑
minuend		subtrahend		difference

Four is the subtrahend.

sum

See also **addend, addition**

The answer to an addition problem. It is the total amount resulting from the addition of two or more numbers (called addends), quantities or magnitudes.

Example

3	+	4	=	7
↑		↑		↑
addends				sum

Seven is the sum.

supplementary angles

See also **complementary angles, cointerior angles**

Two angles which add together to equal 180°.

Example

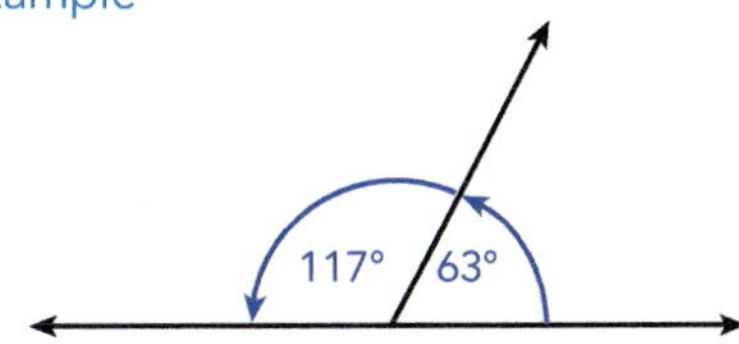

Angles 117° and 63° are supplementary.
Angle 117° is called the supplement of 63°.
Angle 63° is called the supplement of 117°.

surd

See also **irrational number**

An irrational number that can only be expressed exactly by using the root symbol, $\sqrt{}$ (also known as the radical symbol).

Examples

- **i** a single root, such as $\sqrt{29}$ or $\sqrt[3]{10}$
- **ii** a root multiplied by a whole number, such as $2\sqrt{5}$
- **iii** an expression, such as $\sqrt{6} + \sqrt{3}$ or $4\sqrt{11} + 5\sqrt[3]{7}$

surface

See also **area, cylinder**

1 The outside of something.

Example

The surface of a tennis ball is furry.

surface continued ▶

2 The top level of a liquid.

Example

Leaves float on the surface of a lake.

The surface of an object may be flat or curved.

Example

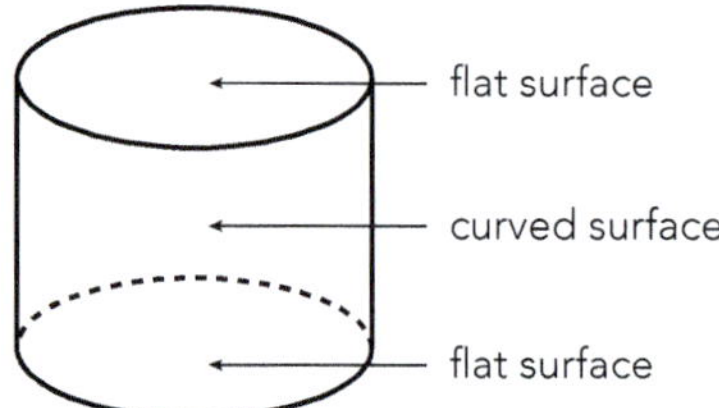

A cylinder has two flat surfaces and one curved surface.

surface area

See also **area, cube, surface**

The total area of the outside of a 3D object.

To find the surface area of a solid, find the area of each of the faces, then find the sum of the areas. A net is useful in identifying all of the faces and finding their areas.

Examples

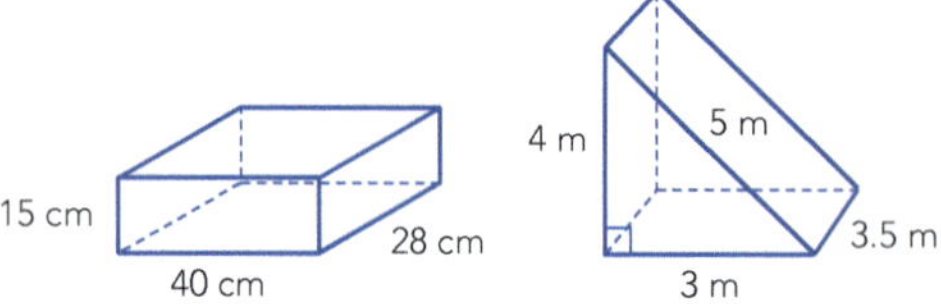

symbol

See also **abbreviation, pronumeral, A list of symbols** on page 186

A letter, numeral or mark which represents something. We do not write a full stop after a symbol.

Examples

1	2	3	+	–	×	÷
=	≠	>	<	≈	%	□
cm	kg	ha	m³	∠		
a	*b*	x^2	2*x*			

symmetry

See also **order of symmetry, reflectional symmetry, rotational symmetry**

Division of an object into two parts identical in size and shape but opposite in orientation. An axis of symmetry can be drawn to show the division.

Examples

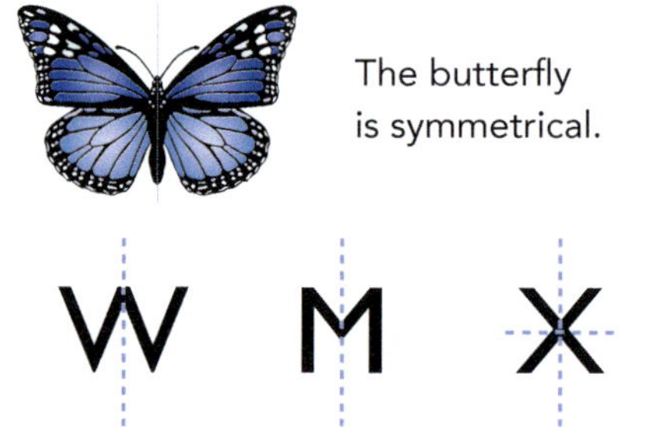

The butterfly is symmetrical.

Système Internationale d'Unités

See **SI**

t

Symbol for tonne.

table

See also **multiplication**

1 An arrangement of letters or numbers in rows or columns.

Example

×	1	2	3	4	5	6
1	1	2	3	4	5	6
2	2	4	6	8	10	12
3	3	6	9	12	15	18
4	4	8	12	16	20	24
5	5	10	15	20	25	30
6	6	12	18	24	30	36

2 When multiplication facts are arranged in order, they are then called multiplication tables.

Example

The multiplication table of nine

$1 \times 9 = 9$
$2 \times 9 = 18$
$3 \times 9 = 27$
$4 \times 9 = 36$
$5 \times 9 = 45$
$6 \times 9 = 54$
$7 \times 9 = 63$
$8 \times 9 = 72$
$9 \times 9 = 81$
$10 \times 9 = 90$

take away

See also **subtraction**

Remove, subtract. It is one method of subtraction.

Example

I had fifteen marbles and I lost seven.
How many do I have now?
15 – 7 = 8 (take away seven from fifteen)

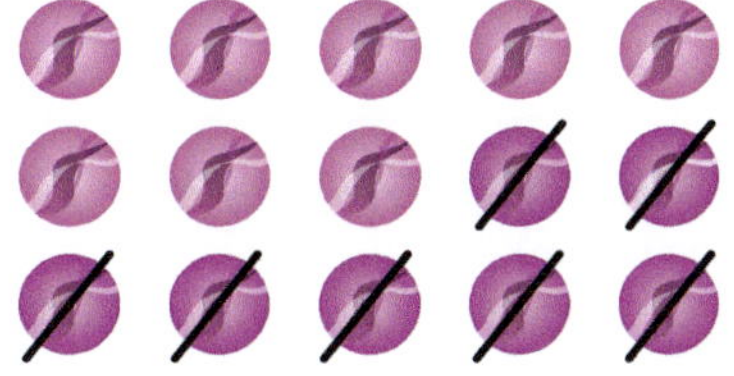

Answer: I have eight marbles now.

tally

A record of items made by placing a mark to represent each item. The marks are usually drawn in groups of five, with the fifth mark in each group crossing the other four, to make them easy to count.

Example

A tally of thirteen items

卌 卌 |||

tangent (geometry)

See also **circumference, radius**

A line that touches a circle at a single point on the circumference. It does not pass inside the circle.

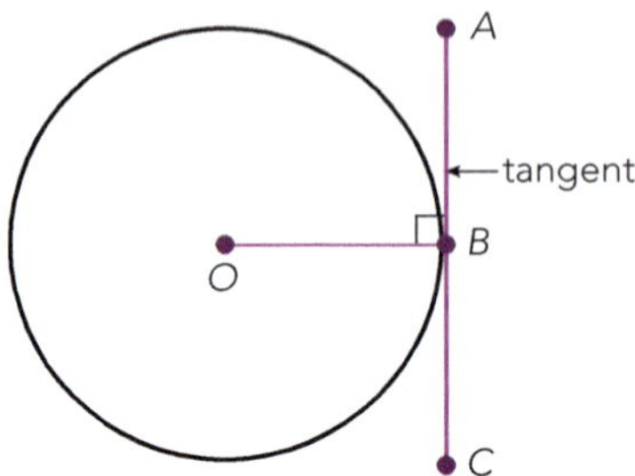

A radius drawn from the centre of the circle to the point of contact between the tangent and the circle is perpendicular to the tangent. In the above diagram, the tangent *AC* touches the circle at point *B*, and is perpendicular to the radius *OB*.

tangent (trigonometry)

(Symbol: tan)

See also **sine, cosine, right-angled triangle, trigonometric ratios**

In right-angled triangles the terms opposite and adjacent always refer to the two shorter sides. The longest side is called the hypotenuse.

The side opposite angle θ is called the 'opposite side'. The side next to angle θ is called the 'adjacent side' (*A*). The side opposite the right angle is called the 'hypotenuse' (*H*). The ratio $\frac{\text{opposite side}}{\text{adjacent side}}$ is called the tangent of θ. It is usually written as $\tan \theta = \frac{O}{A}$. For a specific value of θ, tan θ always has the same value, regardless of the size or orientation of the triangle.

Example

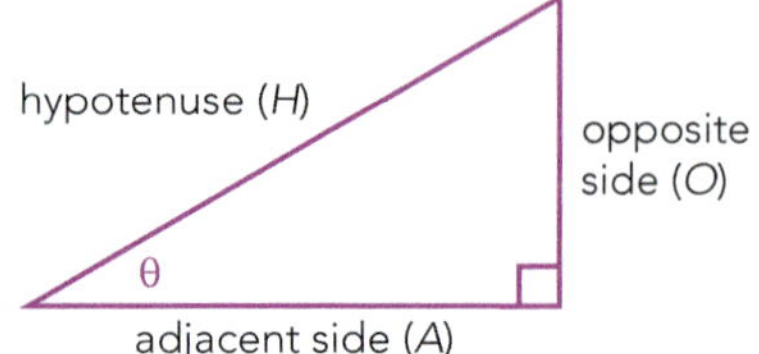

tangram

A Chinese puzzle made up of a square cut into seven pieces that can be rearranged to make many varied shapes.

Example

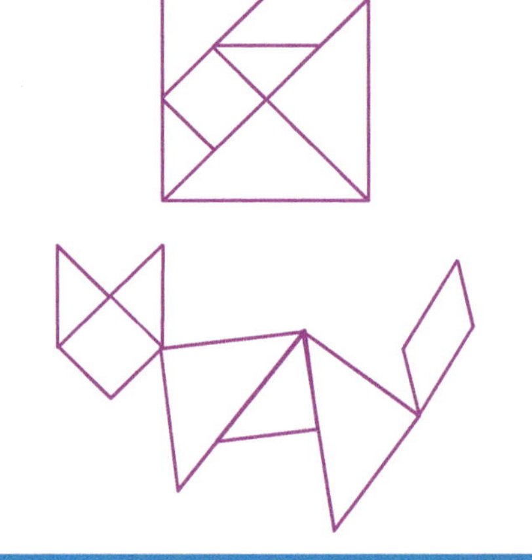

tape measure

See also **measurement, ruler**

A strip of tape or thin metal marked in millimetres, centimetres and metres, used for long measurements such as 6m, 10m or 15m.

tax

See also **gross income, net income, salary, wages**

Money collected by a country's government from its residents to pay for public services such as hospitals, schools, roads and security. In Australia the tax payable is determined by a tax table set by the government and may change from year to year.

Example

Below is an excerpt from the 2013–2014 tax table.

\$37,001– \$80,000	\$3572 plus 32.5c for each \$1 over \$37,000

The tax on \$56 000 (for 2013–2014)

$= \$(3572 + 0.325 \times 19\,000)$
$= \$(3572 + 6175)$
$= \$9747$

temperature

See also **degree Celsius, thermometer**

How hot or how cold something is. Temperature is measured in degrees Celsius (°C).

Examples

i Water freezes (changes to ice) at 0 °C.

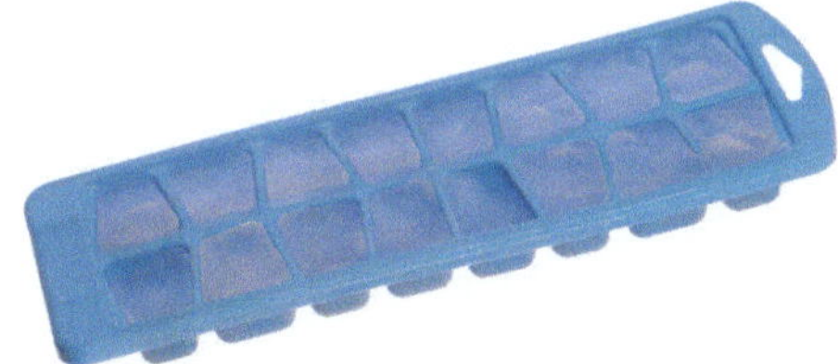

ii Water boils at 100 °C.

iii Normal body temperature is about 37 °C.

template

An instrument for drawing shapes. It may be one of two types:

1 Cardboard or plastic pieces around which we draw.

Example

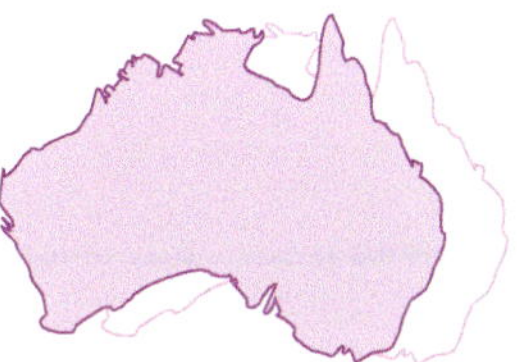

2 A sheet of cardboard or firm plastic out of which shapes have been cut.

Example

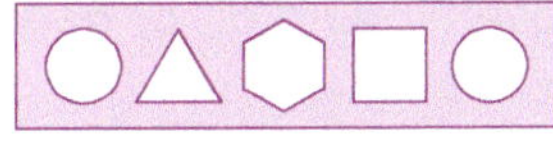

template

term

See also **algebraic expression, algebraic equation, algebraic term**

1 Each of the two quantities in a ratio or a fraction.

Examples

i In the fraction $\frac{3}{4}$, the 3 and 4 are both terms.

ii In 1 : 7, the 1 and the 7 are both terms.

2 Each of the quantities connected by + or – in an algebraic expression or equation.

Examples

i In $3a - 3b$, $3a$ and $-3b$ are both terms.

ii In $a^2 + 3y - 5$, a^2, $3y$ and -5 are all terms.

terminate

See also **terminating decimal**

To come to an end, finish, not to go any further.

terminating decimal

See also **decimal place, recurring decimal**

A decimal fraction that has a finite number of decimal places.

Examples

$\frac{1}{4} = 0.25$

$\frac{1}{8} = 0.375$

$\frac{1}{50} = 0.02$

tessellation

See also **circle, pattern, plane, square, triangle**

A complete covering of a plane by one or more figures in a repeating pattern, with no overlapping of, or gaps between, the figures.

Mosaic and pavement shapes tessellate.

Examples

These shapes tessellate.

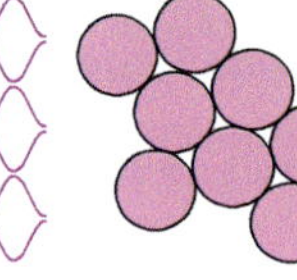

Circles do not tessellate.

Certain shapes will cover a surface completely: squares, equilateral triangles, hexagons, etc. These are said to 'tessellate'.

tetragon

See also **quadrilateral**

A plane shape with four sides and four angles; another name for a quadrilateral.

tetrahedron

See also **polyhedron, regular polyhedron**

A polyhedron with four faces. Also called a triangular pyramid.

A regular tetrahedron has four congruent equilateral triangles as faces and belongs to the group called Platonic solids.

Examples

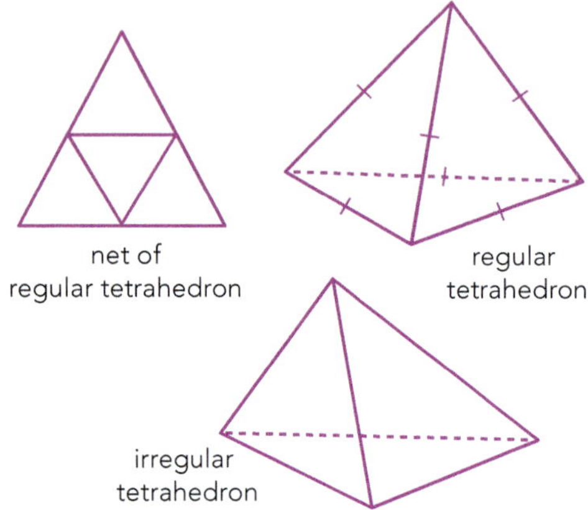

theorem

See also **proof, Pythagoras' theorem**

A rule about a relationship that can be proved to be always true. Once proven, a theorem is known as a property.

Example

Pythagoras' theorem is a famous theorem. The square of the hypotenuse of a right-angled triangle is equal to the sum of the squares of the other two sides.

$c^2 = a^2 + b^2$

B
a
c
C
b
A

thermometer

See also **degree Celsius, temperature**

An instrument for measuring temperature.

Example

This thermometer shows a temperature of 39.8 °C.

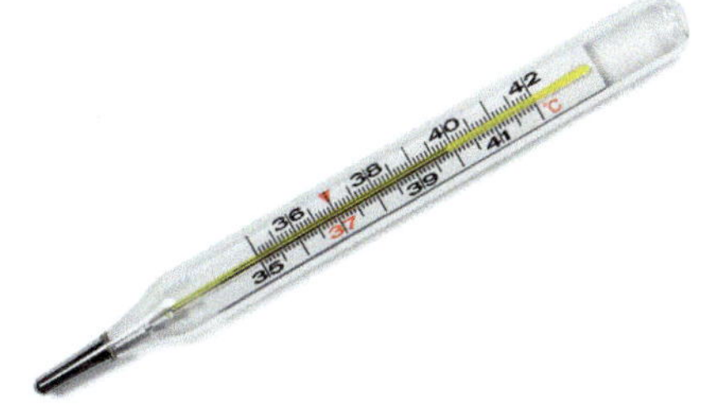

third

See also **ordinal number**

1 The ordinal number which comes after second and before fourth.

Example

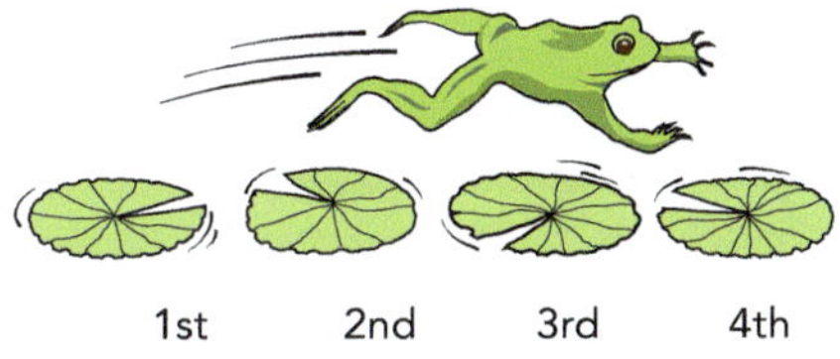

1st 2nd 3rd 4th

2 One third is a fraction that represents one of three equal parts. Written as $\frac{1}{3}$.

Example

$\frac{1}{3}$ has been coloured in 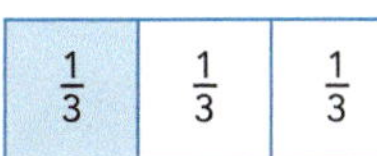

thousand

See also **hundred**

Ten hundreds, written as 1000.

thousand separator

For easy reading, large numbers are divided into groups of three digits either side of the decimal point.

Example

26 375 159.123 45

The correct separator is a narrow space between the groups of three digits, as shown. A comma was used in the past.

three-dimensional (3D)

See also **dimension, solid, sphere**

When an object has three dimensions, length, width and height, then it is three-dimensional. Space figures (solids) are three-dimensional.

Example

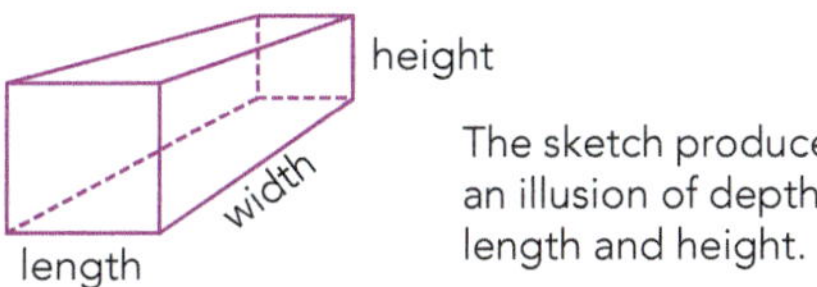

The sketch produces an illusion of depth, length and height.

time interval

See also **unit of measurement**

The time that passes between two events.

Example

The time interval of an aeroplane flight from take off to landing was 12 hours, 35 minutes and 10 seconds.

time line

See also **time interval**

A line on which intervals of time are recorded in chronological order.

Example

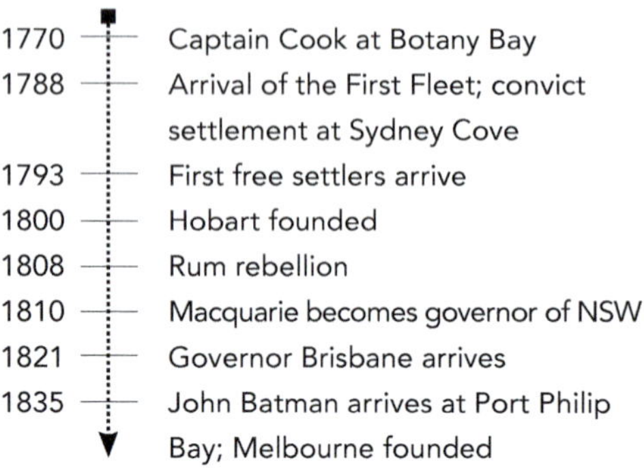

times (Symbol: ×)

A word used for multiplication.

Examples

i When we multiply 3 and 5, we say 'three times five'.

ii In 5(*a* + *b*), we say 'five times' (*a* + *b*).

time zone

See also **time interval**

A region in which all clocks are set to the same time. The world has 24 time zones, which can be represented on a map by vertical columns. The difference between two adjacent standard time zones is usually 1 hour, but sometimes, it is only $\frac{1}{2}$ or $\frac{1}{4}$ of an hour.

Examples

i Western Standard time (used in Western Australia) is 2 hours behind Eastern Standard time (used in Queensland, New South Wales, Victoria and Tasmania) from April to October.

ii South Australia is always $\frac{1}{2}$ an hour behind New South Wales, Victoria and Tasmania.

Sometimes several different time zones use the same time.

Example

China and India use the same time throughout each country, though several time zones run through each of them.

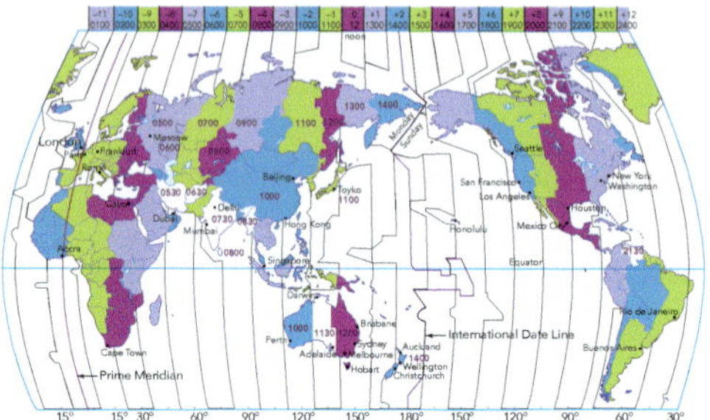

tonne (Symbol: t)

See also **kilogram, litre, mass, metric system**

A tonne is a metric unit for measuring the mass of heavy objects.

$$1 \text{ t} = 1000 \text{ kg}$$

Examples

i The mass of this empty utility is 1435 kilograms or 1.435 tonnes.

ii This water tank contains 1000 litres of water. The mass is 1000 kilograms or 1 tonne.

topology

See also **property**

The part of mathematics that deals with non-measurable properties of things; of insides and outsides, surfaces, shapes and connections.

Topology is concerned with relative positions, not measurement.

Example

Square *ABCD* can be distorted to look like this:

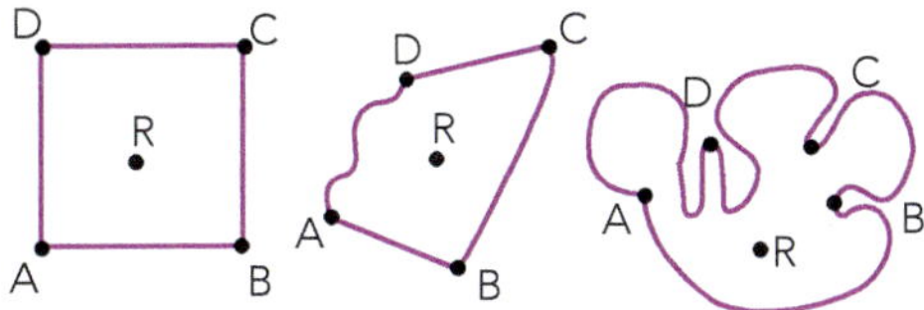

R always remains inside the figure.

Topology is sometimes called 'rubber-sheet geometry'.

torus

A 3D shape, like a doughnut or a tyre tube.

total

See also **add, sum**

1 Sum. The answer when numbers or objects are added together

Example

10 + 20 + 25 = 55
↑
total

2 The whole, complete amount.

Example

The total area of the farm is 80 hectares.

transformation

See also **enlargement, flip, formula, many-to-one correspondence, one-to-one correspondence, reduce, reflection, rotation, slide, translation, turn**

1 The process by which the shape, position or size of an object is changed.

2 The process of rearranging a formula.

Example

The formula for finding the area, $A = l \times w$, can be transformed into: $l = \frac{A}{w}$

3 The process by which a set of numbers (or objects) is associated in one-to-one or many-to-one correspondence with another set of numbers (or objects).

translation

See also **flip, reflection, rotation, slide, turn**

When a shape is moved along a straight line without being rotated or reflected, we say it has been translated. The shape 'slides' along the surface of a plane.

Example

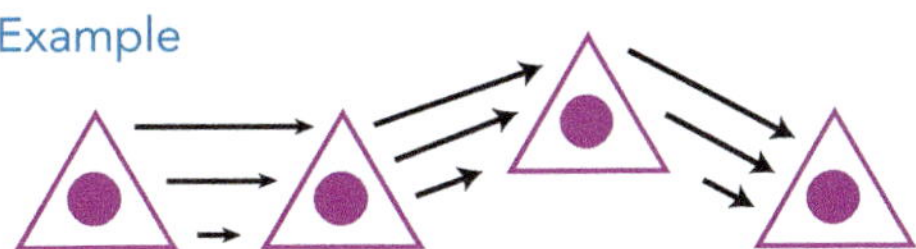

transversal

See also **line, parallel lines**

A straight line crossing two or more lines.

Examples

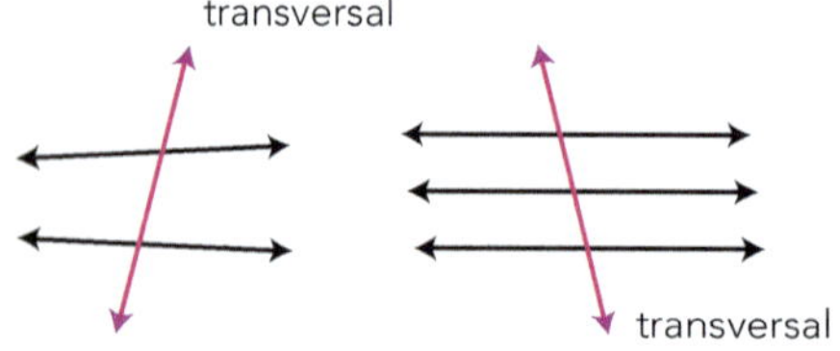

trapezium

See also **isosceles triangle, parallel lines, quadrilateral**

A four-sided figure (quadrilateral) with one pair of sides parallel and the other pair not parallel.

Examples

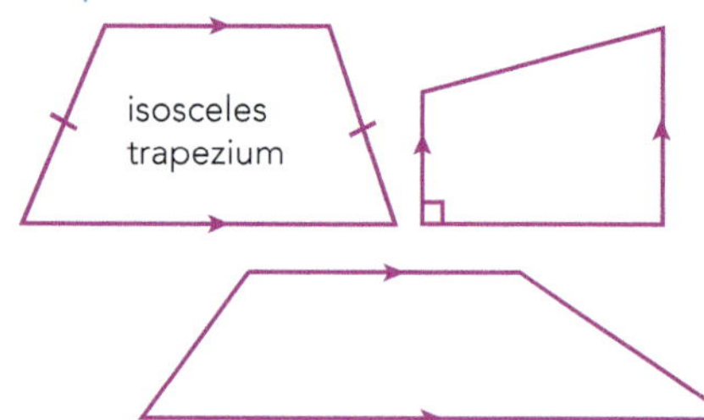

When the two sides that are not parallel are equal in length then the trapezium is an isosceles trapezium. It has one axis of reflectional symmetry. Angles at opposite vertices are equal.

trapezoid

See **trapezium**

traversable

A curve or route is traversable if it can be traced without lifting the pencil or going over any part of the curve more than once.

Examples

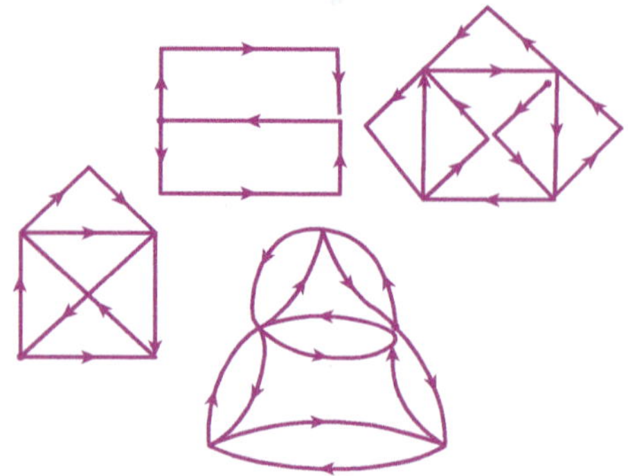

These routes are traversable.

treble

See also **multiplication**

Make three times bigger or multiply by three.

Example

12 trebled is 36.

tree diagram

See also **outcomes, probability, two-way table**

A diagram that has a branch tree-like structure and shows all possible outcomes of a probability experiment.

Example

A family with three children. The first child could have been a girl or a boy, so could have the second and third child.

A tree diagram shows all possible outcomes as follows:

1st child 2nd child 3rd child

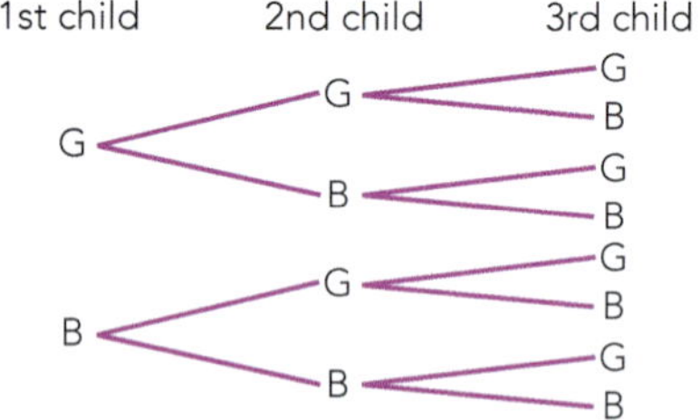

triangle

See also **equilateral triangle, isosceles triangle, plane shape, right-angled triangle, scalene triangle, sum**

A polygon with three sides and three angles. We can classify triangles by sides or by angles.

1 By sides.

Examples

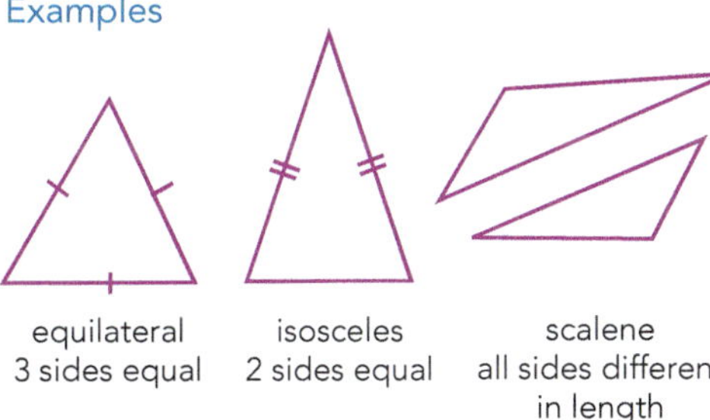

2 By angles.

Examples

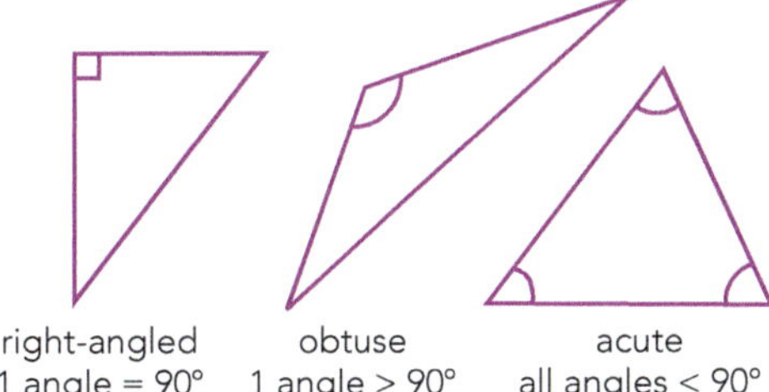

The sum of angles inside a triangle is always 180°.

triangular number

See also **triangle**

A number that can be represented by dots in the shape of a triangle.

A sequence of triangular numbers is created by adding the next consecutive integer.

$1 + 2 = 3$
$1 + 2 + 3 = 6$
$1 + 2 + 3 + 4 = 10$, etc.

Examples

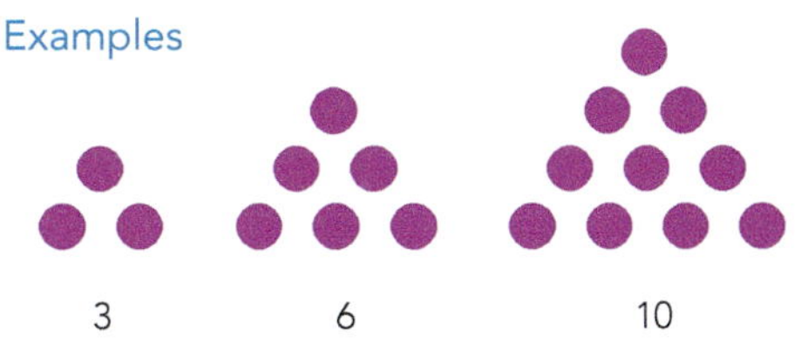

trigonometric ratios

See also **cosine, sine, tangent**

In a right-angled triangle, three basic ratios between pairs of sides can be defined with respect to a reference angle, θ (the Greek letter theta). These three ratios are known as the sine, cosine and tangent of θ, and are usually written as sin θ, cos θ and tan θ.

They are defined as:

$\sin\theta = \frac{\text{opposite}}{\text{hypotenuse}}$ or simply $\frac{O}{H}$.

$\cos\theta = \frac{\text{adjacent}}{\text{hypotenuse}}$ or simply $\frac{A}{H}$

$\tan\theta = \frac{\text{opposite}}{\text{adjacent}}$ or simply $\frac{O}{A}$

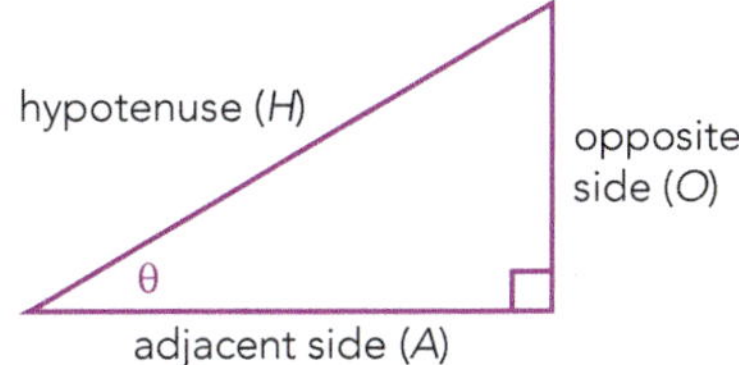

For a given value of θ, these three ratios do not change, regardless of the size or orientation of the triangle.

Example

For θ = 30°:

- sin 30° = 0.5 (i.e. the opposite side is half the length of the hypotenuse)
- cos 30° ≅ 0.866 (i.e. the adjacent side is approximately 0.866 times the length of the hypotenuse)
- tan 30° ≅ 0.577 (i.e. the opposite side is approximately 0.577 times the length of the adjacent side)

These ratios can be used to calculate other side lengths in the triangle, if one is known.

trillion

See also **Large numbers** on page 191

A trillion is a million millions, that is, 1 000 000 000 000, or 10^{12}.

trundle wheel

See also **circumference, metre**

A wheel, 1 metre in circumference, used for measuring distance. The wheel often gives a click sound at each revolution (1 metre), so the number of metres can be counted.

turn

See also **rotation, transformation**

Move. Change position. Rotate.

turning point

See also **gradient, maximum, minimum, parabola**

The point at which the gradient of a curve changes from negative to positive (a local minimum) or positive to negative (a local maximum). A parabola has a turning point that is either a minimum or maximum value.

Example

The point (1, 2) is the minimum turning point of the parabola shown below.

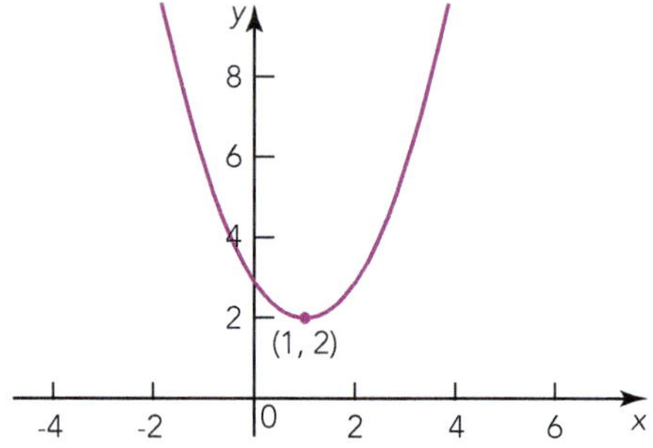

twelve-hour time

See also **a.m., p.m., twenty-four hour time**

A period of one day (twenty-four hours) divided into two halves of twelve hours each.
Twelve-hour time should include a.m. and p.m.

Example

This clock shows either 7.45 a.m. or 7.45 p.m.

twenty-four hour time

See also **a.m., p.m., twelve-hour time**

A period of one day divided into twenty-four hourly divisions, to prevent errors between a.m. and p.m. times.

Examples

A 24-hour clock

12-hour time	24-hour time
1 a.m.	0100 one hundred hours
10 a.m.	1000 ten hundred hours
1 p.m.	1300 thirteen hundred hours
3.40 p.m.	1540 fifteen-forty hours

twice

See also **double, multiplication**

Two times, or double.

Example

Twice six is 2 × 6 = 12

two-dimensional (2D)

See also **dimension, length, plane shape, region, surface, width**

The property of having two dimensions, length and width.
Plane shapes and surfaces have two dimensions.

Examples

Plane shapes have two dimensions.

two-way table

See also **outcome, probability, tree diagram**

A way of displaying all of the possible outcomes in a probability experiment made up of two events.

Example

Tossing a coin and rolling a die

Coin/ Die roll	1	2	3	4	5	6
Heads	(1, H)	(2, H)	(3, H)	(4, H)	(5, H)	(6, H)
Tails	(1, T)	(2, T)	(3, T)	(4, T)	(5, T)	(6, T)

From the two-way table, we can see that there are twelve equally possible outcomes.

undefined

A value that cannot be calculated. Any number divided by zero is undefined.

Examples
$\frac{3}{0}$ is undefined.
tan 90° is undefined.

unequal (Symbol: ≠)

See also **inequality, not equal**

Not equal.

Example
$3 \neq 4$
Read as: 'Three is not equal to four' or '3 and 4 are unequal'.

uniform cross-section

See also **prism, solid**

The unchanged shape formed when some solids are cut in slices parallel to the end throughout the length of the solid.

Example
All prisms and cylinders have a uniform cross-section.

union

See also **element of a set, set**

The combining of two or more sets (groups) to include all the members of all the sets. The sets may overlap or be completely separate (disjoint).

Examples

i Overlapping sets
The union of the set of people who play golf and the set of people who are doctors would contain all golfers and all doctors. As there would be golfers who were doctors, the sets would overlap.

ii Disjoint sets
The union of the set of dogs with the set of cats.

unit

See also **metric system, unit of measurement**

Unit is another name for one.
The unit column (or 'ones' column) in our number system refers to the first column to the left of the decimal point. In 425.0, the unit digit is 5, or '5 ones'.

Example

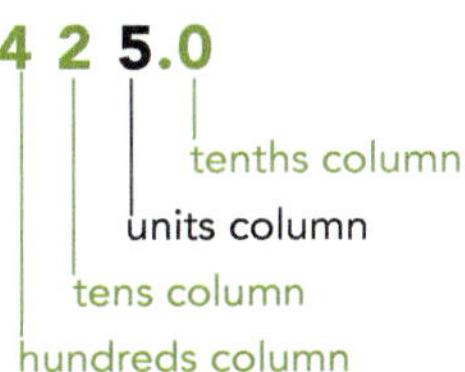

unitary method

See also **unit price, unit ratio**

A way of solving problems, by working out the value of one unit.

Example

Five kilograms of grapes cost $14.50. How much for three kilograms?

5 kg = $14.50
1 kg = $\frac{\$14.50}{5}$ = $2.90
3 kg = $2.90 × 3 = $8.70

unit, basic

See **standard unit**

unit circle

See also **cosine, sine, tangent, trigonometric ratios**

In unit circle trigonometry, cos θ and sin θ are defined as the *x*- and *y*-coordinates, respectively, of a point *P* on the unit circle, where the position of *P* is determined by the angle θ.

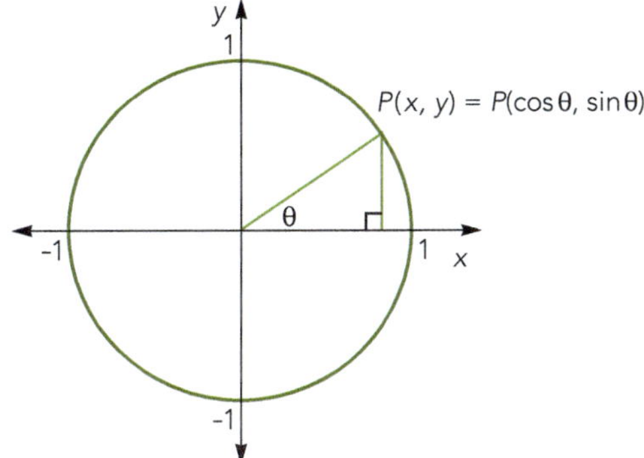

Tan θ is defined as the length of the interval *TM*, where *TM* is part of a tangent that is parallel to the *y*-axis and intersects the *x*-axis at *M*. The length of *TM* is also dependent on the size of θ.

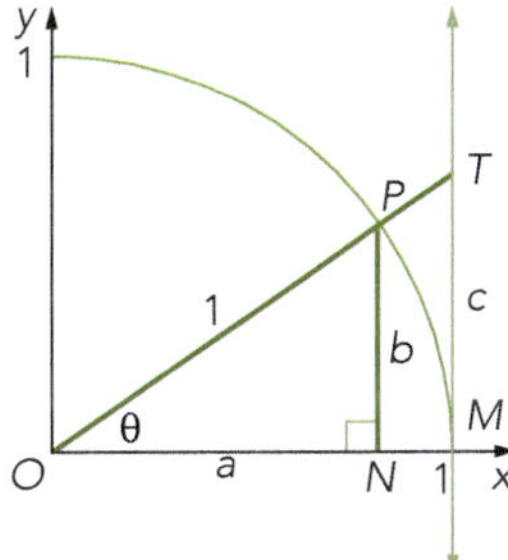

unit fraction

See also **fraction, numerator**

A fraction that has 1 as the numerator.

Examples

$\frac{1}{3}$ $\frac{1}{10}$ $\frac{1}{129}$

unit of measurement

See also **standard unit**

The name given to a standard, defined quantity of something that has been measured, such as weight, length, time or volume.

Examples

kilograms, grams, minutes, litres

unit price

See also **unitary method**

The price per unit of quantity. It allows the price of the same type of goods to be compared easily. The unit is often 100 mL or 1 L, 100 g or 1 kg.

Example

A 375 g can of tomato soup sells for $1.50. The unit price is 40c per 100 g.
A 500 g can of tomato soup sells for $1.95. The unit price is 39c per 100 g.

unit ratio

See also **ratio**

A ratio expressed in the form of a number compared to 1.

Examples

3 : 1,   0.5 : 1

unit square

See also **distance, unit of measurement**

A square with sides of length equal to one unit of length or distance.

Example

A square with sides one metre long has an area of one square metre (1 m^2).

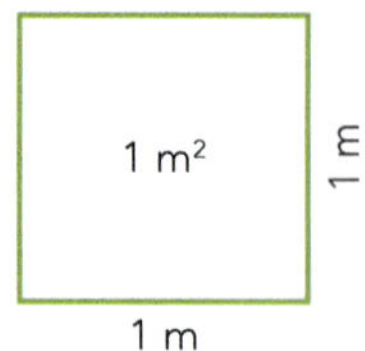

universal set

See also **element of a set, population, sample, set**

The set to which all members or elements belong, symbolised by ξ. It is the population from which a sample can be taken.

Examples

A pack of cards, all the students on a class roll, all the cars in a car yard

unknown value

See also **number sentence, pronumeral, variable**

In number sentences, algebraic expressions or equations, the unknown values are variables. They are represented by pronumerals.

Examples

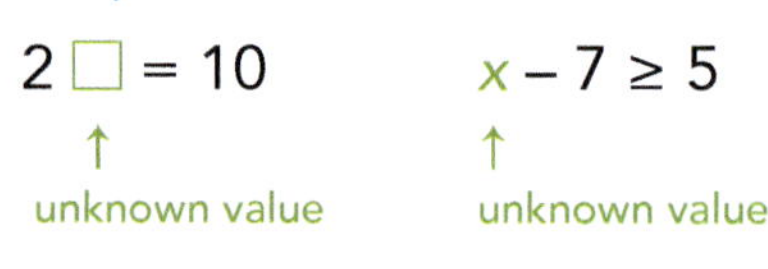

$2a - 2b$

↑ ↑

unknown values

unlike terms

See also **like terms**

In algebra, terms that do not have exactly the same variable and power. Unlike terms cannot be combined or simplified by adding or subtracting.

Examples

V

Symbol for volume.

value

See also **evaluate, place value**

1 When an expression is evaluated, the result is the value of the expression.

Examples

i $\frac{3+5}{2} \times 7$
$= \frac{8}{2} \times 7$
$= 4 \times 7$
$= 28$
28 is the value of $\frac{3+5}{2} \times 7$

ii If we have an algebraic expression, we substitute, then evaluate.

Find the value of $\frac{x+5}{2}$, if $x = 10$.
Answer: $\frac{10+5}{2} = 7.5$
7.5 is the value.

2 The amount of money something is worth.

Example
A smart phone costs $689.
Its value is $689.

vanishing point

See also **perspective**

In perspective, the point or points at which all parallel lines appear to meet.

Example

variable (algebra)

See also **algebraic expression, constant, number sentence, open number sentence, pronumeral, symbol**

1 A symbol or letter representing an unknown value in an algebraic expression. It is sometimes called an unknown.

Example
In $x^2 + 3x + 20$, x is the variable.

variable (algebra) continued ▶

2 A mathematical sentence that has at least one variable is called a number sentence or equation. A value may be found for the variable that will make the number sentence true. This is a solution to the equation.

Example
$x + 3 = 7$ is true only when $x = 4$.
The number 4 is called the solution of $x + 3 = 7$.

If x is replaced by any other number, the sentence will become not true (false).

3 The same variable may have different values in different equations.

Example

If $x + 3 = 5$, $x = 2$

If $x - 1 = 10$, $x = 11$

variable (statistics)

See also **categorical variable, continuous variable, discrete variable, numerical variable**

Some characteristic, behaviour or occurrence that can be observed or measured, and is expected to differ between individuals, or change over time. These differences or changes are recorded as data.

Examples
- i age of students at a school
- ii hair colour of students
- ii number of text messages sent by a student in a day
- iv rainfall for a particular city over a year
- v daily maximum temperature for a city over a month
- vi the preferred brand of shoes worn by 14-year-olds

Venn diagram

See also **diagram, intersection, set, union**

A diagram used to represent sets and relationships between sets.

Example

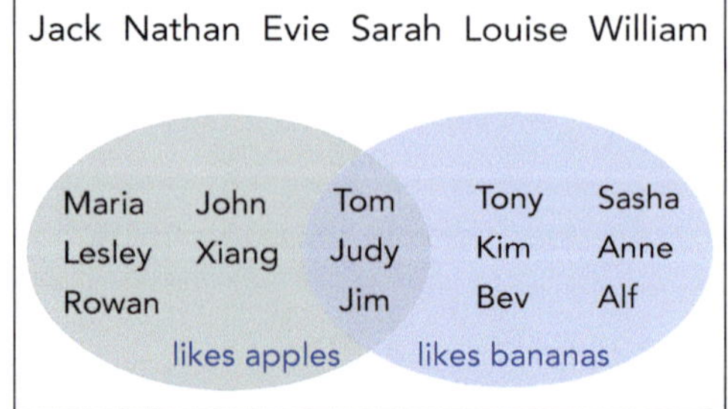

This Venn diagram shows the preferred fruit of class 7A.

There are twenty names inside the rectangle. This is the whole class (the universal set).

There are eight names inside the left circle. These are the people that like apples.

There are nine names inside the right circle. These are the people that like bananas.

There are three names in the region where the circles overlap. These people like apples and bananas. This region is called the 'intersection'.

The total number of names in both circles is fourteen. These are the people that like apples or bananas. This region is called the 'union'.

There are six names inside the rectangle that do not appear in either circle. These are the people in 7A who do not like either fruit.

vertex (Plural: vertices)

See also **apex, arm of an angle**

Top, the highest point.
A point where two or more adjacent lines meet to form an angle or a corner.

Examples

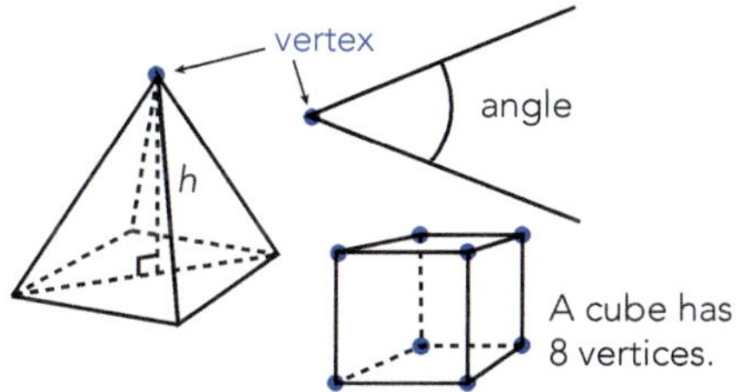

In plane or solid figures, the vertex is the point opposite the base.

vertical

See also **axis, horizon, horizontal, perpendicular, right angle**

A vertical line is perpendicular (at right angles) to the horizon.

Examples

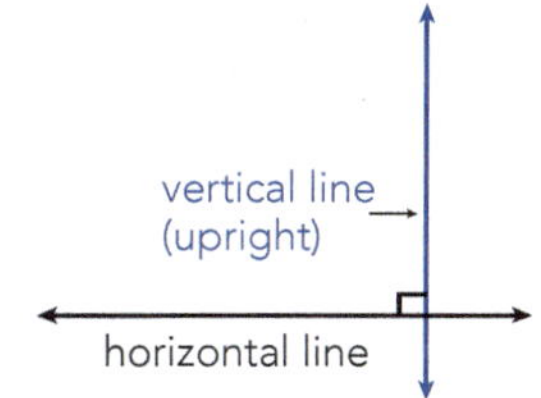

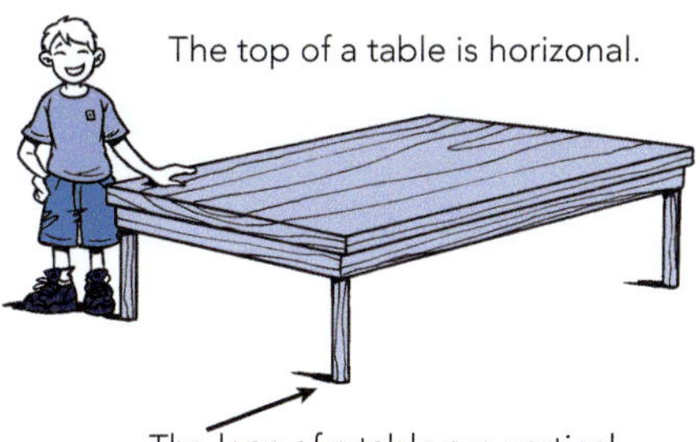

vertically opposite angles

See also **complementary angles, parallel lines, supplementary angles, vertex**

When two lines intersect, they make four angles at the vertex. The angles opposite each other are equal in size and are called vertically opposite angles.

Example

volume

See also **capacity, cubic centimetre, cubic metre, cubic unit, Metric relationships** on page 188, **solid**

The amount of space inside a container, or the actual amount of material in the container.

Example
The volume of this object is 36 cubic units.

Some units of volume are:

- for the volume of solids
  cubic centimetre cm^3
  cubic metre m^3
- for the volume of liquids
  millilitre mL
  litre L
  kilolitre kL
  megalitre ML

wages

See also **income, salary**

Income that is usually based on an hourly rate of pay. The rate may be higher (time and a half or double time) for extra hours worked above the standard number (overtime) or for work done on weekends or public holidays (penalty rates).

Example

A waitress in a café is paid a wage of $12.00 per hour for 40 hours a week, but one week she works 5 hours overtime at a rate of time and a half, and for 3 hours on a public holiday at a rate of double time. Her gross income for that week was

$40 \times \$12 + 1.5 \times 5 \times \$12 + 2 \times 3 \times 2 \times \$12$
$= 480 + 90 + 72$
$= \$642$

week

A period of time: 7 days. There are 52 weeks in a year.

weight

See also **mass**

The force of gravity on the mass of an object. The weight of an object changes if the gravitational pull changes (e.g. on the Moon or a different planet). The mass of an object (the amount of matter the object is made of) remains constant.

Example

Astronauts become weightless in space but the mass of their bodies does not change.

Astronaut on Earth:
his mass = 75 kg
his weight ≈ 75 kgwt (unit is different)

Astronaut in space:
His mass is still 75 kg but he is weightless.

People often speak incorrectly of weight when they really mean mass.

whole numbers

See also **counting number, zero**

Zero together with all counting numbers.

{0, 1, 2, 3, 4, 5, 6, 7, 8, ...}

width

See also **length, measurement**

The measurement from side to side. Also called breadth.

Example

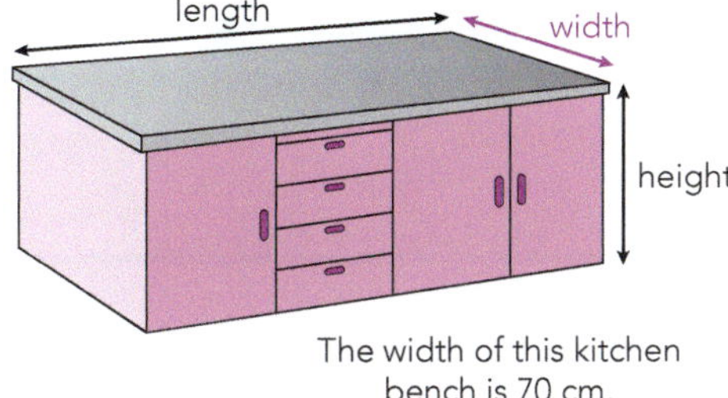

The width of this kitchen bench is 70 cm.

withdrawal

See also **deposit**

An amount of money taken out of an account at a bank or other financial institution.

Example

An account has $200 in it. A withdrawal of $50 is made. The account now has $150 in it.

x-axis, *y*-axis

See **axes, Cartesian plane, coordinates**

x-coordinate, *y*-coordinate

See **coordinates**

x-intercept, *y*-intercept

See **axes, intercept**

yard

A unit of length in the imperial system.

1 yard = 36 inches (≈ 90 cm)

year

See also **day, leap year, revolution**

The period of time it takes the Earth to make one complete revolution around the Sun: 365 days, 5 hours and $48\frac{3}{4}$ minutes. The extra hours, minutes and seconds are put together into an extra day every four years to form a 'leap year'.

zero (Symbol: 0, Ø)

See also **digit,**

The numeral 0 (nought). Nothing. These words all mean zero: nil, nought, none, nix, null, oh, void, empty set, zilch, duck (in cricket), love (in tennis). Rules for working with zero:

- A number + 0 = same number
  $5 + 0 = 5$
- A number – 0 = same number
  $7 - 0 = 7$
- A number × 0 = 0
  $6 \times 0 = 0$
- 0 ÷ any number = 0
  $0 \div 10 = 0$
- A number ÷ 0 has no answer
  $3 \div 0$ is undefined

Example

In the number sixty, 0 shows there are no units and 6 means six tens.

zero power

See also **index, index laws, power of a number**

An index of zero. Any number raised to the zero power is equal to one.

Examples

$2^0 = 1$ $376^0 = 1$ $x^0 = 1$

Useful Information

Units of measurement

length

10 millimetres (mm)	= 1 centimetre (cm)
100 centimetres (cm)	= 1 metre (m)
1000 millimetres (mm)	= 1 metre (m)
1000 metres (m)	= 1 kilometre (km)

area

100 square millimetres (mm^2)
= 1 square centimetre (cm^2)
10 000 square centimetres (cm^2)
= 1 square metre (m^2)
10 000 square metres (m^2) = 1 hectare (ha)
100 hectares (ha) = 1 square kilometre (km^2)
= 1 000 000 square metres (m^2)

mass

1000 milligrams (mg)	= 1 gram (g)
1000 grams (g)	= 1 kilogram (kg)
1000 kilograms (kg)	= 1 tonne (t)

liquid volume

1000 millilitres (mL)	= 1 litre (L)
1 mL (for liquids)	= 1 cm^3 (for solids)
1000 litres (L)	= 1 kilolitre (kL)
1 kL (for liquids)	= 1 m^3 (for solids)

solids volume

1 cubic centimetre (cm^3)
1 cubic metre (m^3)

time

60 seconds (s)	= 1 minute (min)
60 minutes (min)	= 1 hour (h)
24 hours (h)	= 1 day (d)
7 days	= 1 week
365 days	= 1 year
366 days	= 1 leap year
12 months	= 1 year
10 years	= 1 decade
100 years	= 1 century
1000 years	= 1 millennium

symbols

m	metre
g	gram
L	litre
t	tonne
m^2	square metre
m^3	cubic metre
ha	hectare
°C	degree Celsius

Remember: These are the correct symbols.

mm	cm	m	km	
mL	L	kL		
mg	g	kg	t	
mm^2	cm^2	m^2	ha	km^2
cm^3	m^3			
s	min	h	d	

angle measure

1 degree (1°)	= 60 minutes (60')
1 minute (1')	= 60 seconds (60'')
1 right angle	= 90 degrees (90°)
1 straight angle	= 180 degrees (180°)
1 revolution	= 360 degrees (360°)

1 radian = approx 57.3 degrees (57.3°).

A list of symbols

Symbol	Meaning	Example
$+$	addition sign, add, plus	$2 + 1 = 3$
$-$	subtraction sign, subtract, take away, minus	$7 - 6 = 1$
$\times$	multiplication sign, multiply by, times	$3 \times 3 = 9$
$\div$ $\overline{)\ }$	division sign, divide by	$9 \div 2 = 4.5$
$=$	is equal to, equals	$2 + 2 = 1 + 3$
$\neq$	is not equal to	$2 \neq 5$
$\doteqdot$ $\approx$ $\triangleq$	is approximately equal to	$302 \approx 300$
$\leq$	is less than or equal to	$x \leq 12$
$\geq$	is greater than or equal to	$5 \geq y$
$>$	is greater than	$7 > 6.9$
$<$	is less than	$2 < 4$
$\not<$	is not less than	$6 \not< 5$
$\not>$	is not greater than	$3.3 \not> 3.4$
c	cent(s)	50c
$	dollar(s)	$1.20
.	decimal point (on the line)	5.24
%	per cent, out of 100	50%
°	degree Celsius, degree (angle measure)	°C 35 °C 90°
'	minutes (angle measure)	5° 35'
"	seconds (angle measure)	12°05'24"
$\angle$ $\wedge$	angle	$\angle AOB$ $B\hat{O}C$
$\triangle$	triangle	$\triangle$ ABC
$\parallel$	parallel lines, is parallel to	AB $\parallel$ CD
‡ ‖	line segments of the same length	
∟	right angle, 90°	
$\perp$	is perpendicular to, at 90°	$h \perp b$
$\sqrt{\ }$	square root	$\sqrt{4} = \pm 2$
$\sqrt[3]{\ }$	cube root	$\sqrt[3]{27} = 3$
π	pi, $\pi \approx 3.14$	$C = 2\pi r$
$\equiv$ $\cong$	is congruent to	$\triangle ABC \equiv \triangle DEF$
$\sim$ |||	is similar to	$\triangle ABC \sim \triangle DEF$ $\triangle ABC$ ||| $\triangle DEF$
$\therefore$	therefore	$a^2 + b^2 = c^2$, $\therefore b^2 = c^2 - a^2$

Roman numerals

	Thousands	Hundreds	Tens	Units
1	M	C	X	I
2	MM	CC	XX	II
3	MMM	CCC	XXX	III
4		CD	XL	IV
5		D	L	V
6		DC	LX	VI
7		DCC	LXX	VII
8		DCCC	LXXX	VIII
9		CM	XC	IX

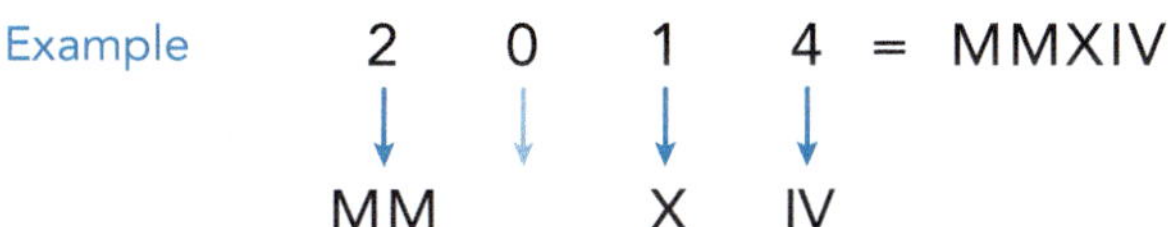

Parts of a circle

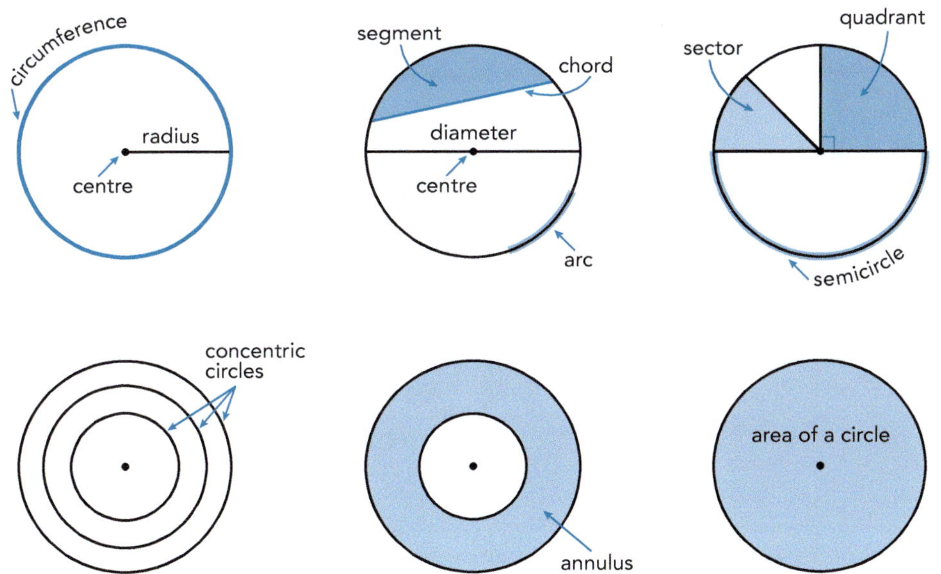

Metric relationships

Length	Area	Volume	Capacity
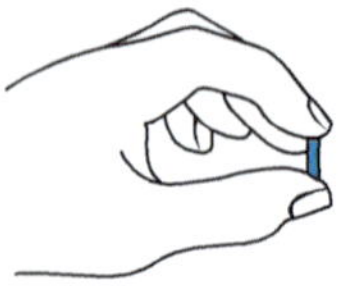	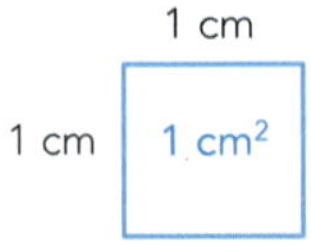 1 cm 1 cm 1 cm^2	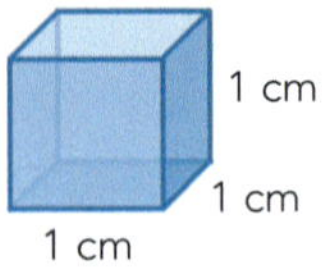 1 cm 1 cm 1 cm	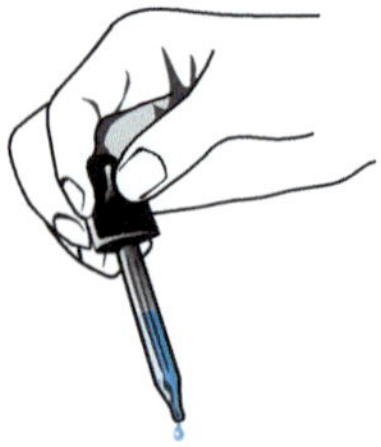
1 cm 10 mm	1 cm^2 100 mm^2	1 cm^3 1000 mm^3	1 mL One 1 cm cube (cubic centimetre) has a capacity of 1 millilitre.
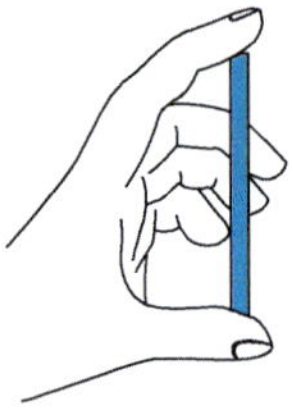	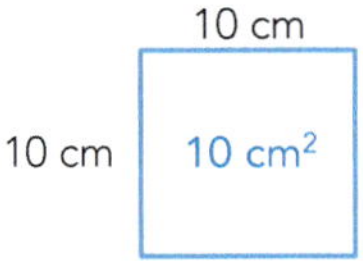 10 cm 10 cm 10 cm^2	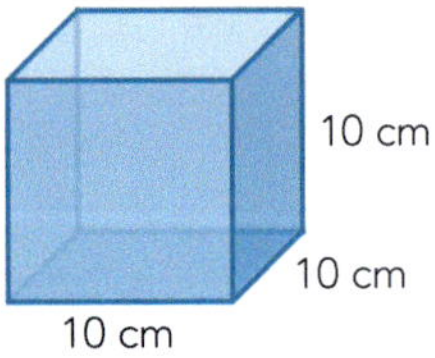 10 cm 10 cm 10 cm	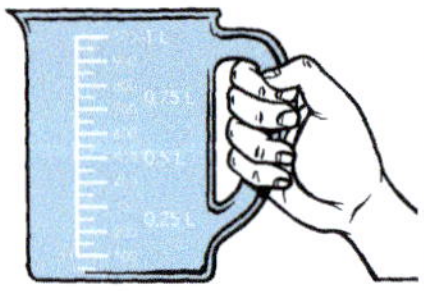
10 cm 100 mm	100 cm^2 10 000 mm^2	1000 cm^3 1 000 000 mm^3	1 L One 10 cm cube (1000 cm^3) has a capacity of 1 litre.
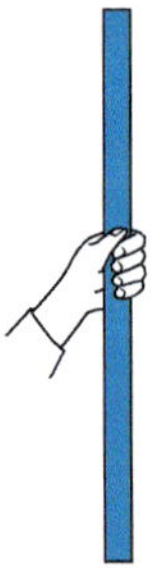	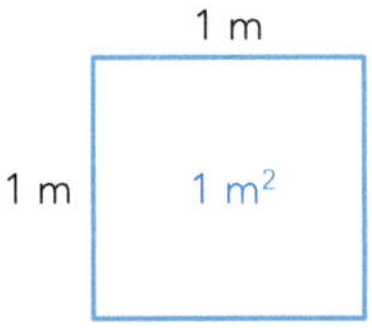 1 m 1 m 1 m^2	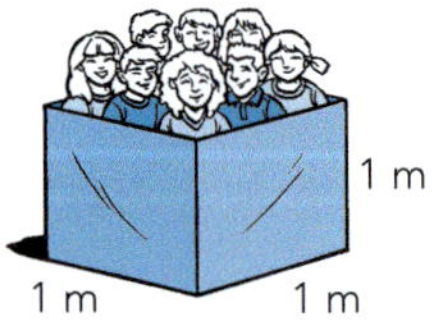 1 m 1 m 1 m	
1 m 100 cm	1 m^2 10 000 cm^2	1 m^3 1 000 000 cm^3	1 kL One cubic metre has a capacity of 1 kilolitre. These 5 drums each hold 1 kilolitre.

Formulae

Plane shapes	Diagram	Area	Perimeter
circle	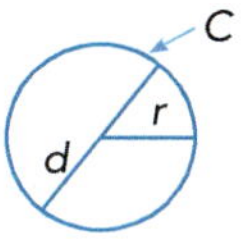	$A = \pi r^2$	$C = 2\pi r = \pi d$
square	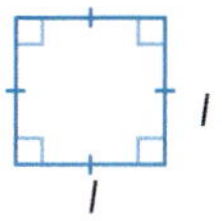	$A = l^2$	$P = 4l$
rectangle	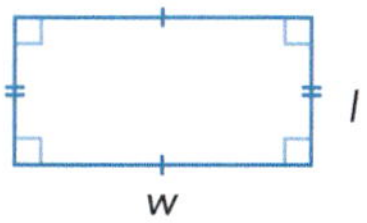	$A = lw$	$P = 2(l + w)$
kite	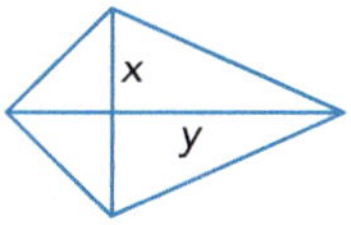	$A = \frac{xy}{2}$	
trapezium	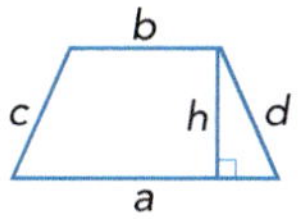	$A = \frac{a + b}{2} \times h$	$P = a + b + c + d$
parallelogram	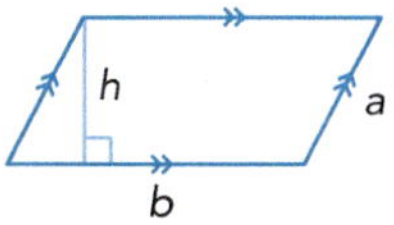	$A = bh$	$P = 2(a + b)$
rhombus	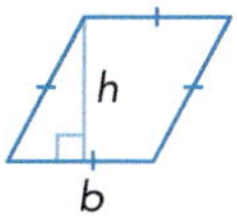	$A = bh$	$P = 4b$
triangle	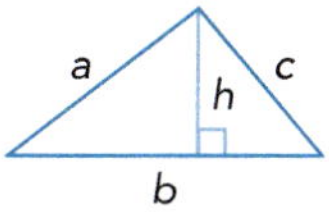	$A = \frac{1}{2}bh$	$P = a + b + c$

More formulae

Solids	Diagram	Volume	Surface area
cube	L L L	$V = L^3$	$SA = 6L^2$
cuboid	H W L	$V = LWH$	$SA = 2(LW + HL + HW)$
pyramid	H	$V = \frac{1}{3}$ base $\times H$	SA = area of base + 4 × Area of △
cylinder	r h	$V = \pi r^2 h$	$SA = 2 \times \pi r^2 + 2\pi rh = 2\pi r\,(r + h)$
cone	h r	$V = \frac{1}{3}\pi r^2 h$	
sphere	r	$V = \frac{4}{3}\pi r^3$	$SA = 4\pi r^2$
Pythagoras' theorem	a b c	$c^2 = a^2 + b^2$ $a = \sqrt{c^2 - b^2}$ $b = \sqrt{c^2 - a^2}$ $c = \sqrt{a^2 + b^2}$	

Large numbers

million	1000 × 1000	10^6
billion	1000 millions	10^9
trillion	1000 billions	10^{12}
quadrillion	million billions	10^{15}

Letters used in mathematics

in sets

I or J	integers
N	natural numbers
Q	rational numbers
R	real numbers
W	whole numbers

in geometry

a, b, c, d, …	sides of polygons
	lengths of intervals
	names of lines
A, B, C, D, …	points, vertices
A	area of polygons
b	base of polygons
C	circumference of a circle
d	diameter of a circle
h	height
l	length
O	origin, centre of a circle
P	perimeter
r	radius of a circle
s	side
S, SA	surface area
V	volume of solids
w	width

Decimal system prefixes

Prefix	Symbol	Value	Value in words	Example	Meaning
pico	p	10^{-12}	one trillionth of	1 pF	picofarad
nano	n	10^{-9}	one thousand millionth of	1 ns	nanosecond
micro	μ	10^{-6}	one millionth of	1 μs	microsecond
milli	m	10^{-3}	one thousandth of	1 mg	milligram
centi	c	10^{-2}	one hundredth of	1 cm	centimetre
deci	d	10^{-1}	one tenth of	1 dB	decibel
			unit		
deca	da	10^{1}	10 times	not commonly used in Australia	
hecto	h	10^{2}	100 times	1 hL	hectolitre
kilo	k	10^{3}	1000 times	1 kg	kilogram
mega	M	10^{6}	1 million times	1 ML	megalitre
giga	G	10^{9}	1 thousand million times	1 GB	gigabyte

Numerical prefixes

Prefix	Meaning	Example
mono	1	monorail
bi	2	bicycle, binary
tri	3	tricycle, triangle
tetra	4	tetrahedron, tetrapack
quad	4	quadrilateral, quads
penta, quin	5	pentagon
hexa	6	hexagon
hepta, septi	7	heptagon
octa	8	octagon
nona, non	9	nonagon
deca	10	decagon, decahedron
undeca	11	undecagon
dodeca	12	dodecagon, dodecahedron
icosa	20	icosahedron
hect	100	hectare
kilo	1000	kilogram
mega	1 000 000	megalitre, megawatt
giga	1000 million	gigabyte

Other prefixes

Prefix	Meaning	Example
anti	opposite, against	anti clockwise
circum	around	circumference
co	together	cointerior, coordinate
geo	earth	geometry
hemi	half	hemisphere
macro	very big	macrocosmos
micro	very small	microbe
multi	many, much	multibase blocks
peri	around	perimeter
poly	many	polygon
semi	half	semicircle
sub	below, under	subset
trans	across, beyond, over	transversal
uni	one, having one	unit

The multiplication square

×	1	2	3	4	5	6	7	8	9	10
1	1	2	3	4	5	6	7	8	9	10
2	2	4	6	8	10	12	14	16	18	20
3	3	6	9	12	15	18	21	24	27	30
4	4	8	12	16	20	24	28	32	36	40
5	5	10	15	20	25	30	35	40	45	50
6	6	12	18	24	30	36	42	48	54	60
7	7	14	21	28	35	42	49	56	63	70
8	8	16	24	32	40	48	56	64	72	80
9	9	18	27	36	45	54	63	72	81	90
10	10	20	30	40	50	60	70	80	90	100

Greek alphabet

The letters of the Greek alphabet are used as symbols for angles, mathematical operations, etc.

Examples

$\alpha, \beta, \gamma, \delta, \ldots \pi \ldots$

Σ sum

∞ infinity

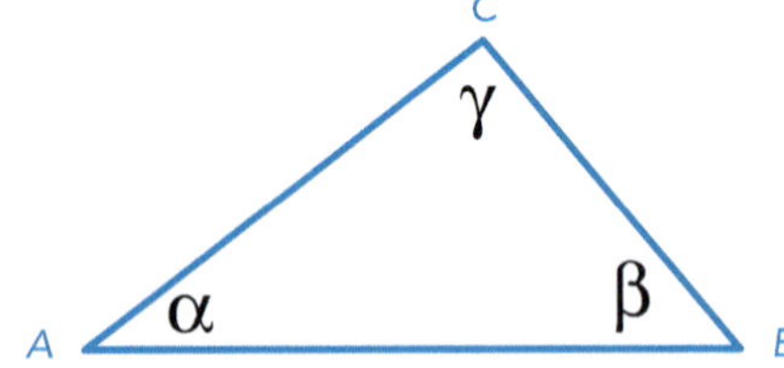

Capital	Lower case	Handwritten	Pronunciation
Α	α	α	alpha
Β	β	β	beta
Γ	γ	γ	gamma
Δ	δ	δ	delta
Ε	ε	ε	epsilon
Ζ	ζ	ζ	zeta
Η	η	η	eta
Θ	θ	θ	theta
Ι	ι	ι	iota
Κ	κ	κ	kappa
Λ	λ	λ	lambda
Μ	μ	μ	mu
Ν	ν	ν	nu
Ξ	ξ	ξ	xi
Ο	ο	ο	omicron
Π	π	π	pi
Ρ	ρ	ρ	rho
Σ	σ	σ	sigma
Τ	τ	τ	tau
Υ	υ	υ	upsilon
Φ	φ	φ	phi
Χ	χ	χ	chi
Ψ	ψ	ψ	psi
Ω	ω	ω	omega

Conversion tables: metric and imperial

length

Metric		Imperial
1 mm		0.03937 in
1 cm	10 mm	0.3937 in
1 m	100 cm	1.0936 yd
1 km	1000 m	0.6214 mile

Imperial		Metric
1 in		2.54 cm
1 ft	12 in	0.3048 m
1 yd	3 ft	0.9144 m
1 mile	1760 yd	1.6093 km
1 nautical mile	2025.4 yd	1.853 km

area

Metric		Imperial
1 cm^2	100 mm^2	0.155 in^2
1 m^2	10000 cm^2	1.1960 yd^2
1 ha	10000 m^2	2.4711 acres
1 km^2	100 ha	0.3861 $mile^2$

Imperial		Metric
1 in^2		6.4516 cm^2
1 ft^2	144 in^2	0.0929 m^2
1 yd^2	9 ft^2	0.8361 m^2
1 acre	4840 yd^2	4046.9 m^2
1 $mile^2$	640 acres	2.59 km^2

mass

Metric		Imperial
1 mg		0.0154 grain
1 g	1000 mg	0.0353 oz
1 kg	1000 g	2.2046 lb
1 t	1000 kg	0.9842 ton

Imperial		Metric
1 oz	437.5 grain	28.35 g
1 lb	16 oz	0.4536 kg
1 stone	14 lb	6.3503 kg
1 hundredweight (cwt)	112 lb	50.802 kg
1 long ton	20 cwt	1.016 t

volume

Metric		Imperial
1 cm^3		0.0610 in^3
1 dm^3 (decimetre)	1000 cm^3	0.0353 ft^3
1 m^3	1000 dm^3	1.3080 yd^3
1 L	1 dm^3	1.76 pt (pint)
1 hL (hectolitre)	100 L	21.997 gal

Imperial		Metric
1 in^3		16.387 cm^3
1 ft^3	1728 in^3	0.0283 m^3
1 fl oz (fluid ounce)		28.413 mL
1 pt	20 fl oz	0.5683L
1 gal	8 pt	4.5461L

temperature

to convert from Celsius to Fahrenheit:

$$F = \frac{9}{5} \times \text{Celsius} + 32$$

To convert from Fahrenheit to Celsius:

$$C = \frac{5\,(\text{Fahrenheit} - 32)}{9}$$

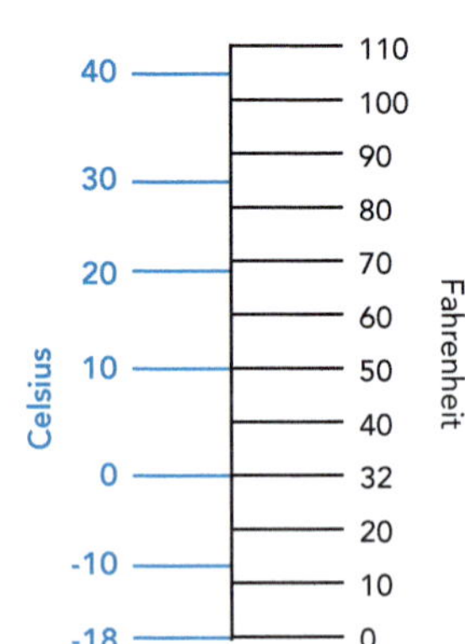

Computing terms

Boolean function

Mathematical logic used for searching computer databases. Common Boolean functions include AND, OR and NOT.

Example
Database Search: first name = 'John' AND age = '20'
This will only return all people with the first name of John who are aged 20.

Database Search: first name = 'John' OR age = '20'
This will return all people with the first name of John and all people who are aged 20.

Database Search: first name = 'John' NOT age = '20'
This will return all people with the first name of John who are not 20 years old.

CPU (Central Processing Unit)

See **hertz, kilohertz, megahertz, gigahertz**

The central part of the computer which controls all of the processing of data. It is situated on the motherboard of a computer system and its speed is measured in hertz.

gigabyte (Gb)

See **bit, byte, kilobyte, megabyte, terabyte**

A measurement of computer-based storage.

1 gigabyte = 1024 megabytes

gigahertz (GHz)

See **CPU, hertz, kilohertz, megahertz**

One billion cycles or electrical pulses per second of a computer CPU.

1 GHz = 1000 MHz = 1 000 000 Kz = 1000 000 000 Hz

hertz (Hz)

See **CPU, megahertz, gigahertz**

A measurement of clock speed of a computer CPU. It is also used to measure sound frequencies for hearing aids and radio transmission.

1 hertz = 1 cycle or electrical pulse of a CPU per second

hexadecimal

See **binary, decimal, octal**

Containing 16 parts or digits. It is a base 16 number system that is made up of 16 digits. The digits represented by this number system are 0 to 9 and then A to F. This number system is used primarily by computer systems, particularly by the programming languages that control computer hardware. It is also the number system used to represent colours on web pages.

Example
Digits represented:
0, 1, 2, 3, 4, 5, 6, 7, 8, 9
A = 10 B = 11 C = 12
D = 13 E = 14 F = 15

kilobyte (Kb)

See **bit, byte, megabyte**

A measurement of computer-based storage.

1 kilobyte = 1024 bytes

kilohertz (KHz)

See **CPU, hertz, gigahertz**

One thousand cycles or electrical pulses per second of a computer CPU.

1 KHz = 1000 Hz

megabyte (Mb)

See **bit, byte, kilobyte, gigabyte**

A measurement of computer-based storage.

1 megabyte = 1024 kilobytes

megahertz (MHz)

See **CPU, hertz, kilohertz**

One million cycles or electrical pulses per second of a computer CPU.

1 MHz = 1000 KHz = 1 000 000 Hz

octal

See **binary, decimal, hexadecimal**

Containing 8 parts or digits. It is a base 8 number system that is made up of 8 digits. The digits represented by this number system are 0 to 7. This number system is used primarily by computer systems, particularly by certain programming languages.

Example

Digits represented: 0, 1, 2, 3, 4, 5, 6, 7

RAM

(Random Access Memory)

See **byte, kilobyte, megabyte, gigabyte, terabyte**

The primary memory of a computer system. When a computer system is turned off, all contents in RAM are lost. The capacity of RAM is measured in bytes.

resolution

A measurement of the quality of a digital image. It is calculated by multiplying the number of dots (pixels) horizontally of the image by the number of dots (pixels) vertically of the image.

Example

Resolution of an image with 1024 horizontal pixels by 768 vertical pixels:

Resolution = 1024 × 768 = 786 432 pixels

1 000 000 pixels = 1 megapixel

terabyte (Tb)

See **bit, byte, kilobyte, megabyte, gigabyte**

A measurement of computer-based storage.

1 terabyte = 1024 gigabytes